ANDRÁS SIKLÓS

REVOLUTION IN HUNGARY AND THE DISSOLUTION
OF THE MULTINATIONAL STATE
1918

STUDIA HISTORICA

ACADEMIAE SCIENTIARUM HUNGARICAE

189.

Edited by

F. MUCSI

REVOLUTION IN HUNGARY AND THE DISSOLUTION OF THE MULTINATIONAL STATE

1918

by

ANDRÁS SIKLÓS

AKADÉMIAI KIADÓ · BUDAPEST 1988

Translated by
ZSUZSA BÉRES

Translation revised by
EMMA ROPER-EVANS

ISBN 963 05 4466 0

CONTENTS

6

INTRODUCTION

The purpose of this book is to give a comprehensive study of the Hungarian revolution in 1918, the events leading up to it, its outcome and its aims.

The history of the Hungarian revolution, which followed World War I and the dissolution of multinational Hungary were closely connected. Therefore, as well as describing these problems, this book also gives a detailed account of the events leading up to the end of January 1919, by which time most of the new frontiers had emerged and though the final decision was yet to come, the process of dissolution appeared to have been completed.

Up to November 1918, according to the Compromise of 1867 the Hungarian state was part of the dualist Austro–Hungarian Monarchy. Obviously, events in Hungary, up to the time when the country became an independent state were closely connected with the events which took place beyond the River Leitha, that is, the Austrian half of the Habsburg Empire. They were also strongly dependent, during the final phase of the war, on the developments regarding to defence and foreign affairs which were common to both countries.

An in-depth account of these events which so vitally influenced developments in Hungary is beyond the scope of this book. To make up for this deficiency the Introduction has been used to give only a brief chronological outline of the Austrian events. The author has done this on the assumption that the history of Austria will, perhaps, be better known to the reader than that of Hungary, which is not only a more distant country, but also owing to the language barrier less accessible.

The Austro–Hungarian Monarchy declared war at a time when its internal political situation was unsettled. Torn by bitter internal strife, it hoped to consolidate its weakened position by a speedy and victorious military campaign. As the war dragged on and as hopes of final victory faded it became increasingly clear that these expectations were totally unfounded ones. Instead of alleviating the empire's grave social and national conflicts, the war, which caused the death of millions of people and brought about great suffering, only exacerbated an already explosive situation.

With the passage of time it became increasingly obvious that the Monarchy, now on the brink of disaster, could only be saved by an immediate peace. However, things took a different turn during the winter of 1917–1918. Following the breakthrough at Caporetto, i.e. the victory in northern Italy and the withdrawal of Russia from the theatre of war (the armistice and later the peace treaty were signed in Brest-Litovsk on December 14, 1917 and March 3, 1918, respectively) tipped the balance in favour of those who demanded the continuation of the war and victory. The position of the "peace party" became hopeless. In the spring of 1918 the secret negotiations initiated and backed by the Emperor entered a deadlock; the Sixtus affair, which had been provoked by Foreign Minister Czernin, facilitated the "deepening" of the alliance with Germany and made the support of the "decisive" German offensive launched in March on the western front inevitable. Under orders from Germany, the Austro–Hungarian Monarchy opened a great offensive in northern Italy (the "Battle of Piave", June 14–23, 1918). Despite great efforts the offensive was repelled and the Monarchy suffered serious losses. As István Burián, the Monarchy's new Foreign Minister noted in his diary on June 22: "Wicked carelessness and recklessness ... is there still scope for politics making?"[1]

The internal situation of the Monarchy and the state of the *hinterland* was alarming during the preparation and execution of the great offensive.

Economic difficulties became increasingly insurmountable: shortage of raw materials, the catastrophic drop in industrial output—including the war industry—the total breakdown of transportation, inadequate supplies and starvation in the major cities.

Coupled with the economic difficulties, news of the Russian Revolution sparked off a new wave of organised strikes, which were also linked with the bread riots of the urban population and the resistance movement of the peasantry against requisitions. The Austrian Minister of the Interior's confidential reports covering the period between March 1 and June 30, 1918 speak of 436 strikes and 193 other actions in the areas beyond the River Leitha.[2]

The desperate situation of the Monarchy and the policy change of the Allied Powers—now openly supporting the secession of the nationalities—sharpened nationalistic conflicts within the empire and gave new impetus to the national movements led by the middle classes.

Decay soon spread to the army. This factor was of decisive significance as the joint army had been the main sustaining force of the conflict-ridden Habsburg empire—in times of both war and peace. Signs of disintegration ranged from simple cases of violation of discipline to outright desertions, from the alarming behaviour of those returning from revolutionary Russia to open mutiny.

Historians put the number of deserters at about 230,000 in the spring of 1918, adding that the actual figure was probably far higher.[3] The official but incomplete statistics of the Ministry of National Defence list 30 cases of mutiny between April 11 and July 16, 1918. Reports speak of hundreds, indeed in some instances about over a thousand participants (Judenburg, Rumburg, Radkersburg, Pécs, Kraguevac).[4]

---

[1] *Archives of Reformed Universal Convent*. Burián legacy. Diary, June 22, 1918.
[2] *HHSt. Kab. Arch*. Geheim, Tagesberichte des M. d. I., K. 37.
[3] *Plaschka,* Bd. II. p. 101.
[4] *KA KM Abt*. 5–1918–64–50/91. Statistik der Heimkehrermeutereien.

Initially only the *hinterland* divisions were hit by the symptoms of decay. However, following the failure of the Italian offensive, they spread to the frontline units as well. According to the official military statistics, effective force of the fighting army totalled 406,000 on July 1, 1918, which had dropped to 238,900 by October 1.[5]

In mid-September the Macedonian offensive of the Entente Powers (Dobropolje, September 14, 1918) led to the collapse of the Balkan front. The disintegration of the front was coupled with the defection of Bulgaria and the Bulgarian revolution (the soldiers' uprising in September, 1918). For the second time, the imperialist war had triggered off civil war, a warning to those who advocated the continuation of the war.

In an increasingly hopeless situation, the leadership of the Monarchy tried to stave off imminent collapse with desperate measures.

The extremely vague peace memorandum of September 14, which was made public despite opposition from the Germans, was rejected. France's reply, which was passed on to the Monarchy's embassy in Switzerland referred to Clemenceau's speech in the Senate, September 17: "There is no possibility for a compromise between crime and law ... Forward to outright victory."[6]

On October 4, the Monarchy, now unopposed by Germany, put forward a proposal for an immediate ceasefire and peace negotiations based on President Wilson's Fourteen Points. However, there was no response for quite a while.

The Emperor published an Imperial Manifesto on October 16. As a last desperate attempt to save the situation the Manifesto proclaimed Austria a federal state. However, the nationalities unanimously rejected it and declared it a belated and inadequate offer.

Washington's eventual reply to the peace proposal of October 4 made it unequivocally clear that the government of the United States no longer stood on the Fourteen Points platform. Whereas the Fourteen Points advocated autonomy for the national minorities under the sceptre of the Monarchy, the American reply of October 21, acknowledged the Czechoslovak National Council as a belligerent government and also gave full recognition to South Slav aspirations for national independence.

On October 24, the Entente opened its meticulously prepared offensive on the Italian front. A few days after the launching of the offensive the Austro–Hungarian army showed signs of total disintegration.

The armistice signed in Padua on November 3, which meant that the majority of the army were made prisoners of war, was seen as a diplomatic victory for the Monarchy. It implied the recognition of the continued existence of the empire in some form or other. However, the end was nigh. At the time when the armistice was signed the Austro–Hungarian Monarchy had been practically nonexistent and on

---

[5] *Ö-U. Letzter Krieg* Bd. VII. p. 361.
[6] *Journal officiel* du 18 Septembre 1918. Session ordinaire du Senat.

its territory the outlines of new, independent successor states, who broke totally with central power, began to emerge.

In Poland, the Warsaw Regent's Council issued a proclamation on October 7, in which, making reference to the acceptance of Wilson's Fourteen Points, they announced the formation of an independent unified Polish state, covering all previous Polish territories.

On October 28, a Coalition Liquidation Committee was formed by the representatives of the Polish parties in Austria, which demanded power over Galicia. Field Marshal Benigni, commander of Cracow's *Militärkommando*, offered no resistence when his HQ was taken over on October 31.

In the liberated Polish territories amidst the confusion of the hectic events of late October and early November, a people's government was set up in Lublin on November 7 and a Workers' and Soldiers' Council was formed in Poznan on November 9. Thus the vital question was no longer concerned with the retention of ties with the Monarchy, but, basically, with the struggle between the various political trends in a new, unified Poland. Would the Polish leaders be able to preserve their privileged position, would the Polish landowners and capitalists be able to retain their economic and political power, or at least part of it in the face of the intensifying revolutionary aspirations of the workers and the peasantry?

In the eastern parts of Galicia the Ukrainians attempted to form an autonomous Ukrainian state. On November 1, Ukrainian troops occupied Lemberg, took the military commander as an "honorary prisoner" and called on Count Huyn, the governor of Galicia, to hand over power. The Ukrainians also demanded areas beyond the Carpathian Mountains inhabited by Ukrainian people as well as the northern district of Bukovina. In Eastern Galicia the Ukrainian demands met with resistance from the Poles and in southern Bukovina from the Romanians living in the area.

In Bohemia power passed into the hands of the Czech National Council after a demonstration which erupted in Prague on October 28, and after the occupation of the *Militärkommando* in Prague on October 30. The creation of a new independent state was announced in the first law passed by the National Council on October 28. Amongst the signatories of the law were Vavro Šrobar, the representative of the Slovak National Party who was on an unofficial visit in Prague. By involving Šrobar, the National Committee (Narodny Vybor) wished to stress that the law of October 28 signified the formation of the Czechoslovak and not merely the Czech state.

The separation and proclamation of an independent Czechoslovakia sealed the fate of the Habsburg Empire. Although the existence of the Monarchy was not threatened by the loss of Galicia, the triangle Vienna–Budapest–Prague formed the basis of the Habsburg geometry.

On October 29 the Croat National Assembly, the Sabor, which gathered in Zagreb, announced with all solemnity the creation of the independent states of Croatia, Slovenia, Dalmatia and their joining to the common state of the Slovenes, Croats and Serbs. As a result of this resolution, which discreetly avoided taking a stand on the question of dynasty, power in Croatia passed into the hands of the South Slav National Council. The military commanders accepted the take-over and put up no resistance, nor did the public officials. In Ljubljana the Slovenian National Council took over on October 31, as the Bosnian National Council did in Sarajevo on November 1. Like in Zagreb, they met with no resistance whatever.

In Vienna, the German deputies of the *Reichsrat* gathered on October 21 for consultations at the seat of the Lower Austrian diet. At this meeting the German Social Democratic Party, the Christian Socialist Party and the parties of "German nationalism" proclaimed themselves a provisional National Assembly and adopted a resolution about the creation of an independent German–Austrian state. On October 30, the provisional National Assembly adopted a provisional constitution, which gave no rights or any kind of sphere of executive authority for the Monarch. In German–Austria, from October 30 onwards the governing and executive power was vested in the executive committee of the provisional National Assembly, the twenty-member German–Austrian State Council.

In Hungary the process of revolution and disintegration ran parallel with the developments in Austria. In the final days of September, news of the collapse of the Balkan front gave an unexpected impetus to this process, which will be the substance of this book.

1. POLITICAL CRISIS—REVOLUTIONARY SITUATION

FIRST NEWS FROM THE BULGARIAN–MACEDONIAN THEATRE OF WAR

The first account of the turn of the tide in the Balkans was published in the Budapest dailies on September 27, almost a fortnight after the launching of the Entente offensive. According to a brief communiqué released by the Hungarian News Agency the Bulgarian front had collapsed on September 14 and the Entente forces were subsequently able "to extend" their breakthrough. As the report put it "owing to unfavourable terrain and bad roads the Bulgarian troops suffered substantial losses of both equipment and prisoners of war in the course of their retreat. The Bulgarian retreat is still in progress. Efforts by Austro–Hungarian troops to extend help were seriously hampered by bad road conditions. These events of the Macedonian theatre of war are bound to affect the military position of the Austro–Hungarian troops in Albania. Given this state of affairs, military command must learn from the situation lest our positions there be endangered".

Since the Bulgarian armistice talks were already under way at this time and as Bulgaria's break with the war seemed imminent, the report, released in Vienna, tried to prepare public opinion for this eventuality: "The possibility of certain political consequences evolving from the developments of the military situation in the Balkans is not to be dismissed."[1]

On September 28, the newspaper headlines reported that "Bulgaria has left the alliance of the Central Powers. In accordance with the wishes of the King and the people, the government of Bulgaria has requested a ceasefire from the Entente and has put forward a proposal for peace".[2]

These alarming reports caused apprehension in the *hinterland,* where the situation had already been tense and was almost reaching breaking point. Almost everyone in Budapest started to read the newspapers—on the tram, on street corners and even while walking through the streets. "Sheets of white newspaper fluttered in the air like sea-gulls prior to a storm."[3]

Prime Minister Sándor Wekerle, who had returned to Budapest on the 28th, after the meeting of the Crown Council the day before, made no attempt to conceal the hopelessness of the situation at an eagerly awaited press conference, held in the evening. His statements and cynical answers to journalists' questions made it

---

[1] *Pesti Napló* (Pest Diary), September 27, 1918. "Serious Situation on the Bulgarian–Macedonian Front."
[2] *Pesti Napló*, September 28, 1918.
[3] *Ibid.*

perfectly clear to those present that the war was now drawing to an ignominious end and that the fate of the regime responsible for the defeat now hung in the balance.

During the last days of September the stock exchange was a hive of feverish activity. Minimum exchange rates were introduced to stop prices plummeting and later the stock exchange was closed temporarily. All to no avail. Wekerle issued a statement to clarify his earlier pronouncements. However, the statements published in the press, from the 29th onwards was to the effect that "We have taken the necessary steps to protect our front" ... "Our line of defence may be regarded as being fully protected on all sides" failed to alleviate mounting tensions."[4]

CABINET CRISIS

News of the speedy retreat of the German army, the collapse of the Balkan front and the change of government in Germany at the end of September stirred up a hive of activity on the political scene. A new situation emerged in the tug-of-war between the two political trends dominating the Hungarian ruling classes, the National Party of Work and the moderate opposition.

In the summer of 1918 it became apparent that after more than a year in power the constantly reshuffling minority government would move even further to the right. In the brief lull which followed the June strike and the Piave fiasco, Wekerle's greatly diminished "'48 Constitution Party"—already abandoned by Apponyi, Andrássy and Vázsonyi—continued to negotiate a merger and the appointment of National Party of Work ministers with the National Party of Work, despite the fact that the German offensive had ground to a halt. There were even rumours of Tisza's return as Prime Minister. Collapse seemed imminent and it finally became clear that these plans were not feasible. In early October Tisza once again came out with the plan of "national concentration", calling upon the right wing and the moderate opposition—which was also conservative albeit willing to make certain concessions and carry out modest reforms—to join forces. To help bring about an agreement Tisza was willing to back certain politicians who, in his judgement, still held a comparatively clean record.

On October 10, the Monarch demanded Wekerle's resignation on account of his double-dealing in the South Slav issue.[5]

---

[4] *Pesti Hírlap* (Pesti Daily), September 29, 1918. "Wekerle's Statement." October 1, 1918. "The Stock Exchange." A statement issued by Wekerle was read out by Elemér Horváth.

[5] According to a memorandum drawn up on October 12 by Wekerle for the Cabinet office, the dismissal of the Ban of Croatia (Mihajlovics) was the issue which had brought matters to a head. Referring to the intolerable state of affairs in Croatia, the Monarch had demanded the Ban's dismissal. It fell upon Wekerle to carry out his wish. Meanwhile the Ban travelled to Vienna to drum up support. Relying on the information they had received from him, the Ban's supporters made a statement to the effect that it was Wekerle's own wish that the Ban be dismissed. Refusing this accusation, Wekerle made the following statement: "His majesty raised the issue, demanding an immediate change of regime."

The Cabinet crisis which subsequently erupted was followed by a series of audiences and negotiations. However, these seemingly endless talks bore no fruit.

Tisza, who felt that with a majority in parliament he still held the reins of power, remained intransigent in regard to suffrage and democratic reforms. The only concession he was willing to make was to accept the appointment of Andrássy as joint Foreign Minister, which he had previously opposed. Under these circumstances the moderate opposition rejected cooperation with the National Party of Work, still the Monarch was reluctant to appoint a new government against its wishes.

As a result of the negotiations and planning which dragged on until mid-October Wekerle retained his position. This, however, was merely a procrastination and did not resolve the crisis. The retention of the government, on the one hand, reflected the total intransigence and blind opposition to reform of those in power, and, on the other, it clearly indicated the deadlock which emerged in the wake of efforts by the ruling circles to mutually obstruct each other's aspirations. At the same time at the root of the crisis lay not only the stubborn resistance of a recanting National Party of Work but, also—which those concerned did not wish to acknowledge—that during those days Andrássy and his liberal supporters, the so-called "centre-left" were no longer capable of carrying out a political initiative similar to the Bulgarian, German or any other model.

A year and a half of political wrangling, of which the Cabinet crisis of early October was only yet another phase, had undermined the confidence of the masses not only in Tisza and the strongly anti-reform National Party of Work, but also in the moderate opposition and the activity of those minority governments who took over from Tisza. Instead of working off mounting tensions, Wekerle's promises, Andrássy and Apponyi's incompetence, Vázsonyi's promises "to clamp down" and Szterényi's "to overrun" achieved just the opposite, they only intensified impatience, hatred and lack of confidence.

The signs of impending catastrophe paved the way for politicians whose integrity had not been undermined during this period of political crisis. Attention now turned to the left wing groups of the opposition.

MIHÁLY KÁROLYI AND THE INDEPENDENCE AND '48 PARTY

An outstanding political personality was leading the left wing of parliamentary opposition—Mihály Károlyi (1875–1955).

(*HHSt. Kabinetsarchiv,* K. Z. Akten 2519/1918. Ung. Min. Präsident Wekerle 12/10 berichtet betreffend den Banuswechsel in Kroatien–Slavonien.)

According to Szterényi, the Monarch had made the following statement on October 10, in his presence: "I can no longer stand this constant covering up in my name, everyone wants to be good, but wants to leave all the responsibility to me" ... "I do not wish to continue with Wekerle for another twenty-four hours..." (*Szterényi,* pp. 126–127.)

The son of the landed aristocracy, Mihály Károlyi's political career began in the Liberal Party. Following the 1905 elections he joined the Independence Party and acted as president of the Hungarian National Agricultural Association (OMGE) between 1909 and 1912. During the years leading up to World War I Károlyi, leaning towards Justh's party, began to adopt a gradually sharper position against the reactionary politics of the Hungarian ruling classes which were embodied by István Tisza. Following the merger in June 1913 of the independence factions, Károlyi became chairman of the United Independence Party. In the summer of 1914 he made a lecture tour in the United States, on his return he was caught in France by the outbreak of the war, where he was interned for a short period. After his return home Károlyi expressed his support for the war and volunteered for active service. As the war dragged on Károlyi's pacifist conviction and anti-German sentiments grew stronger, he pressed for reforms, the extension of legislation governing suffrage and criticized the opportunism of the Independence Party which was under Apponyi's influence. In the summer of 1916 Károlyi broke with Apponyi and founded a new party called the Independence and '48 Party which also came to be known as the Károlyi Party. True to the traditions of the left wing of the independence movement, the new party demanded greater independence (a common monarch for Austria and Hungary, a national army, an independent tariff area, an independent bank), democratic reforms (universal suffrage, secret ballot, freedom of the press, association and assembly) and social welfare measures (support for social welfare institutions and that the system of large landed estates be rectified). Just as important were the new party demands for the conclusion of war and "a rapid peace agreement to protect territorial integrity".

On paper, Károlyi was the leader of a small and apparently insignificant party, with only twenty MPs—mostly from traditionally anti-Austrian electoral districts—supporting him in parliament. These MPs (landowners, lawyers, journalists and public servants) accounted for only a fraction of the National Assembly. However, the weight of Károlyi's appearance on the political scene and the power of his programme were not determined by the internal balance of power of a parliament elected eight years earlier.

Károlyi had close links not only with his own party, but also with the radical intelligentsia and certain leaders of the Social Democratic Party. In the spring of 1917 these links were lent an organized structure by the formation of the Suffrage Block and the ties of friendship were not severed even when, in early 1918, the party alliance broke up owing to the split with Vázsonyi.

During the June strike Károlyi stood by the striking workers. At the same time he disregarded the attacks and machinations of the right by taking stand against "strengthening" the alliance with Germany. On September 8, he addressed an open letter to his Cegl;éd constituents. In this letter Károlyi made a conspicuous and sharp attack on Tisza's warmongering, a position which allowed no room for compromise. On September 16, Károlyi, in a speech addressed to the Cegléd delegation which came to greet him, criticized Burián's peace memorandum. Instead of meaningless and ineffectual memoranda, Károlyi suggested the acceptance of Wilson's Fourteen Points and urged the drawing up of a concrete peace proposal.

News of the collapse of the Bulgarian front reached Károlyi in Transylvania, on his father-in-law, Gyula Andrássy's Dubrin estate. On hearing the alarming news he immediately interrupted his holiday and returned to Budapest on the first train. "Peace, democracy, independence." This was how he summed up his programme for the delegation greeting him at the railway station. By peace Károlyi meant a peace of compromise, in which a new, pro-Entente orientation would pave the way to breaking the alliance with Germany. By democracy, he meant democratic reforms, by independence "personal union" (a common monarch for Austria and Hungary).

When the Cabinet crisis erupted Károlyi demanded a new governing party made up of members of the opposition with clean records and in which political parties with no representation in parliament, that is, the Radical Party and the Social Democratic Party would also be given a place.

Following Wekerle's resignation the King received Károlyi who put forward the plan outlined above, backing it up with the argument that the Entente "would prescribe much harsher conditions if those responsible for anti-Entente policies were to retain the reins of power".[6]

In the new government Károlyi wished to ensure a place for the representatives of the national minority parties as well. In early October he met and conducted negotiations on several occasions with Slovak, Romanian and Serb politicians. He believed that the national minority leaders could be won over by a more liberal nationality policy and that they would support his ideas.

On October 15 in Vienna at the last session of the foreign affairs sub-committee of the Hungarian delegation, Károlyi declared the Austro–Hungarian Monarchy responsible for having started the war. In a passionate speech he attacked the pro-German leaders, blaming them for not taking any of the opportunities which could have taken Hungary out of the war. "We have lost the war because of you", he said. "And if you remain, we shall lose peace as well . . . Out with you, so the people can negotiate for the management of their own fate, their peace, future, independence and liberty."[7]

As a result of his bold and resolute stand, Károlyi's popularity increased daily. His demands: a speedy end to the war, lasting peace, that the political leadership should answer for their actions, independence, liberty and common law, gave voice to the desires of the masses fed up with the war.

A growing body of opinion held that a change of regime would help Hungary withdraw from a lost war without serious consequences. Some of Károlyi's statements, including the repeated assertion that Wilson's Fourteen Points did not contradict the country's territorial integrity, further strengthened the unfounded

---

[6] *Károlyi, 1923*, p. 408.
[7] *Világ* (World), October 16, 1918. In: *Károlyi 1968*, p. 217.

hope that if independence was achieved, a multi-national Hungary would survive intact, too.

The pacifist programme of the Károlyi Party which drew on nationalism, aimed to change and radically transform a regime in crisis, but at the same time wanted to preserve it. The ruling circles rejected it. Not only Tisza and the National Party of Work opposed Károlyi's programme, powerful opposition also came from Andrássy's moderate conservative-liberal opposition who considered the radicalism of the independent left as dangerous.

THE BOURGEOIS RADICALS

In the autumn of 1918 the bourgeois radicals shot to prominence with a speed that took even the party's own leadership by surprise.

This movement, which started during the first decade of the century, established itself as the Bourgeois Radical Party in 1914, just a few months before the outbreak of World War I. At the party's statutory meeting, Oszkár Jászi, the party chairman, outlined its three basic goals: land reform, the solution of the nationality issue and public education. The programme put forward a whole series of proposals for extending public liberties, developing the economy, resolving the nationality issue, ensuring the country's independence and preserving peace. This programme remained valid during the war years, the only change being made that the twelve-point programme published at the end of the war substituted "pacifist and free-trade foreign policy" for the original protectionist trend. The Bourgeois Radical Party believed that this could be achieved "by eliminating the economic and political walls separating peoples, the creation of a system of alliance among states belonging to the European culture on the basis of general disarmament and peace without annexation and war-reparations".[8]

From the outset there were three distinct trends and, accordingly, three groupings within the Bourgeois Radical Party. A liberal grouping, one sympathising with Marxism and one calling itself the "free socialists", which was situated between the other two. The liberals were willing to support measures against "feudalism" (the system of large landed estates, the Church); they would not, however, hear of the struggle against working capital. Belonging to the group calling themselves "Marxists"—headed by lawyer Pál Szende, secretary-general of the National Hungarian Commercial Association—were such intellectuals who considered the revolutionization of the bourgeoisie as their task, and using this as a pretext, avoided joining the Social Democratic Party. Headed by Oszkár Jászi, the "free socialists" called for democratic reforms, and adopted several social welfare demands put forward by the social democrats. However, they openly rejected the fundamental precepts of Marxism (including the theory of class struggle).

---

[8] *PI Archives,* Leaflet Collection II. 13/13. "What Does the Radical Party Want?", *O. Jászi,* "What is Radicalism?", Title-page.

The Radical Party, which comprised a relatively narrow circle of the urban petite bourgeoisie and intellectual strata, did not represent a substantial organized strength. The root of its weakness lay not only in the fact that the war broke out shortly after the party had been established and without doubt hampered organization, but also by the internal division of the party leadership, who were highly adept at writing and teaching and regarded the propagation of their ideas as their fundamental task.

The party chairman, Oszkár Jászi, was an expert on the nationality issue. Regarding Jászi's and the Radical Party's stand on the nationality issue during the last year of the war, mention must, first of all, be made of the debate which unfolded on the pages of *Huszadik Század* (Twentieth Century) in the summer of 1918, and secondly, to Jászi's *A Monarchia jövője* (The Future of the Monarchy), which was published in early October.

The debate in *Huszadik Század,* the radicals' journal, was linked with a study analysing the issue by Mihály Réz, the ideologist of the National Party of Work. In the debate, to which several contributions were made, Jászi rejected Mihály Réz's theory which advocated national self-interest (history as a series of racial struggles, force being the only means of resolving conflicts), as such an "unscientific and barren conception of the destiny of humanity which no aspiring and creative intellect can ever accept". Jászi pitted the self-interest of the individual against the self-interest of the race as the decisive psychological and historical factor. In contrast with Mihály Réz's views, he characterised history as "a vast assimilating levelling up and democratizing process", the meaning of which was "the creation of broader cultural and co-operative units".[9]

Written in early 1918, *A Monarchia jövője* was published only in the autumn of 1918—a detrimental delay. In this book Jászi outlined his ideas regarding the practical solution of the national minority issue within the Austro–Hungarian Monarchy. As Jászi envisaged it, five federal national states would be created within the Monarchy, linked together by common ministries. The remaining nationality problems would then be resolved within the new, separate states, within the framework of cultural and administrative autonomy. Every "reasonable" demand of the national minorities would be granted in the course of internal democratization which Jászi regarded as a precondition for the whole plan. The five federal states would have been Austria, Hungary, Bohemia, Poland and Illyria (uniting the Monarchy's South Slav population). According to the book in these states "aristocratic dualism" would have been replaced by "democratic pentarchy" with the further prospect of this new federal state would later attract the countries of the Balkans, set an example for the creation of supra-national states, and ultimately, it would lead to the creation of a federal state encompassing the entire world.

At the time when he wrote *A Monarchia jövője* Jászi envisaged Hungary's future within the framework of a reorganized Monarchy. He agreed with the secession of

[9] *Nemzetiségi kérdés,* 3., p. 28.

2*

Croatia-Slavonia, but thought that the power of the Hungarian state could be retained over the national minorities with the guarantee of cultural and reasonable administrative autonomy for the Romanian, Slav and German population of the national minority areas.

Jászi's conception, which he backed up with ample arguments, was undoubtedly one of the outstanding plans among those which, in steadily increasing number, had been put forth since the turn of the century.

Its greatest weakness—at the time it was written, and more importantly, when it was published—was that it was based on erroneous assumptions. On the one hand the radicals exaggerated the weight and influence of the liberal, Wilsonian forces in the United States and in the Entente countries, and on the other, the power and viability of the Monarchy. (Jászi envisaged his democratic confederation under Habsburg rule, within the framework of a constitutional monarchy.) Consequently, they also overestimated the possibility of a peace based on understanding and compromise, on which the whole plan hinged.

Jászi also underestimated the likelihood of the Russian Revolution and its impact and failed to grapple with the problems arising from intensified class struggle, which fundamentally determined the events which followed. He believed that inasmuch as he offered the "Danube Federation" as a counterbalance to the "German and Russian millstone" his plan would become desirable to the bourgeoisie who feared revolution and rejected German hegemony regardless of their nationality. Counting on understanding and support from the bourgeoisie, Jászi failed to take into account the fact that the chaos which followed the losing of the war, the fear of revolution and the change in the balance of power turned the bourgeoisie of the national minorities—the leading social stratum of the emerging successor states— away from former oppressors, the formerly ruling nationalities. Instead of reaching a compromise with the latter they were far more likely to stir up nationalist desires and passions and to opt for the—apparently easier, simpler and more advantageous—break with the Monarchy.

The fact that, instead of an internal federation, Jászi promised cultural and administrative autonomy at only county level for the national minorities, and, more importantly, his insistence on the territorial principle, "the historical boundaries",—a fundamental concept of the book—signified a concession to Hungarian nationalism, which paved the way to a more profound co-operation with Károlyi's 48 and Independence Party. Insistence on territorial integrity could, in this respect, have appeared as a realistic conception. However, insofar as Jászi had thought that such a solution would satisfy the national minorities, his assessment of the existing situation was wrong.

When A Monarchia jövője was published in October 1918, Világ, the Radical Party's paper, backed up Jászi's conception by stressing that Hungary's territorial integrity "could only be preserved and protected in this way".[10]

---

[10] Világ, October 13, 1918. L. Biró, "The Danubian United States. Jászi's New Book."

This reasoning (which, no doubt, gave prominence to a part of Jászi's book but did not include the substance of his idea) helped the radicals strengthen their influence and broaden their mass appeal in the weeks leading up to the revolution. When, later on, this success and the illusions it engendered were confronted with the realities, it inevitably backfired. But few would have thought in October 1918 that it would turn out like this. The radicals' star was, for the moment, rising, they were powerful, their influence greater and greater and, following a long period of political inactivity, life was returning to their organizations. The party's appeals and posters began to appear in the streets, membership rose steadily and new organizations were formed.

On October 14, the long-awaited congress of the radicals was opened in the crowded session-room of the former Lower House. Well-known leaders such as Oszkár Jászi, Pál Szende, Lajos Biró, Géza Supka and Marcell Benedek addressed the conference which adopted three resolutions. The first demanded a new government, the second put forward a foreign policy programme, the third outlined domestic policy issues.

The congress made a bid for a new democratic government "brave and resolute in its actions", as only such a government "could save Hungary's territorial integrity and protect society from the convulsions of revolution".

The resolution proposed a foreign policy programme, took the stand that Hungary's territorial integrity "neither contradicts the justified demands of the national minorities, nor the national aspirations of the emerging states".[11]

The most urgent domestic political and economic tasks were summed up in twelve points. Most of these points contained the aforementioned radical demands: suffrage, freedom of the press, agrarian reform, support for commerce and small industry, improvement of the situation of public servants and private employees. However, they also contained new ideas and topical issues: provision for the soldiers returning from the war, the dismantling of the war economy, a one time wealth tax, the nationalization of monopoly industrial plants, etc.

At the congress, the poet Endre Ady was also elected as a member of the party's executive committee. Prevented by illness, Ady was unable to attend the congress, instead he sent a telegramme in which he expressed his greetings to the participants: "... We try to expiate the feudal and nationalist sins. Let us save the Hungarian people—and similarly all the peoples living in Hungary. The time for peoples' rights and peoples' association has arrived..."[12]

[11] *Világ*, October 15, 1918. "Congress of the Radical Party."
[12] *Világ*, October 16, 1918. "Greetings to the Radical Party."

THE HUNGARIAN SOCIAL DEMOCRATIC PARTY AND ITS
LEFT WING OPPOSITION

The Hungarian Social Democratic Party played an important role and represented a decisive force among the ranks of the opposition which rallied against the reactionary and conservative forces in the autumn of 1918. Trade union membership statistics clearly reveal the growth of the SDP's strength and influence during the final years of the war. From 1916 onwards trade union membership rose continuously and at a rapidly growing pace. According to the Trade Union Council, figures rose from 55,338 in 1916 to 215,222 in 1917; in the autumn of 1918 it was—unofficially—estimated at 300,000.[13]

At the beginning of the war the SDP considered the war to be a "defensive" one and, accordingly, only demanded economic and social welfare reforms in line with the war conditions. Later on, however, it modified its stance demanding negotiations for a rapid peace and the relinquishing of the original war aims. The SDP pointed out that as long as the Entente was unwilling to negotiate peace, the social democratic parties of the Central Powers should continue to support their governments' war efforts. As regards domestic matters, however, the SDP returned to its former electoral policy. The chief representative of this policy was Ernő Garami, who played a leading role within the party leadership.

In June 1917 the Electoral Block was formed on the initiative of the social democrats; in return for promises of electoral reform the SDP supported the Esterházy government and, later, Wekerle's coalition Cabinet for a fairly long period of time.[14]

Following the February Revolution, which toppled Tsarism in Russia, and simultaneously with the emergence of German independents, a central faction began to take shape within the Hungarian party, headed by Zsigmond Kunfi who was an excellent orator.

In the course of the struggle for electoral reform, Garami became closer to Vázsonyi, the moderately liberal opposition. At the same time Kunfi was trying to establish an alliance with Károlyi. Although the extraordinary party congress held in February 1918 adopted a decision to "break the formal and organizational links" with the bourgeois parties, ties with Vázsonyi, namely with the moderate opposition and with Károlyi and the left wing of the parliamentary opposition remained intact.

The old left wing opposition within the party drew strength from the October Revolution. Headed by Béla Vágó, Béla Szántó, László Rudas and others, it

---

[13] *A szakszervezeti mozgalom,* p. 106. The Trade Union Council's statistics always refer to the situation on December 31. Reference to the autumn of 1918 figures is made by J. Landler at the October 13 extraordinary congress *MMTVD/5,* p. 480.

[14] On June 15, 1917 Count Móric Esterházy became Prime Minister following Count István Tisza. The short-lived Esterházy Cabinet was changed on August 20, 1917 for the Wekerle government. This cabinet was on more than one occasion altered completely. Until October 30, Wekerle was the head of it.

provided a new source of inspiration for the shaping of new left wing trends. At the beginning of 1918 the outlines of a new left wing began to take shape (Jenő Hamburger, Jenő Landler, György Nyisztor, Jenő Varga). The old and new left wing within the Social Democratic Party relied primarily on the constantly growing group of revolutionary shop stewards among the organized workers (Ede Chlepkó, Rezső Fiedler, Antal Mosolygó, Rezső Szaton). The new blue and white collar workers flooding the trade unions extended the social base of the left wing and enabled the establishment of new organizations and organizational forms.

The sharply-worded propaganda campaign of the revolutionary socialists, who organized illegally outside the framework of the SDP and who were given considerable help by Ervin Szabó, did not leave the balance of power within the movement unaffected. The group, whose work was lead by Ottó Korvin following the strike of January 1918, comprised of opposition workers, intellectuals and students of the Galilei Circle. Their illegal leaflets advocated the following of the Russian example.

In the summer and autumn of 1918 publications of communist prisoners of war in Russia—the *Kommunista Könyvtár* (Communist Library) series, the weekly *Szociális Forradalom* (Social Revolution)—became known in Hungary. The founding of the Hungarian communist organization in Russia and the appearance of its publications in Hungary was a significant event, despite the very brief account published by the official party press.

The struggle for electoral reform bore no fruit, despite the workers' powerful actions in January, March, April and June 1918. The promises remained unfulfilled. Following almost a year and a half of wrangling a bill was passed which was in almost every respect in accordance with the position of the National Party of Work.

In the summer of 1918, following the huge political strike in June, there appeared to be calm in the *hinterland*. The Social Democratic Party leadership and the Trade Union Council strove to preserve this calm. The trade union congresses which convened late in August discussed economic and organizational issues. The single topic on the agenda of the shop stewards' public meeting on September 23, was "the question of social welfare public food provision".

News of the collapse of the Bulgarian front and the political changes in Germany broke the precarious calm and inertia of the movement with force. Following a period of total inactivity the new situation was suddenly characterized by "feverish activity".

On October 1, the daily newspaper *Népszava* (People's Voice), in a sharply worded editorial urged the dismissal of Wekerle, Tisza and Burián and a radical break with "the prevailing system of class rule"—citing Germany, who "had embarked upon new paths", as an example.

On October 3, the party newspaper published details of the peace conditions demanded by the Austro–German social democrats. On October 5, it reported a statement by Austro–German social democrat MPs on the right to self-determination, which, among other things, pointed out the following:

"The representatives of the German workers in Austria acknowledge the right to self-determination of the Slav and Romanian people living in Austria and demand similar rights for the German people living in Austria..."

"We are ready to negotiate, on this basis, with the representatives of the Czech and South Slav people, about how Austria could be transformed into a federation of free national communities. Should the representatives of the Slav nations reject these negotiations... then the German people of Austria will assert their right to self-determination by every means."

Commenting on the above statement, *Népszava* called for the equality of the national minorities in Hungary and argued that in this area, "where different peoples live in such a confusion that is worse than anywhere else in the world... the only way out of the situation is the traditional socialist solution, namely the vast federation of the peoples of the Monarchy and the Balkans". "Any other solution would faciliate the emergence of new irredentists, new oppressed people and minorities who would desire to break away." *Népszava* expected initiative in this field to come from the King and summed up the tasks ahead as follows: The King should appoint a new government which would include representatives of the nationalities. The new government should, without delay introduce universal suffrage with secret ballot. Following immediate elections legislative assembly should be convened. This would regulate "the relationship between Hungarians and the nationalities living in Hungary and between the newly emerging states in the neighbourhood of Hungary within the framework of a federal state based on equality which would include the largest possible area".[15]

On the issue of alliance with the bourgeois political parties the party newspaper did not clarify its position in the early days of October. It published not only Károlyi's and Jászi's speeches and statements, but also those of Andrássy and Vázsonyi. With the passage of time, however, it became clear that neither Andrássy, nor Vázsonyi could compete with Károlyi's constantly growing popularity. Vázsonyi's earlier outbursts, which threatened "to clamp down" the left, made him unpopular with the working class. Also his nationalistic views could not, in the given situation, be reconciled with the stance of the social democrats on the national minority issue.

It was in the autumn—so full of promises and hope—of 1918 that Ervin Szabó, the outstanding ideologist of early-twentieth century socialist labour movement died. Indicative of the changing times was the fact that *Népszava,* the paper which only a few months earlier had called Ervin Szabó "a dry as dust scholar moving around in a void", on the occasion of his death, praised his activity and spoke highly about his achievements. His burial became an important socio-political event and, justly or unjustly, paved the way for co-operation between the Social Democratic Party and the left wing opposition. At his graveside Zsigmond Kunfi and Oszkár Jászi delivered the funeral address, and over the crowd of mourners towered the slender figure of Mihály Károlyi.

[15] *Népszava,* October 5, 1918. "Where does the Road Lead to?"

On October 8, 1918, *Népszava* published the appeal "To the People of Hungary", which summed up the most urgent tasks in ten points. The first point demanded a new government comprising of representatives "all the democratic classes of the country" and of "every nation". The second proposed the dissolution of the Lower House and the convocation of a new national assembly on the basis of universal suffrage, women included, with secret ballot. The other points elaborated the duties of the new government: peace on the basis of the Russian Revolution and the Wilsonian principles; the total democratization of public administration; freedom of association, assembly and organization; fundamental and radical land reform; the nationalization of industrial plants that have expanded beyond single-handed management; fair taxation; labour safety and social welfare measures; preparation for the introduction of an eight-hour working day; compensation for soldiers returning from the war, for the disabled, for widows and orphans. Regarding the national minority issue the proclamation called, on the one hand, for the abolition of the system which oppressed the nationalities and for the unrestricted use of the mother-tongue. On the other hand, it outlined prospects for the creation of "a Hungary based on the association, the federation of equal, free and democratic nations".

On October 13, a few days after the proclamation was published the party convoked an extraordinary congress with a single point on its agenda: "Peace and the Future of Hungary". This involved the assessment of the situation and the outlining of the tasks which faced the party amid the rapidly changing situation. By convening this congress the party leadership hoped to obtain an endorsement for the Proclamation of October 8. Its two main goals were as follows: 1. To change and invalidate the February resolution which banned association with the bourgeois parties; 2. To induce the national minority committees to adopt a resolutely pro-SDP stance.

In a dynamic speech, Zsigmond Kunfi, the speaker at the party meeting explained that external circumstances had toppled the two external pillars of the existing system: dualism and the German alliance. However, the two internal pillars, the oppression of the nationalities and class oppression remained. To topple these is a task of historic significance. Although Kunfi did not openly advocate the declaration of a republic, he did point out that the party did not support the idea of a common monarch for Austria and Hungary—royal power had proved to be weak—but he said that the form the government would take, would be "determined by Hungary's future constitutional assembly".

In regard to the national minority issue Kunfi stressed that the SDP acknowledged the right of every nation to self-determination and all that this entailed. The SDP did not wish to keep peoples who do not want to remain here by force, but hoped that should Hungary become "a federal people's state based on free co-operation", then secession would not come about.

Concerning the issue of alliance with the bourgeois political parties, Kunfi put forward the pro-alliance argument that this was necessary because the working class could not carry out the planned programme on its own, it was not strong enough to take over political power single-handedly. As regards the substance of this co-operation, he strove to disperse doubts. They did not wish to form an alliance with the moderate opposition (Vázsonyi) but with those who had adopted the SDP's action programme.

Kunfi's opening address was followed by contributions from the representatives of the national minority committees,who, unlike on previous occasions, were also seated in the congress' presidium. The spokesmen for the Romanian, Slovak, Serb and German sections assured the SDP of their support. However, it also became clear that they opposed the proposal suggesting the establishment of an alliance with the bourgeois parties, as they did not trust the Hungarian bourgeois political parties, the so-called "historical parties". "I fear", said the head of the Romanian section when commenting on the proposal suggesting the renewal of an alliance with the bourgeois parties, "that should the congress accept this, the SDP would win even less support from the Romanian nationality than it otherwise could". Concerning the issue of whether they belonged to Hungary or not, the national minority sections evaded adopting an unequivocal stand. The reason for this lay in the fact that the right wing leaders of the Slovak and Romanian committees had, by this time, established close links with the bourgeois parties of the national minorities. On seeing the turn of events, these leaders argued that if the Hungarian workers entered into alliance with Hungarian nationalism i.e. the Hungarian bourgeois parties, then they too were entitled to do the same.

The speakers for the national minorities were followed by the representatives of the trades, district and rural organizations. Their contributions to the debate also revealed that the working class opposed the idea of entering into alliance with the bourgeois parties and had strong reservations about it. In spite of this the SDP leadership upheld its proposal, though, as a concession to the atmosphere of the conference, it accepted Jenő Landler's modifying motion which made the acceptance of the "the programme outlined in the party proclamation" a precondition for co-operation.

With this wording—which did not alter the substance of the proposal—the SDP succeeded in invalidating the former resolution which discontinued the alliance with the bourgeois parties and, thus, paved the way to the renewal of this alliance.

The ways and means of implementing it did, however, remain an open issue. The modified form of the proposal favoured an alliance with the Károlyi party and the Radical Party. At the congress Garami and the right wing did not even attempt to justify and defend its former policy of co-operation with the moderate opposition. Garami's silence did not, however, mean that he had broken with his earlier conception. Regarding the issue of alliance with the bourgeois parties opinions differed in the party leadership and the party committee (to whom the congress had entrusted the implementation of the resolution) and those who opposed co-operation with Károlyi could point out that the Károlyi party had not openly declared whether or not it would accept the October party programme without reservations.

While the right wing of the SDP kept silent and withdrew at the congress, the left wing put up a powerful appearance, submitting a host of proposals. Referring to the developments in Russia and taking as their point of departure the fact that a revolutionary situation had arisen in Hungary, the left wing opposition regarded the October proclamation unsatisfactory and halfhearted. It was convinced that the goals laid down by the SDP lagged behind the opportunities offered by such favourable circumstances.

In his speech József Pogány suggested that against "the programme of the radically chauvinist Hungarian political parties calling for personal union with Austria, an independent tariff zone and an independent army" must be pitted the demand for the declaration of a republic, free trade and the setting up of a workers' militia. In the name of 32 delegates he put forward a motion in which they called for an independent proletarian policy and to accomplish this, the setting up of a workers' council.

In the name of Pál Zádor, György Nyisztor and other congress delegates, Pogány asked for the acceptance of the "Thirteen points proposal" as a resolution. This proposal, among other things, contained demands which went beyond the official party programme: the abolition of the Upper House; the immediate transformation of public administration, the setting up of popular organs to monitor this; the distribution of ecclesiastical estates, entailed property and eventually every estate "which the owner and his family are unable to cultivate on their own"; the establishment of agricultural co-operatives with strong state support; the nationalization of industrial plants, primarily heavy industry, mining, food, clothing and building material manufacturing plants, with the effective participation of blue and white-collar workers; the nationalization of banks; wealth tax to cover war costs and state expenditure; the rationing of food and clothing to increase and improve production and to ensure fair distribution; the solving of the housing problem, that is the linking of living space to the number of occupants.

These proposals gave prominence to the demands of the imminent democratic revolution, but also went beyond it; they also reckoned with the possibility of a socialist revolution.

On the issue of alliance with the bourgeois political parties Pogány pointed out that this would upset the self-consiousness of the national minority workers as well as the Hungarian workers. "You cannot pursue two tactics simultaneously", stressed Pogány. The SDP should not seek alliance with the national minority bourgeoisie or with "the historical parties" who "stand on the basis of territorial integrity", but with the hundreds of thousands of unorganized workers, with the millions of unorganized peasants, with the tens of millions of foreign workers and with the Russian Revolution.

The aim of the SDP, said Pál Zádor, should be that "the proletariat of every nationality living in Hungary take over the management of the country's destiny".

THE HUNGARIAN COMMUNIST GROUP IN RUSSIA

Led by Béla Kun, the group of Hungarian communists in Russia also put forward its position on the SDP's October programme and the resolution adopted by the congress.

Béla Kun was born in the village of Lele in Transylvania on February 20, 1886. His father was the village notary. His secondary school studies took him to Zilah and later to Kolozsvár where he attended the Calvinist college. He joined the Social Democratic Party at the age of 16. During his university years he became a journalist and later worked as clerk in the local workers' insurance bank. When World War I broke out Kun was called up and sent to the Russian front. He was a prisoner of war from 1916 onwards, and he started to organize the prisoners of war revolutionary movement at the camp in Tomsk. He was among the first to join the Bolsheviks—before the victory of the October Revolution. At the end of 1917 he went to Saint Petersburg where he met Lenin. Following the founding of the Hungarian section of the Russian Communist Party (March 24), of which he became the leader, the Federation of Socialist Prisoners of War elected Kun their president. In February 1918 he fought against the Germans and later on the Perm front. In July he participated in the suppression of the left wing socialist revolutionaries in Moscow.

The communist prisoners of war rejected the goals of the SDP as a whole and were ready to arrive at appropriate conclusions in regard to organization as well. The Hungarian Bolsheviks pointed out that the new phenomena of historical development: imperialism, the world war, the establishment of the dictatorship of the proletariat in Russia had created a fundamentally new situation for the labour movement, so they put the possibility of a socialist revolution, of the seizing of power on the agenda. Thus, under these circumstances, a bid for bourgeois democracy as the immediate objective no longer meant progress and the path to liberation, but was a means "to save the disintegrating bourgeois state organization against Bolshevism and the proletarian revolution".[16]

On the basis of this the group's weekly, *Szociális Forradalom,* denounced the SDP's October proclamation as a document of treason and accused the party with opportunism, conspiracy with the ruling class and of relinquishing the class struggle. The main criticism which *Szociális Forradalom* levelled at the SDP was the total lack of perspectives for the proletarian revolution and secondly, their disregard for the important demands of a democratic transitional programme.

Instead of a revolutionary struggle, the proclamation advocates the equality of classes before the law. It wished to conclude peace on the basis of the conflicting principles of the Russian Revolution and Wilson's peace proposal. Calling for disarmament, it forgets about the general arming of the people. It makes no mention of the international unity of the proletariat, but does on the other hand,

---

[16] *Szociális Forradalom,* October 23, 1918. B. Kun, "The Judgement of the Bolsheviks."

advocate peaceful co-operation between bourgeois states. It suggests a constitutional assembly instead of a republic of councils of workers and the landless
peasantry. The proclamation does not call for the confiscation of wealth
accumulated during the war and does not speak of the abolition of private property.
There is no mention of secularization and the nationalization of church schools.
The proclamation only wished to prepare for the eight-hour working day and,
instead of progressive income tax, it only recommends a fair tax policy.

The ten points of the proclamation do not only stray from the path of class
struggle and miss existing opportunities for revolution, but, at the same time, they
also renounce the provisional programme of the SDP in which the demand for a
general arming of the people and the confiscation of church estates was
unequivocally present.

Regarding the slogan of an independent Hungary, *Szociális Forradalom* ran an
elaborate article in which it said that this demand in the programmes of the
bourgeois political parties only meant that "the Hungary of the imperialist German
alliance" would be replaced "by the Hungary of a counter-revolutionary pro-
Entente sentiment".[17]

Commenting on the disintegration of the Monarchy, the paper takes a stand
against national division, which, in the given situation, "is the obvious aspiration
and interest of the national bourgeoisie", but does not serve the interests of the
exploited and oppressed masses, regardless of their nationality.

Since these masses were "still under the influence of those social patriots who had
struck an alliance with the petite bourgeoisie" this process could not be obstructed.
However, parallel to the emergence of the bourgeois national states and with the
termination of the national bourgeois revolution in the Monarchy, the revolution
of the Monarchy's proletariat progressed. Soon "another phase of the revolutionary process will arrive, where Hungarian, Czech, South Slav, Romanian and
German armed revolutionary masses will express their will . . . it is not a democratic
independence, but the revolutionary dictatorship of the workers and peasants, is
not a league of nations, but a republic of councils united in alliance".[18]

The necessity of establishing a new party clearly followed from the sharp
criticism levelled at the SDP. To prepare this "the Hungarian members of the
foreign language groups of the Russian Communist Party held a meeting" in
Moscow on October 24. (In a second floor room at the Hotel Dresden was this
famous meeting; in those days the room also served as the centre for the group of
Hungarian communists in Russia.)

Béla Kun, one of the speakers at the meeting, said the following: the SDP had
"deviated from the path leading to socialism . . . therefore . . . the question of
forming a communist party must be raised. I am not led by any kind of
revolutionary fervour in this instance. I do not think that we shall have power in our

---

[17] *Szociális Forradalom*, October 16, 1918. "Independent Hungary."
[18] *Ibid.* "The Disintegration of the Monarchy."

hands tomorrow, but I believe that the Hungarian proletariat will take over power. And we must be prepared for this. . ."[19]

The Hungarian, German, Romanian, South Slav, Czech and Slovak communists attending the conference turned "to the working people of Hungary" with an appeal. Delineating the existing revolutionary situation, and pointing out the opportunism of the SDP, they called on the workers, soldiers and poor peasantry to stage an armed insurrection and seize state power. "Sign the peace with your fellow workers on the opposite side, suffering in the trenches. Leave the trenches and the occupied areas and return home with your arms. Conclude the fraternal alliance of workers, which cannot be broken up by the aggressive war of the great powers of the world." The appeal also summed up the most pressing tasks in 10 points and it was there that the designation "Communist Association of Hungary" first appeared.[20]

PUBLIC MOOD IN EARLY OCTOBER

It is very difficult to describe the public mood in Hungary in early October. Retrospectively, it is hard to determine what and how much people had understood of the news depicting royal audiences, of the heavily censored reports on congresses, how many people had participated in passionate debates about the possibilities and tasks of the future and how many were able to get hold of the circulating illegal publications arriving from Russia.

When Ervin Szabó was buried on October 2, work stopped for 10 minutes at Csepel and in several industrial plants in Budapest.

On October 8, almost one hundred thousand workers in over seventy factories attended rallies presenting the SDP proclamation.

From the Press Committee's prohibiting order it is known that on October 10 there was a demonstration in front of the HQ of the National Party of Work, which ended with the breaking of the building's windows.

There were demonstrations and strikes in some of the provincial towns as well.

Numerous factors indicated an agitated and inflamed atmosphere; however, no large-scale action involving the whole of the country and the workers took place in the first half of October.

Amongst the bourgeoisie the feeling of panic was replaced by a temporary optimism following the publication of the peace proposal. After October 4 even the stock exchange seemed to relax for a while and rates began to rise again.

---

[19] *Sarló és Kalapács* (Sickle and Hammer), 1932. No. 4. Gy. Szamuely, "The Preparation of the Hungarian Communist Party."

[20] *Párttörténeti Közlemények* (Party History Bulletin), 2/1964, pp. 164–169. Gy. Milei, "The Hungarian Group of the Russian Communist Bolshevik Party for the Setting-up of the Hungarian Communist Party."

THE LAST SESSION OF THE NATIONAL ASSEMBLY

On October 16, Parliament convened to debate issues of domestic and foreign policy. Although there appeared to be a surface calm, the situation was already explosive.

The emergency session of Parliament was initiated by the Károlyi Party, immediately after news of the events on the Bulgarian front were received. However, the government and the parties supporting it—who regarded the circumstances as unfavourable—did not think it important to respond quickly to this demand.

After much wrangling, the days following the reappointment of the Wekerle government and the days preceeding the imperial proclamation finally seemed an appropriate time for the government to enter into a debate in Parliament.

In accordance with the old political routine, Wekerle believed the wisest tactic would be to give prominence to national demands in the given situation. He thought that this would take the wind out of the opposition's sails and thereby divert attention away from unresolved issues and increase the popularity of the King and the existing regime.

The fact that a similar manoeuvre in January 1918—following the announcement of a promise of an independent army—failed to produce the desired effect did not stop Wekerle. For in the course of the negotiations on the issuing of the Imperial Manifesto Wekerle had obtained the Emperor's approval to announce the personal union. Thus, he was able to produce a trump card, the old slogan of the independence parties, the promise of the abolition of common ministries between Austria and Hungary.

At the October 16 session Wekerle immediately rose to speak. He announced— referring to the Imperial Manifesto issued at the same time—that as Austria had been attempting to resolve its domestic affairs on a federal basis, it was inevitable that "we too, should adopt the stand of personal union". In the rest of his speech he promised individual rights to the nationalities and the revision of the Compromise of 1868 to the Croats. "Let us all unite not only in the proclamation of an independent Hungary, but also in its creation",[21] said Wekerle, in conclusion. Wekerle's policy of unleashing nationalist sentiment to provide an outlet for discontent and thus stem the tide of revolution closely resembled the policy which the Slav and Romanian bourgeoisie had applied successfully in the course of the emergence of the states which grew upon the ruins of the Monarchy. Whereas, however, in the neighbouring countries the representatives of this policy came mostly from the ranks of the opposition, in Hungary exactly the opposite happened. Politicians like Wekerle and his associates, who, at the last moment, tried to win public support with new, radical independence slogans, had already lost the confidence of the working class and the peasantry through their aggressiveness,

---

[21] *Képviselőházi napló* (Parliamentary Proceedings). XLI. pp. 275–276.

their policy of exploitation and non-fulfillment of promises. They were, justly, regarded as being among those responsible for the war.

Mihály Károlyi, who rose to speak after Wekerle, saw clearly not only the aim of the government's manoeuvre, but also its weakness. He rejected the Prime Minister's announcement on the grounds that those who had been staunch advocates of dualism yesterday should not declare personal union today. He reminded his audience that Wekerle had often made promises which he later failed to fulfill. He expressed his opposition to all procrastination. "We have lost the war", he said. "Now it is important that we ought not lose the peace." Károlyi presented a list of factors which he saw as necessary to achieve a good peace settlement: a new orientation in foreign policy (break with Germany, the adoption of a pacifist stand); a radical and democratic direction in domestic policy (universal and equal suffrage with secret ballot, democratic land policy); a new approach to the handling of the nationality issue "in order to protect Hungary's territorial integrity".[22]

During Károlyi's speech, the still bellicose right wing made an attempt to intimidate the opposition supporting him. When Károlyi said that "the day of reckoning has arrived", i.e. that the nation will take to task those responsible for what had happened, someone from the ranks of the National Party of Work interrupted: "This is Entente talk." Károlyi brushed this aside by replying "then give a German speech". Another leader of the party, Márton Lovászy was, however, not satisfied with this and interjected: "Take cognizance of the fact that we are Entente sympathizers!". Another Károlyi Party MP, János Vass, backed him up: "So are we!".[23] Following Lovászy's naive and overly candid interjection a huge storm erupted in the House. Derogatory remarks—"traitors, scoundrels",— and threats—"slap him in the face!"—were exchanged. The session was suspended for ten minutes though the pandemonium continued even during this interval.

Following this scene the right wing felt almost in control of the situation. When, in his interpellation, László Fényes—who supported Károlyi—talked about the fact that "the soldiers did not want to fight for German interests any longer", emotions, once again, flared up. Defence Minister Sándor Szurmay rejected this "slanderous accusation" with an air of superiority: "Our armed forces ... will carry out their duties faithfully to their sacred oath."[24]

Excitement which was generated by the Parliamentary debate was further increased when an attempt was made to assassinate István Tisza, who after leaving the session was about to sit in his car. The assassination attempt was organized by a group of revolutionary socialists who believed that the physical elimination of Tisza, who had embodied a warmongering policy, would spur the still inactive masses on to action: "It will provide the spark for the great and inevitable explosion". Although meticulously planned, the assassination attempt failed. At

---

[22] *Ibid.*, p. 280.
[23] *Ibid.*, p. 279.
[24] *Ibid.*, p. 289.

the decisive moment the weapon in young János Lékai's hand misfired. Notwithstanding, the attempt stirred up considerable excitement. The papers carried detailed reports, quoting what Lékai told Tisza following the assassination attempt and what he said later during police interrogation. ("I wanted to kill that man and together with him, the idea which was one of the main causes of the conflagration of the world... I'm terminally ill and my life's not worth much anyway.")[25]

It was after such precedents that István Tisza addressed the House on the following day, October 17. From Tisza's speech the National Party of Work expected guidelines and encouragement. The speech, however, failed to come up to these expectations. Although Tisza's voice was as calm and resolute as ever before, his sentences concise and to the point, the content of what he said was uncertain and held little hope for his supporters. Regarding the issue of a "personal union", Tisza not only endorsed Wekerle's stance, but went even further than the Prime Minister's statements—correcting and formulating them in a more resolute manner. "This personal union", he said, "must not be either just a playing with words, or a half measure".

Tisza then went on to say that the maintaining of the alliance with Germany was superfluous. He argued that "this alliance had been necessitated by the need to put up a defence against the aspirations of the aggressive and autocratic Russian Empire", now a past danger "because the Tsar's empire had collapsed in the war".

Due to the pressure of the events, Tisza changed his stance on the dual monarchy and the alliance with Germany. Regarding the national minority issue, however, he stated that there was no need for far-reaching changes as "we have never been the oppressors of the national minorities" and only "a tiny minority" in Hungary opposes "the fundamental idea of the nation state". Tisza also turned against demands urging the democratization of the country, the extension of suffrage. "We need not adopt the stand of democratization, since we already accomplished that a long time ago." It was what he said about the war that created the greatest stir. "I do not want to juggle with words. I recognize what representative Count Mihály Károlyi said yesterday, namely that we lost this war..."

This announcement caused havoc. Admittedly, Tisza only repeated what Károlyi had already said, but coming from a political leader who had always talked about a victorious peace up until then, advocating perseverence to the end, and who, as late as the end of September, had wanted to negotiate with the South Slavs from a position of strength, such a statement sounded quite different from the speech of an opposition politician who had, in any case, never made a secret of his views on the subject.

Realizing the excitement and amazement he stirred up, Tisza himself realized that he had perhaps said more than he should have. He immediately—and also in the course of a subsequent speech—tried to explain and justify his words. "We have lost it not in the sense that we were unable to continue to put up strong and heroic

---

[25] *Pesti Napló*, October 17, 1918. "Assassination Attempt on István Tisza."

3 Siklós András

resistence . . . we have lost it in the sense that . . . we have no hope of winning it . . . In my view, to conceal this serious truth would be just as wrong as to give it a panic-stricken and extreme interpretation such as it does not possess."[26]

However, no explanation could alter the facts. Tisza's announcement spread like fire and its impact was incalculable. It was then that the bourgeois and petite bourgeois strata came to realize that there was serious trouble and the unsuspecting were caught completely unawares by Tisza's statement.

Following Tisza's speech—on the same day—several others also expounded their views, though very little attention was paid to them. It was in front of half empty benches that MP János Benedek of the Independence (Bizony) Party delivered a lofty speech about the salvation of the nation, the preservation of the territorial integrity of this beautiful, one thousand year old country. In a low-key address, Sándor Giesswein spoke of how "both '67 and '48 were outdated concepts, that . . . the idea of the nation must be brought into closer contact with humanity's ideal that . . . so long as nations regard themselves as an end in themselves, this kind of tragedy will inevitably recur".[27] (Giesswein was the most prominent figure of the democratic wing of the christian socialists; by the end of the war he had established contact with Ervin Szabó.)

In reports published about the sessions of Parliament, the nationality issue and the stand adopted by the nationality parties was somewhat overshadowed by the battle between Tisza and Károlyi.

Early in October the movement and organization of the nationality parties seemed an issue of secondary importance. There was almost nothing about it in the papers and any reports that were published were incorrect and biassed. The national minority parties were represented in Parliament by 40 Serbo-Croatian, 4 Romanian and 2 Slovak MPs. The tiny number of Romanian and Slav MPs in Hungarian Parliament (which totalled 400 MPs) was sufficient to prove in itself that the national minority issue was—as opposed to Tisza's view—far from being resolved.

Although they were expected to attend, the Serbo-Croatian MPs stayed away, thereby letting the government know that they regarded their links with Hungary as terminated.

In the name of the Romanian National Party Sándor Vajda addressed Parliament. He announced that the Executive Committee of the Romanian National Party had held a meeting at Nagyvárad on October 12, at wich it adopted a proclamation. The proclamation, which he then proceeded to read out, demanded the right to self-determination for Romanians living in Hungary and Transylvania and questioned the right of the Hungarian government and Hungarian Parliament to speak in the name of the Romanian nation.

The Romanian National Assembly in Transylvania was to possess the sole right to represent Romanians in the future and until the national assembly convened the

[26] *Képviselőházi napló*, XLI. p. 292.
[27] *Képviselőházi napló*, XLI. p. 308.

Executive Committee of the Romanian National Party had the right to represent them.

Vajda disputed the palliative statements of Wekerle and Tisza, taking them to task for the grievances of the recent past: "The prisons were and still are full of nationalities". "Eight courts have been passing sentences for the past two years. . ." "Our schools are being closed down by the hundred."[28]

Although the declaration and the remarks accompanying them went quite far, they nonetheless carefully avoided the issue of secession and union with Romania. Vajda did not make any mention of the problems of social progress and democratic transformation either. In regard to these issues he expressed the stand that the nationality issue had to be resolved first "because it is only on a national basis and within the framework of the nation that social rectification can develop in a normal direction".[29]

In the name of the Slovak National Party Nándor Juriga expounded his stand a day later, on October 19. In the name of the "National Council of the Slovak People Living in Hungary", he read out a statement, which, like the Romanians, demanded the right to self-determination for the Slovaks. Juriga stated that the Slovak people wished to create their own state community on their settlement territory; that they did not recognize the right of the Hungarian Parliament and government to regard itself as the representative of the Slovak nation; he stressed that apart from the Slovak National Council no one had the right to negotiate in Slovak affairs.

In his long speech Juriga expounded that he had no confidence in the Károlyi party either; in regard to Hungary the Károlyi party, too, rejected the principles of federation which the Emperor's proclamation had already adopted in relation to Austria. Juriga stated that in regard to the national minority issue his opinion of the Károlyi party was no better than that of the National Party of Work. "It is six of one and half a dozen of the other, they only employ different tactics."[30]

In the course of their history the Slovak people had suffered equally from both the Kuruc and the Labanc. When either the Kuruc or the Labanc came to Trencsén County they kept asking the people whether their sentiments lay with the Kuruc or the Labanc. In the end they replied: "Don't ask us whether we are Kuruc or Labanc, just go ahead and beat us up, the poor have always been beaten up."[31]

At the same time Juriga praised the bourgeois radicals Oszkár Jászi and Lajos Biró; ". . . even amongst the Hungarians there are excellent intellects and warm hearts; however they are still not apparent. . ."[32]

When asked about the composition and the HQ of the Slovak National Council he had mentioned, Juriga gave an evasive reply. However, there could be no doubt that he, and not the Slovak members of the National Party of Work represented the views of the Slovak bourgeois leaders in this situation.

[28] *Ibid.*, p. 317.
[29] *Ibid.*, p. 353.
[30] *Ibid.*, p. 353.
[31] *Ibid.*, p. 354.
[32] *Ibid.*

3*

The last two days of the parliamentary session, October 22 and 23, were also marked by numerous speeches that created stirring and exciting scenes.

On October 22, Mihály Károlyi requested leave to speak again and urged peace, if necessary immediate separate peace. Speaking passionately, he declared: "the country is in a mood of repressed revolt". "We must act", he continued, then added that if the government failed to act "I will".[33]

Tisza in a lengthy defence tried to clarify his role in the outbreak of the war. He read out excerpts from hitherto unpublished documents to prove that the Monarchy did not want war and that, at least during the early stages, he personally was decidedly opposed to the idea. Tisza's reasoning, his attempt to avert responsibility, was not very convincing. He failed to supply an answer to the question of why he later changed his position. He had concealed the fact that other leaders in the Monarchy had supported the war from the very beginning. He failed to explain the impact of the German militarist position on the decision to start the war and to send an ultimatum to Serbia.

On October 23, Aladár Balla of the Károlyi party responded to Tisza's arguments. During his speech the excitement reached fever pitch. Balla had barely been through a few sentences when the slightly tipsy Zoltán Meskó (Independence Party MP, who later founded an Arrow-Cross Party during the Horthy period) interrupted: "Even now the Gotterhalte is being sung in Debrecen!"[34]

This was a reference to a visit on that same day to Debrecen by Charles IV, in connection with which an afternoon daily had reported that the military band played the Austrian national anthem when the King arrived.

The excitement had hardly died down (the incident was also denounced by House Speaker Károly Szász of the National Party of Work after the suspension and re-opening of the session), when Károlyi handed over a telegramme to the speaker: "We have just received this, read it out."[35] The telegramme contained news of the military insurrection in Fiume. Another storm erupted and the session had to be suspended once again.

During the lengthy interval the opposition MPs held an impromtu meeting in the vaulted hall after which the party leaders assembled for a conference in the Prime Minister's room. Gyula Andrássy, who had returned from negotiations in Switzerland the day before, also attended the meeting. Under the influence of the heated atmosphere Andrássy supported the view that the government should resign. Tisza also supported this proposal. He believed that, under these increasingly chaotic and hopeless circumstances, it would be better for the moderate opposition to take over the handling of the situation. He hoped that following the resignation of the government with his party's support the "left of centre" Andrássy–Apponyi duo would be able to seize the reins of power and would put an end to threats coming from the left. In order to enhance co-operation with

---

[33] *Ibid.*, p. 359., p. 362.

[34] *Ibid.*, p. 442.

[35] *Ibid.*, p. 446.

the moderate opposition Tisza, at this point, was willing to endorse the extension of suffrage.

As a result of these negotiations the Wekerle government resigned and this announcement also marked the end of the session of Parliament. However, before the Speaker could adjourn the meeting, opposition journalists gathered on the gallery to stage a demonstration against censorship, loudly cheering for the freedom of the press.

2. A VICTORIOUS REVOLUTION—THE HUNGARIAN REPUBLIC

THE FINAL DAYS

The government crisis which had erupted at the beginning of October and was only staved off but not resolved, renewed due to the resignation of the Wekerle government.

While in early October the National Party of Work and the moderate opposition had wrangled over political leadership, now, following the merger of the National Party of Work and the '48 and Constitution Party—as a result of which the former lost its leading position—the struggle for power was concentrated on Andrássy and Károlyi. In this new, cut-throat struggle Andrássy was in a better position because the King, following the advice of Prince Windischgraetz, had meanwhile appointed him common Foreign Minister. It followed from this appointment, which was effective as of October 24, that any government formed after the resolution of the crisis had to be endorsed by Andrássy, who, in this case, undertook the role of "chancellor".

The setting up of a government which would ensure a leading role for the moderate opposition parties was a difficult task. The candidates for the office of Prime Minister, above all, János Hadik, a good friend of Andrássy's, were reluctant to undertake a task which promised little hope of success. The substance of the difficulty lay in the fact that amid mounting tensions it seemed a hopeless undertaking to form a government with the exclusion of and against the opposition which rallied around Károlyi. At the same time it was also predictable that Mihály Károlyi would not take a subordinate role because of his rising popularity throughout the nation. Some SDP leaders—among them Ernő Garami—would have been willing to participate after having been persuaded by Andrássy and his supporters who spared neither time nor energy. However, they were reluctant to say yes, without an endorsement from Károlyi or against his wishes, as they were well aware that they could not make their agreement acceptable to the working class. The bourgeois radicals, too, opposed co-operation with Andrássy. They believed that the presence of nationalist politicians who had compromised during the war, in a new government would create an unfavourable situation in relation to the Entente and would eliminate any chance of co-operation with the national minority parties.

Thus, at the first go Andrássy's plan proved to be unsuccessful. On October 25, Andrássy travelled to Vienna without having formed the new government he had so eagerly pressed for. At the same time his efforts helped those whom he wanted to exclude from power to join forces and rapidly conclude efforts by the opposition parties to form an alliance.

On the eve of October 23, representatives of the Károlyi party, the bourgeois radicals and the SDP gathered for a meeting at the Károlyi Palace. Participants agreed that there being no other alternative: the three political parties had to form the Hungarian National Council. On October 25, when it became obvious (at least it seemed so on that evening) that for the time being Károlyi's appointment as Prime Minister was not to be expected, the National Council was officially formed.

The three political parties announced the forming of the National Council in a proclamation. This was published in full on October 26 in the Budapest dailies which, by that time, had completely disregarded censorship. Drawn up by Jászi and revised by Kunfi, the proclamation comprised a detailed political programme summed up in twelve points.

The goals formulated by the proclamation reiterated—sometimes in a less direct manner—the demands of the SDP's October 8 proclamation: the ousting of the government; the dissolution of the Lower House; universal suffrage with secret ballot; radical land and extensive social welfare reforms; the right to self-determination and "the fraternal federation of equal peoples"; territorial integrity based not on coercion, but on common sense and on common economic and geographical bonds. To the SDP programme the proclamation added some of the radical demands of the Károlyi party and the Radical Party. It also incorporated a number of new demands raised by more recent developments: complete independence for Hungary; the withdrawing of military units from Hungary; the repudiation of the German alliance; the invalidation of the treaties of Brest and Bucharest; an immediate cessation of hostilities; the delegation of democratic politicians to the peace conference; the forging of economic and political links with the neighbouring states; general amnesty for political prisoners; freedom of association and assembly and the abolition of censorship.

A few days after its formation the National Council set up specialized departments as well as a twenty-member Executive Committee presided over by Mihály Károlyi. A list of the Executive Committee members was published in the daily press on October 30. In the Executive Committee the Károlyi party was represented by Mihály Károlyi, Dezső Ábrahám, Tivadar Batthyány, János Hock, Zoltán Jánosi, Márton Lovászy, the SDP by Vilmos Böhm, Ernő Garami, Sándor Garbai, Zsigmond Kunfi, Jakab Weltner and the more or less outsider József Díner-Dénes; the bourgeois radicals by Lajos Biró, Oszkár Jászi, Lajos Purjesz and Pál Szende. Other council members were Mrs. Ernő Müller of the SDP women's committee, Róza Bédy-Schwimmer representing the feminists, Lajos Hatvany on behalf of the press and László Fényes as an independent.

By issuing its proclamation the National Council made a claim for power as a rival government. In its appeal it called upon "all foreign peoples and governments . . . to seek direct contact with the Hungarian National Council instead of the present government on every issue pertaining to Hungary".[36]

---

[36] *Pesti Napló,* October 26, 1918. "The National Council Has Been Set Up." For the list of Executive Committee members *cf. Pesti Napló,* October 30, 1918.

When the leaders of the National Council later wrote in their memoires that they "had not wanted revolution, but evolution", and that they regarded the National Council not so much as a revolutionary organ, but, rather, one designed to avert revolution, they obviously spoke the truth. Despite the intention of its leaders, the setting up of the National Council was in itself a revolutionary deed.

In the territories beyond the River Leitha, national councils comprising of the representatives of the *Reichsrat* functioned as legal national councils. Not only were these acknowledged by the Imperial Manifesto of October 16 but were in fact encouraged by it with a view to guiding and preparing the new statal communities and the new governments. In Hungary the situation was different. For many decades Hungary had possessed features of independence which the Imperial Manifesto was now promising to the newly liberated nationalities living in Austria. Hungary already had its own Parliament and its own government. Under the circumstances the Hungarian National Council did not possess a legal foundation and this was openly acknowledged in the press commentary accompanying the publication of the Manifesto on October 26: ". . . there exists no legislation which states the setting up of such a national council . . . the very existence of the national council is a law unto itself . . . if the Ukrainians, the Poles, the Czechs and the Slovenians may form their own national council on the basis of an imperial edict, then the Hungarian National Council must be set up on the basis of the will of the people".[37]

Within a short period of time the National Council became the rallying point for all those who wanted to break with the existing system. In addition to the moderate opposition this centre included—whether the leadership wanted it or not—those who insisted that the imminent transformation should be carried out at all cost, by force if necessary. The National Council served as an umbrella organization for revolutionary groups whose goals went far beyond anything the leadership had envisaged.

On October 26, on the day when the proclamation of the National Council was issued, the negotiations—already under way—on forming a new government continued at Gödöllő. According to contemporary memoires, on this day politicians marched to the King in ridiculously large numbers. Amongst them were representatives of the Christian Party with Károly Huszár at the helm, Vilmos Vázsonyi representing the democrats, István Nagyatádi Szabó and János Mayer of the Smallholders' Party and the independents led by Apponyi, representing every shade of the political spectrum. Oszkár Jászi represented the radicals and, for the very first time, SDP delegates Ernő Garami and Zsigmond Kunfi presented themselves before the King. Moreover, the Monarch also received Lehel Héderváry, MP for the Gödöllő district and resignedly he admitted everyone to his presence.

Prime Minister designate János Hadik was waiting in the antechamber; István

---

[37] *Pesti Napló*, October 26, 1918. "The Hungarian National Council Has Been Set Up."

Bárczy who was mayor of Budapest for a time also sat with him, as a substitute candidate for the post.

Late in the afternoon Mihály Károlyi appeared unexpectedly, following a hurried summons saying that the King would be willing to appoint a Károlyi government on the condition that a number of vital Cabinet posts would go to the moderates. During his audience with Károlyi it seemed for a moment that the Monarch, utterly confused by so much advice, would be able to come to a decision after all and resolve the crisis by appointing Károlyi as Prime Minister. "Ich hab mich entschlossen, Sie zu meinem ungarischen Ministerpräsidenten zu ernennen" (I have decided to appoint you as Hungary's Prime Minister),[38] announced the King finally in a tired voice. However his decision lasted only until he was called to the telephone. Speaking from Vienna, Gyula Andrássy was on the line and a conversation with him made the whole situation uncertain once more. During that night Károlyi and the King travelled to Vienna, to no avail. Yielding to resistance from Andrássy and others, the Monarch did not appoint Károlyi Prime Minister. Instead, he sent the Archduke Joseph to Budapest on October 27, to continue negotiations for the resolution of the crisis as *homo regius* (the representative of the king).

The eruption of the government's crisis and the fact that it kept dragging on gave impetus to the fledgeling mass movement.

On October 24, several hundred college students, among them many reserve officers on study leave, marched to the Károlyi Palace where Károlyi addressed them with words of encouragement and handed over a flag to the demonstrators.

The next day the students held a meeting in the Museum Gardens, where they marched in closed ranks to the Royal Castle to submit their demands to the King or the ministerial council. A police cordon gave way to demonstrators at the Chain Bridge and the military guard allowed them access to the Castle. However, in the Castle courtyard mounted police charged them and blows were dealt with the flat of the sword causing many injuries.

While the demonstration was taking place in Buda, the right wing student organizations marched to the Andrássy mansion on the bank of the Danube and listened to spokesmen from the moderate opposition. This was the first and last effort, after October 23 staged by the pro-Andrássy right wing.

During the evening in Parliament Square and later in front of the Károlyi party centre in Gizella Square initiative again passed into the hands of the left wing. Following the meeting in Parliament Square the leaders of the Galilei Circle proceeded, accompanied by a huge crowd, to the Anker Mews where they took over possession of the circle's closed premises. (The headquarters of the Galilei Circle had been shut down during the January 1918 strike.)

"The daily press proclaimed freedom of the press, the students proclaimed freedom of assembly and now the members of the Galilei Circle are proclaiming the

[38] *Károlyi 1923*, p. 454.

freedom of association",[39] proclaimed the young people who addressed an enthusiastic and applauding crowd from the balcony.

Later that night a students' council and a soldiers' council was formed to recruit and organize students and soldiers. Led by Airforce Captain Imre Csernyák, the Soldiers' Council was set up by reserve officers who had participated in the demonstration in the morning and several of whom had only recently returned from Russia where they had been prisoners of war. The formation of the Soldiers' Council was a significant event as the officers who rallied around it soon began to exert influence over the vast majority of military units stationed in Budapest.

Another important factor was that through Béla Szántó, who served as a reserve second-lieutenant at the Ministry of Defence at the time, the Soldiers' Council established contact with the left wing of the SDP, the revolutionary socialists and with the opposition shop stewards working in the factories. It was this fledging organization which later on, consciously prepared for revolution and hammered out a plan for an armed uprising, despite the disapproval of the National Council.

While the Soldiers' Council was still only in its embryonic stage, the government, in response to erroneous (or misunderstood) information to the effect that the outbreak of revolution could be expected that night, placed the armed forces concentrated in Budapest on the alert and appointed General Lukachich, who was known for his firmness, as Budapest's military commander, during the late hours of the 25th.

On Sunday, October 27 the National Council staged a rally in Parliament Square. Speakers at the rally, in which almost 100,000 people took part, outlined the demands of the National Council and called upon the crowd, who were cheering the republic, to keep calm and observe order.

Following the rally, in response to the announcement that Mihály Károlyi would arrive by the evening train from Vienna, a huge crowd occupied the vicinity of the Western Railway Station. Whilst Károlyi was received with a standing ovation, it was with the utmost difficulty that the police could whisk the Archduke Joseph, who arrived on the same train, away through a side entrance.

As Károlyi alighted from the train, he was greeted by a welcoming committee headed by Márton Lovászy, who said the following: "If you have not become Prime Minister due to the will of the King, we shall make you Prime Minister due to the will of the people."[40] It was very difficult to move ahead amid the enthusiastic crowd. When Károlyi finally managed to get into his car the demonstrators unharnessed his horses and drew the president of the National Council along the Teréz Boulevard.

In the afternoon of October 28 a huge crowd gathered in front of the Károlyi party's Gizella Square headquarters in response to a rumour that the representatives of the National Council were planning to make an important announcement. At first the speakers were able to keep the crowd at bay, later however,

---

[39] *Pesti Napló,* October 26, 1918. "The Galilei Circle Has Re-Opened."
[40] *Magyarország* (Hungary), October 29, 1918. "The Arrival of Count Mihály Károlyi."

sensing their growing impatience, they announced "Let's go to Buda". Following this proposal the leaders of the Károlyi party who were present at the rally, István Friedrich, Barna Buza, János Vass and László Fényes, decided to lead the procession of demonstrators to the Archduke Joseph in Buda and demand Károlyi's appointment as Prime Minister. The group of soldiers positioned at the mouths of the roads leading to the Chain Bridge allowed the demonstrators to pass, however, the armed police concentrated in front of the Chain Bridge blocked their way. The mounted police rode into the crowd and the gendarmes at the bridge-head fired into it.

The toll: 3 dead and several wounded. (The papers carried the names and occupation of 52 of the injured. 25 were workers, 10 were students, 5 were tradesmen, 4 were office workers, 7 were of other occupations and 1 was a Russian prisoner of war.)[41]

Following the bloody events of October 28, the so-called "Battle of Chain Bridge" brought the tension to a head. On the 29th workers staged a half hour protest strike and the National Council was flooded by applications for membership.

Two events that day underlined that the hours of the old order were numbered. First the news coming from an arms factory in Soroksári Street that during a protest strike the workers occupied the arms depot and took possession of rifles, pistols and ammunition. (A contemporary newspaper report mentions 5,000 arms. According to a later testimony by the Chief of Police, László Sándor in the Tisza-trial: "They took away 1,200 rifles and 500 revolvers.")[42]

When the armed police arrived on the scene, they were helpless and even the detectives sent out to investigate the case were unable to trace the missing weapons.

Another vital piece of news was that the police had joined the revolution. Poorly paid and inadequately supplied, the rank and file of the police force, who had reached exhaustion point from around the clock duty, staged a revolt on the 27th at the police barracks in Mosonyi Street. Police arriving from the meeting in Országház Square refused to carry out further orders and demanded the improvement of their situation. Although this incident was successfully settled, following the "Battle of Chain Bridge" the body of civil servants and the detective corps also joined the discontented. Fearing the consequences of the police discharge, the majority of police officers decided to join the National Council and tried to persuade the chief of police to accept their proposal. When their efforts failed, they sent their own delegation in the evening to the Hotel Astoria to announce their intention to join the National Council.

Meanwhile, following one and a half days of negotiations, the Archduke Joseph appointed János Hadik as Prime Minister. On the 29th Hadik had appeared in the

---

[41] *Az Est* (The Evening), October 30, 1918. "There are 3 dead and 55 injured following the Battle of Chain Bridge." *Az Est* reported on those who received first-aid from the ambulance.

[42] Testimony by Dr. László Sándor, former chief of police for the Budapest Hungarian Royal Police, at the trial of the murderers of Count István Tisza. *Cf. Batthyány*, p. 165.

evening hours at the premises of the People's Party, where the leaders of the
Apponyi and the Bizony group, the representatives of the People's Party, the
Democratic Party and the Smallholders' Party were holding a confidential meeting.

The bulletin containing the programme of the new government promised a great
deal: a speedy ceasefire and peace negotiations, the withdrawal of Hungarian
troops, complete independence for Hungary, universal suffrage with secret ballot,
radical land reform and a settlement with the national minorities.

At the same time Hadik sent a report on the situation to the Monarch in Vienna.
In it Hadik asked for the dismantling of common organs, and above all, the setting
up of an independent Hungarian Ministry of Defence under the present Minister of
Defence. In addition to the army, every joint unit stationed in Hungary as well as
every Hungarian military institution in Hungary and the Hungarian military
industry in its totality would belong under the authority of the independent
Ministry of Defence. The most important point of the proposal was that the
Archduke Joseph would be appointed commander in chief of the armed forces in
Hungary.[43]

News of the Archduke Joseph's appointment as commander in chief of the
independent Hungarian army was also reported by the press who quoted "well-
informed circles" adding that "the Parliament will elect the archduke as
Palatine".[44]

The National Council acknowledged Hadik's appointment and adopted a wait-
and-see attitude. On October 30 the left wing bourgeois press and *Népszava* wrote
that they would keep an eye on Hadik, who had appropriated the programme of the
National Council. The right wing press acknowledged this with satisfaction and
added that the National Council "had a right to do this".[45]

On October 30 the Social Democratic Party issued a manifesto to the workers
which ended with the following admonition: "everyone should get ready, but no
one should allow himself to be provoked".[46]

Unlike the National Council, which wished to continue with its policy of wait and
see, the Soldiers' Council and the leaders of the revolutionary left believed that
under these circumstances no more time could or should be wasted. Following the
"Battle of Chain Bridge" and considering that events had speeded up, they decided
to change their original plans according to which the date of the uprising was fixed
for November 4. The new decision called for an immediate armed insurrection on
the basis of earlier plans.

The substance of their plan was the following: two assault battalion were to
march to the city centre along Rákóczi Street and Üllői Street and on the way, to

---

[43] *KA. MKSM. 1918. 69–27/9.* Bericht Graf Hadiks über "den moralischen Zusammenbruch des
Hinterlandes". October 29, 1918. 16.00 hrs. The following note may be read on the last page of the
lengthy petition: "Laut Meldung des Flügeladjutanten S. M. Oberstleutnant Brugier seitens Seiner
Majestät an Graf Hadik telephonisch Ah. genehmigt."

[44] *Pester Lloyd,* Morgenblatt, October 30, 1918. "The Programme."

[45] *Alkotmány* (Constitution), October 31, 1918. "The Programme."

[46] *Magyar Hírlap* (Hungarian Daily), October 31, 1918. "Manifesto to the Workers."

persuade the soldiers of the Üllői Street Barracks to join the uprising. Machine gun units were to be positioned in front of the Astoria and on Oktogon Square. They were to take over the square HQ and the military command. They would occupy the public buildings, the main post office and telephone exchanges. Two monitors would advance along the Danube. A battery would point its guns on the city and a marine detachment was to capture the Parliament. Lukachich would be arrested and if necessary the government as well.

Early on the morning of the 30th, the plan by the Soldiers' Council and the revolutionary left was revealed to Károlyi by Imre Csernyák, president of the Soldiers' Council. Károlyi tried to talk Csernyák out of this plan, taking a firm stand against it.

THE VICTORY OF THE REVOLUTION

On October 30, the two opposing camps were positioned as follows: János Hadik, the Archduke Joseph's Prime Minister managed, after strenuous efforts, to put together a new government in which the members of the moderate opposition shared the ministerial portfolios and undersecretary of state posts. (The various trends of the People's Party were represented by Károly Huszár, István Rakovszky and Jenő Czettler, the independent groups supporting Hadik by János Benedek, Samu Bakonyi, and Nándor Urmánczy. Constitution Party member Lajos Návay also became a member of the new government and so did István Nagyatádi Szabó of the Smallholders' Party, Miksa Fenyő, director of the Confederation of Industrialists (GYOSZ) and Baron Lajos Kürthy, who was close to Tisza.)

Hadik had a big majority in Parliament, which under the given circumstances, was of little consequence as the new government could not count on the sympathy of the masses. Although at the last moment the right wing, which enjoyed the support of the Church, experimented with the setting up of a new mass organization called the "National Defence Federation", which was supposed to counter the National Council and which was ridiculed by the left wing press as a "pogrom council". However, this move was taken too late and the mass majority were unaware of its existence.

The force on which the "legal government" could rely was the army and the armed police who were concentrated in Budapest. Some sources put the strength of the military units in Budapest at 18,000, while others speak of a far greater number. To enforce law and order and to suppress possible riots there were 81 specially trained armed police companies and 37 machine-gun units.[47] The armed police also

---

[47] *Lukachich*, p. 64. In an article, Hogyan lettem forradalmár? (How I Became a Revolutionary?) written for a publication entitled *A diadalmas forradalom könyve* and in a later book entitled *Kell-e a katona* (Is a Soldier Needed?), p. 95., Linder puts the strength of the military stationed in Budapest at 80,000. A similar figure, "70–80,000 strong garrison" is quoted by L. Magyar: *A magyar forradalom* (The Hungarian Revolution, p. 222.). According to L. Bús Fekete: "there were eighteen thousand people at Lieutenant General Lukachich's disposal". (*Katona forradalmárok*, p. 34.)

lined up units which they considered highly reliable: they included a trainee regiment of would be junior officers and Bosnian battalions trained to obey all instructions without question.

In times of peace these forces would have easily suppressed any kind of revolutionary action. Following a four-year war, however, when the Monarchy was coming apart at the seams, the situation was quite different. Fed up with the endless hardships of war—inadequate accomodation and poor clothing—the rank and file soldiers became receptive to revolutionary ideas all the more so as they came into repeated contact with the population, moreover with its most discontented and most active section. Reserve officers, who were assigned for duty with the armed police in large numbers also developed a feeling of sympathy towards the National Council. The majority of active officers and the higher leadership were ready to take steps against the mass movements and, if necessary, to carry out orders to this effect. However, the great majority of commanders were of non-Hungarian nationality. Under different conditions the presence of officers who could not even speak Hungarian could have been distinctly advantageous for those in power. However, in October 1918 the German, Czech and South Slav field officers who were attached to the HQ of the city commander and to other military HQ were no longer interested in how they could prevent or suppress a revolution in Hungary, but, rather, in being able, as soon as possible, to return to their own homeland and ensure their future in the coming era.

It did not improve matters when, at the last moment, on October 26, General István Bogát, the military commander of Budapest and Colonel Karnitschnig, his chief of general staff, were relieved of their duties. It has already been mentioned that Bogát was replaced by Géza Lukachich, a young, rough general who became notorious, hated and feared for the death sentences he passed on deserters. However, the new commander found himself in an unknown area with which, owing to the rapid turn of events, he was unable to get properly acquainted.

Prospects of the new government further deteriorated due to the aforementioned behaviour of the police, the fact that the majority of police officers joined the National Council. Although on the 30th the chief of police tried to reverse the tide by issuing threats on the one hand and promising a pay rise and extra bonuses, on the other, his efforts bore little fruit. The fact that the police went over to the National Council was of great importance because the police were to have been the principal means of suppressing a possible uprising against the government. The fact that the police force ceased to function, that on the 30th police could not be seen in the streets except among the ranks of demonstrators, obviously influenced the behaviour of those military contingents and gendarmes brought to Budapest, who were the most fit to fight.

The constantly deteriorating situation of those in power and the isolation of the new government was indicative of both the growing power of the National Council and the sudden advance of the revolutionary forces rallying around it. On October 30, the overwhelming majority of the population rallied behind the National Council. The National Council was supported by the organized working class, part of which was waiting in arms for the signal. Comtemporary sources put the number of armed workers in Budapest at around 30,000.[48] Deserters also rallied for whom a change of regime was a matter of life and death. (According to the testimony of the Chief of Police László Sándor in the Tisza-trial the number of deserters was around 40–50,000.)[49] The Soldiers' Council set up the so-called counter-military police from the ranks of deserters who were partly organized by it.

The marines constituted an interesting factor within those forces preparing for revolution. The marines who were either on leave, deserted or brought to Budapest because they were unreliable, were lead by a Serb, Sándor Horvát (Horvatsanovics), who prior to this had taken part in the uprisings of Cattaro and Pécs. (When asked by the National Council whether or not the marines would be reliable since many were of foreign nationality, Horvát replied with self-assurance: "nationality is irrelevant to sailors—the main thing is that there should be an uprising".)[50]

On October 30, the telephone operators also joined the revolution—in response to a call from the National Council (led by Margit Rományi, there had been contact between the telephone exchanges and the left for some two years). The participation of the telephone operators meant that by being able to tap phone calls the National Council was, on the one hand, able to obtain knowledge about government plans and military commands in advance, and, on the other, it could, at the decisive moment, paralyse telephone contact between these organs.

According to contemporary sources, 80–90 companies of the garrison and the military contingents stood at the disposal of the Soldiers' Council on October 30.[51] Although it is possible that the Soldiers' Council's estimates of strength are exaggerated, the debate over it is purely academic. For it is beyond dispute that, under the circumstances described above—and with due consideration for the actions which could be expected of the working class, the benevolent neutrality of the armed forces which had not yet openly joined, and the joining of the police force—even a nominal number of companies would have been sufficient to trigger off and carry out an armed uprising.

In the morning of October 30 all appeared calm in the streets of Budapest. Work started as usual in the factories and impromptu meetings were held only during the lunch-break. At these meetings social democrat speakers spoke out against the "Wekerle–Tisza mafia" and proposed the forming of a workers' council. The

[48] *A diadalmas forradalom könyve*, p. 146.

[49] *Batthyány*, p. 162.

[50] The scene is described in: *A diadalmas forradalom könyve*, p. 192.; *Katona forradalmárok*, p. 26.; *Mrs. Mihály Károlyi*, p. 278.

[51] *Katona forradalmárok*, p. 78. According to L. Magyar they expected to rely on 40 companies. (*A magyar forradalom*, p. 9.). In his memoires T. Sztanykovszky writes that up until October 27 over half of the 1,800 strong armed police joined. (*A katonatanácsról*, p. 86.) István Kató considers the figure of 80–90 companies exaggerated. *Cf.* "Az 1918. évi magyar demokratikus forradalom előzményeinek és győzelmének néhány kérdése" (Some Questions Pertaining to the Events Prior to, and the Victory of the 1918 Hungarian Democratic Revolution". *Párttörténeti Közlemények*, 1/1956, p. 12.)

proposition adopted by those present pointed out that the workers "are ready for an all-out struggle", and would not rest until "they had achieved immediate peace, total democratic rule and self-determination and liberation of every oppressed nation and class".

The proposal to set up a workers' council constituted a concession on the part of the party leadership to the left wing. For the official social democratic stand, even at the October 13 party congress had been that such an organ would be superfluous because the party's body of shop-stewards was basically synonymous with a workers' council. Regarding the task of such a new organ the draft resolution and the commentary accompanying it confined itself to stating that the Workers' Council will serve to complement and co-ordinate existing organizations, it will be "the internal organizing link of the workers waging the struggle and as such it will function alongside the National Council". The draft proposal ordered the factory's body of shop-stewards to elect the members of the workers' council.[52]

Following the relative calm the scene livened up on the streets in the afternoon. There were demonstrating groups, handing out leaflets. One of these leaflets, which found its way into the barracks in the early morning, contained the message of the Soldiers' Council: "Soldiers! . . . The National Council releases you from your old oath. From now on you owe your allegiance to the National Council. . . The National Council orders you to join!"[53] On other leaflets, which came out of *Népszava*'s printing press in Hungarian and in German translation contained Zseni Várnai's inspiring poem *To My Soldier Son*. Enthusiastic officers toured the coffee houses and restaurants, calling on everyone to join the revolution. From the Hotel Astoria a modest procession set out in the direction of Rákóczi Street and by the time it reached Gizella Square via the Nagykörút (Great Boulevard) and Andrássy Street, it had grown into an overwhelming crowd. Here, in front of the Károlyi party's HQ soldiers, officers and marines gathered. The crowd also included the postmen who had joined the National Council, all in compact formation, in lines of four, like the police. (The police arrived from the Café Gresham, where they had held a meeting during the afternoon and formed, with the participation of several hundred policemen, the free organization of state police employees.) From Gizella Square shortly after nine o'clock the masses marched again to the Astoria under red-white-green and red flags, singing revolutionary songs. Armed soldiers on bicycles led the procession, they were followed by some eighty officers with drawn swords. The officers were followed by marines dressed in blue and over a thousand soldiers and masses of demonstrators. By this time, public transport had come to a halt on Museum Boulevard, the automobiles and trams became stuck amongst crowds numbering many thousands.

In Gizella Square and in front of the Hotel Astoria the leaders of the National Council strove to calm down the excited crowds, who were demanding immediate

---

[52] *Népszava*, October 31. "The Workers' Council Has Been Formed."

[53] *A katonatanácsról*, p. 89. The leaflet is published in facsimile by A. Siklós: *Az 1918–1919. évi magyarországi forradalmak*, p. 111.

action. Speakers tried to convince demonstrators that there was no need for violence and bloodshed. In any case, power would pass into the hands of the National Council in a day or two. When news arrived that the masses were about to set free the imprisoned soldiers they immediately announced that the soldiers had already been released from the Conti Street Division Court Jail. The officers, who had already removed their cap buttons, took the oath again and again. The masses applauded and cheered. Despite repeated warnings, no one dispersed. Rank-and-file soldiers and ordinary workers delivered speeches from the top of cars or lampposts to provoke action, to settle accounts and were given a far more favourable reception than the professional orators who appeared on the balcony.

During that night the Hotel Astoria was the centre of the revolution. Not only because on its first floor was situated the crowded premises of the National Council's Executive Committee and Bureau, but also because in the evening the representatives of the Soldiers' Council and the revolutionary left also moved their headquarters to the hotel.

It had already been reported to the National Council and the Soldiers' Council that the military command had received orders to remove certain unreliable troops from Budapest. Those concerned sought advice from the Soldiers' Council who suggested that they should refrain from open resistence for a day or two, however it offered help to the deserters and hid them. When, during the night, news arrived that two marching companies of the 32nd Infantry Brigade were waiting to depart at the Eastern Railway Station, Béla Szántó issued an order of insubordination. Szántó, who on this night took over the control of the uprising "as the commander in chief of the revolution", in a short speech delivered from the balcony of the Hotel Astoria, called upon the demonstrators to go to the railway station and stop the transportation of the marching companies. Some ten thousand people set off on Rákóczi Street, headed by Ottó Korvin and some Soldiers' Council officers—among them Árpád Korvinyi, who had returned from Russian captivity as a revolutionary. The meagre guard at the railway station did not even attempt to resist, and the soldiers even handed over their arms and joined the demonstrators, who forced their way through the locked gates and broke into the wagons containing arms and ammunition. The soldiers who had joined the uprising accompanied by armed civilians, began to make their way back. Part of the procession left the main body of demonstrators at the National Theatre and made its way down the Nagykörút, to the Üllői Street Barracks to call upon the soldiers stationed there to join the revolution and free the prisoners.

At this point the leaders of the National Council intervened and tried to alter the course of events and to halt the uprising. Upon receiving the news that the soldiers who had joined the uprising and the armed police lining up at Üllői Street could clash at any moment, the Károlyi party politicians: László Fényes, Márton Lovászy, Dezső Ábrahám, Jenő Landler, József Pogány and Imre Csernyák, president of the Soldiers' Council hurried to the scene. With great difficulties they persuaded the masses marching against the barracks to turn back. However they could not reverse the tide. While they prevented a clash in the Nagykörút, at the

Astoria the soldiers arriving at the scene attacked and occupied the headquarters of Budapest's Military Command, which was situated nearby. The guard put up no resistance and the battalion of military police standing in the courtyard joined the uprising. General Albert Várkonyi, the military commander of the town was taken prisoner and escorted to the Hotel Astoria.

Várkonyi's appearance amongst the members of the National Council not only caused surprise, but also stirred up anxiety when it became clear that the aged general, despite a friendly reception and much persuasion, was not willing to take the oath. Following the occupation of the City Command Béla Szántó issued orders to two platoons to seize the telephone exchanges. The occupation of the Teréz Telephone Exchange (in Nagymező Street) caused no problems as the guard joined the insurgents. The situation at the József Telephone Exchange (in Mária Terézia Square) was more difficult as the commander of the guard tried to force negotiations while secretly asking for reenforcements. However, all of this was of little consequence as from two in the morning the telephone operators put through calls only for the National Council and obeyed only their orders, regardless of the decision the guard would eventually make. At 2.30 a.m. the police officers who had joined the National Council occupied the police headquarters. At 4 a.m. the marines in line with their promise, were anchoring between Chain Bridge and the Elizabeth Bridge with two monitors. On Landler's orders the trains bound for Budapest were stopped lest the military command should order enforcements from the countryside. In the early morning the Soldiers' Council, following the arrival of a military police battalion sent troops to enforce the bridges and railway stations. Two platoons occupied the building of the Austro–Hungarian Bank. The guard of the main post office sent a request to the National Council for a commissioner to take over office.

Lukachich, Budapest's military commander stood helpless while the insurrection successfully progressed. During the afternoon the contingents of the trainee regiment sealed off the building of the school in Reáltanoda Street and captured the deserters gathering there. When, however, during the same evening a colonel began demanding identity papers in the Astoria, the military police who should have enforced this action deserted their commander. The colonel and the few soldiers who remained loyal to him looked on helplessly as those arrested were freed in the street.

When, at 1.30 a.m. the occupation of the City Command was reported, Lukachich issued an order to the Bosnian soldiers on the alert at the Károly Barracks in Falk Miksa (today Néphadsereg) Street that two companies should set off for the City Command immediately and recapture it. When they encountered resistance, the Bosnian unit said that they had been fired on from the Lobkowitz Barracks adjacent to the City Command and refused to obey orders. Breaking up into smaller groups they returned to their own barracks.

From 2 a.m. onwards Lukachich could only operate through delegates and messengers. At 2.30 he gave an order to General Károly Hodula, who served at headquarters, to take ten companies—two from the Sapper Barracks and eight from the Károly Barracks—and attack and recapture the City Command and the József Telephone Exchange. Lukachich sent news of this, via a messenger, to the contingents of the trainee regiment, pointing out that he would send further orders in regard to the timing of the coordinated attack. General Hodula did not obey his orders because those contingents allocated, simply refused to carry out the task set for them. Lieutenant Colonel Aladár Szepessy, the commander of the trainee regiment having waited in vain for the promised signal went over personally to Buda Castle in the morning to report that the outcome of an attack would be doubtful since his soldiers were unreliable.

By this time the Archduke Joseph had already been reviewing his position—he was negotiating with Károlyi over the phone—Lukachich received orders in the early hours of the morning to hold out. At this point the Buda side and the Castle vicinity was still under his supervision, several barracks had not yet joined the insurrectionists and the Ministry of Defence in Vienna had sent a promise of immediate help. Only, would anything ever come of these promises?

An important momentum in this situation was that in the small hours *Népszava*'s printing press began to print leaflets—at the suggestion of a young journalist, János Gyetvai. "The revolution is on!"—thus began this famous appeal, which, outlining the events of the night, called upon the workers to join the revolution. "Workers! Comrades! Now it is your turn! No doubt the counter-revolution will attempt to regain power. Stop work! To the streets!"[54]

In the early morning hours leaflets were taken to the factories by volunteers.

Work did not start on October 31; the workers, singing revolutionary songs, marched to the centre of the city.

While the streets came to life the armed contingents of the revolution forced their way into the closed barracks to persuade thousands more soldiers to join the revolution.

At around seven in the morning Károlyi, in response to a request from the Archduke Joseph, arrived at the archduke's palace accompanied by Jászi and Kunfi. Hadik announced his resignation and the archduke informed those present that he had been authorized by the King to appoint Károlyi as Prime Minister and to ask him to form a new government. Both Károlyi and Kunfi promised to guarantee law and order provided that Lukachich would not resist further and would order his soldiers to return to their barracks.

During the morning the National Council's Executive Committee moved its HQ to the Town Hall. On Károlyi's return it was there that the new government was formed after brief consultations.

In the new Cabinet the Independence and '48 Party was represented, in addition to Mihály Károlyi, by Tivadar Batthyány, Márton Lovászy and Barna Buza, the

---

[54] *PI Archives*, Pamphlet and Leaflet Collection/II, 11/1918/X/4254. The leaflet is published in facsimile in: A. Siklós: *Az 1918–1919. évi magyarországi forradalmak*, p. 111. The appeal was probably worded by Jakab Weltner, deputy editor-in-chief of *Népszava* and as he put it, "unknown to the party leadership". (*Weltner*, p. 57.).

social democrats by Ernő Garami and Zsigmond Kunfi, the bourgeois radicals by Oszkár Jászi and, as Undersecretary of State, by Pál Szende. The three independent members were: Béla Linder (Minister of Defence), Ferenc Nagy (Minister of Food) and Dénes Berinkey (Minister of Justice, as of November 4).

The members of the Cabinet took the oath in front of Archduke Joseph. Following this the first Cabinet meeting was held in Buda Castle at the Prime Minister's office. Károlyi summed up his programme in the following points: The enactment of legislation for independence. Suffrage (in local government and villages as well). Immediate amnesty for soldiers and civilians. Immediate release for the foreign internes. Freedom of the press. Common jury. Freedom of assembly and association. Decisions about war and peace are to be the right of the National Assembly. The setting up of a Ministry for Labour and Welfare. Radical land policy to distribute land amongst the masses. Immediate appointment of a Hungarian Foreign Minister, the commissioning of the Prime Minister to head the Hungarian Foreign Ministry. To prepare for legislation to set up an independent Hungarian Foreign Ministry. The publication of a codus that could be used at any time for the dissolution of parliament. Károlyi also added that "considering the present overexcited atmosphere and the general pro-republic mood, the incorporation of personal union into the government's programme could be dangerous"; however, "we declare to His Majesty that His Majesty is our King and we do not object to his being the Monarch of other countries as well, but only if this does not interfere with Hungary's full independence..."[55]

On the 31st, the victory of the revolution was celebrated with a show of ecstatic joy in the streets. On the main roads military trucks, requisitioned automobiles and wagon carts rolled by, crowded with soldiers and civilians cheering the revolution and firing into the air. Not only did they remove their cap-buttons, but they also cut off the officers' insignia of rank. Torn-off rosettes were replaced by frostflowers or bands in the national colours. Tram traffic stopped, the shops remained closed, as did the restaurants and offices. Armed soldiers appeared in front of the prisons and jails and, in accordance with the order issued by the National Council, freed political prisoners.

At the same time alarming news, which later turned out to be partially true, arrived that the stocks of the military depots were being taken away, that railway stations were being attacked and that wagons full of goods were being forced open. The armed police and the police tried to intervene, but "the restoration of law and order" claimed several victims.

During the afternoon armed soldiers appeared in István Tisza's villa in Hermina Street. They dismissed the gendarmes ordered to guard the villa and shot Tisza dead after a brief verbal exchange.

In the wake of the Budapest events, violent protests erupted in the afternoon and evening hours of the 31st in some of the provincial towns, where the public mood

---

[55]OL K 27. Minisztertanácsi jegyzőkönyvek (Cabinet Minutes), October 31, 1918.

had already been highly excited. Workers staged strikes, workers, students and citizens marched in the streets, cheering the National Council.

News of the revolution had been brought by soldiers arriving from Budapest. Soldiers from contingents travelling on trains passing through Hungary to and from the front rapidly joined in, the revolution spread at the rate in which the wagons crowded with soldiers firing into the air arrived at the railway stations. Together with much of the population, the soldiers forced open the freight cars laden with goods and equipment and took away the stocks from the military depots. The gendarmerie was helpless. Reactionary officials, mayors and chiefs of police fled the public wrath not even waiting to be dismissed.

Terrified, the local governments quickly declared their allegiance to the National Council, local organs of which were being formed everywhere.

From the cities, the revolution spread to the villages. Wherever possible the village poor conducted an onslaught on the mansions of the landed landowners, broke into granaries and drove away livestock. In many areas rural merchants and caterers who had become rich in the course of the war were also robbed. Notaries, district administrators and indeed parish priests who had abused their power during the war were driven away. Often even parsonages were wrecked. These peasant actions spread throughout the whole country; they were extremely violent on the Great Plain and even more so in nationality areas.

On November 1 a rally in Tisza Kálmán Square demanded an immediate proclamation of the republic and several large factories adopted resolutions to this effect, too.

Upon receiving the alarming news from Budapest and, even more so, from the countryside, the Cabinet meeting, which was held in the morning, came to the following decision: "Gauging the republican movement, the disconsolate state of the country and the excited public mood", it requested its release from the oath taken the day before. At the same time it announced its resignation in case its request was not granted.

Following a certain amount of wrangling—and several excited phone conversations—the King "did not accept the resignation"; however, he "released the government from the oath and its consequences".[56]

The members of the Cabinet took new oaths, this time to János Hock, who took over the presidential post of the council from Károlyi. In regard to the constitutional form, the Cabinet adopted the position that within the following six weeks a legislative assembly would decide and that this legislative assembly should be elected on the basis of universal suffrage with secret ballot.

On November 1 the government made another important decision: it empowered the Minister of Defence to order an immediate cessation of hostilities. Linder made the government's decision known to the public via a proclamation and, during the same night, he passed the relevant decree to the commander-in-chief and to the various army group commanders.

[56] *OL K 27. Cabinet Minutes,* November 1, 1918

The aim of the capitulation order, which was later—though not then—strongly criticized by the counter-revolution, was to persuade a still reluctant supreme command to negotiate a cease-fire immediately. The government believed that the cessation of further hostilities, of the senseless shedding of blood was the most important precondition to attain calm and to tone down violent passions.[57] At the same time the capitulation order also served more distant goals: to prevent soldiers returning home from the war armed, "from totally upsetting the internal order" which had already been shaken, and thereby channel the revolution in an undesirable direction. Another consideration was to prevent the turning of certain contingents under the leadership of officers with counter-revolutionary sentiments against the government. Finally, the government believed that the immediate declaration of the desire for peace and the break with the war policy would internationally be to Hungary's advantage.

The supreme command did not obey the order to call upon the Hungarian troops to capitulate. However, the issuing of the order and Linder's constant pressing helped to convince the AOK – which had also been forced by the German–Austrian government to act similarly, because they were afraid of the consequences of the total disintegration of the front and of that that the armed soldiers returning home were no longer under their control,—to issue, twenty-four hours later, an order to cease all hostilities. This order, however covered the whole army, not only Hungarian troops.

By withdrawing the oath to the King and by taking a new oath the government gave up its previous stand, which held that personal union with Austria was necessary. Its new stand: a complete break with Austria.

The victory of the revolution and the resolution outlined above finalized the dissolution and collapse of the Monarchy, hopes attached to the survival of the House of Habsburg and dynasty expired.

THE FIRST DAYS OF THE REVOLUTION

The highly important events of October 1918 took place in Hungary relatively peacefully, just as in other areas beyond the River Leitha. For reasons similar to those in Austria, the old order refrained from entering into armed conflicts in Hungary.

At the same time, as the result of a more complex situation, and of the privileged position of the country, the *ancien régime* was more powerful and more resistent on this side of the Leitha than in the other half of the empire. In Hungary the anti-secession and pro-Monarchy forces were stronger (despite the advocation of

---

[57] "Raging tempers, which were at exploding point, had to be vented. There was no alternative but to capitulate, everywhere, immediately, at home and at the fronts." (Linder, *cf. A diadalmas forradalom könyve*, p. 14.)

independence and the appeal of its slogans) than in the Austrian provinces which had not possessed even the minimum requisites of independent statehood. Partly for this reason the turning point in Budapest came later than in Cracow, Prague, Zagreb or, say, in Vienna where there had been strong hopes for an *Anschluss*. It was primarily due to this that the Hungarian National Council did not so much fight for the country's independence, but rather as a result of a process affecting the whole of the Monarchy, Hungary received it as a gift. Thus, the final break with Austria was not the intention or even part of the programme of the Hungarian National Council, it was indeed contrary to its own goals and was declared only under pressure from external events.

Though somewhat belated, the social content of the Hungarian revolution was not of less value than the events which took place in Bohemia, Austria or the South Slav regions. While the first people's law issued in Prague on October 28 and the provisional constitution adopted in Vienna on October 30 stressed that the laws and decrees of the Monarchy would remain in force until further notice, and the new Southern Slav state had not declared itself a republic, the Hungarian National Council had, from the very beginning, advocated extensive reforms. The "people's government" which was later formed from the political parties of the National Councils began—in its own way—to realize these reforms.

Historians have still not come to an agreement on the issue of whether there had been a revolution at all in German Austria. Regarding Hungary the generally accepted view is that a bourgeois democratic revolution took place in the autumn of 1918. This revolution was bourgeois in the sense that power passed into the hands of the liberal bourgeoisie who had struck an alliance with the Social Democratic Party. Despite their promises of extensive reforms, the new possessors of power did not wish to go beyond the framework of the eighteenth and nineteenth century bourgeois revolutions. The coalition government which was formed as a result of the victory of the revolution did not wish to topple the bourgeois order. On the contrary, by eliminating the remnants of feudalism, it wished to create a bourgeois Hungary to strengthen capitalism via reforms.

Regarding the issue of the driving force behind the Hungarian revolution, contemporary analyses reveal that some people ascribe prominence to the bourgeoisie and within it to the progressive bourgeoisie. Others attribute greater significance to the joint struggle of the bourgeoisie and the working class. Still others, and this is the most widely held view, emphasize the role of the army with the openly declared intention of thereby accentuating the bourgeois character of the revolution.

Perhaps the right approach to the issue is to regard the popular character of the revolution as its principal distinctive feature. The fact that, despite the bourgeois character of the revolution the actual driving force behind the events was not the bourgeoisie, but, rather the working class and the other strata and classes which joined it must also be taken into account. Credit must go to the workers and the soldiers for the victory of the revolution in Budapest. Their success was complemented by rural mass movements and the actions of the peasantry.

Some may argue that during the night of the revolution it was not the workers, but the soldiers, the contingents of the Budapest Garrison which finally determined the course of events, the general strike of workers came only afterwards. However, it must be taken into consideration that the majority of the soldiers themselves were workers and peasants, the contingents which joined the revolution were directed in the crucial hours by the left wing opposition of the SDP.

Indicative of the distinctively democratic and popular character of the revolution was that following its victory various popular organs—workers' councils, soldiers' councils and people's councils—mushroomed throughout the country with amazing speed. These organs emerged as independent political factors alongside the bourgeois democratic government brought to power by the revolution, and they potentially represented a truly popular worker–peasant power.

The spontaneous revolutionary intentions of the popular organs engendered by the popular movements ran counter to the ideas of the government. Their goals went beyond the aims of central power and accordingly, encountered resistance from it. All those who advocated power to the proletariat and wanted to emulate the example of the Russian working class became confronted with a new government which intended to protect and strengthen the bourgeois order.

Under these circumstances, the first days of the revolution were characterized by two tendencies which were to determine the course of events in the future. First, the excitement it aroused and the formation of independent popular organs. Second, in reaction to this, efforts by the government and remnants of the old apparatus to suppress the surging masses, to divest the popular organs of their power and to subordinate them.

As early as October 31 the government and the organs supporting it had called on the workers to take up work, on the soldiers to return to their barracks, and on the population to respect private property. They claimed that victory had been complete and that "we have attained everything we had wanted to".[58] On November 1, at the Town Hall meeting which was to endorse the government's stand regarding the constitutional form, Zsigmond Kunfi, representing the SDP, delivered a passionate speech which he concluded by saying that until the final decision was made "for six weeks we do not wish to resort to class struggle and class hatred".[59] On November 1 and 2 several appeals were issued calling for the surrender of arms in "unauthorized hands". In a speech, also delivered on November 2 (in front of the officers of the Budapest Garrison), the new Minister of Defence Béla Linder, made the following—often quoted—statement: "There is no longer need for an army! I do not wish to see soldiers ever again!"[60] This statement not only reflected a general pacifist mood, but also the intention to uphold domestic law and order.

---

[58] *A diadalmas forradalom könyve*, p. 198.
[59] *Népszava*, November 2, 1918. "Comrade Kunfi's Speech."
[60] *Pesti Hírlap*, November 3, 1918. "The Officers of the Budapest Garrison Take the Oath."

Following the signing (on November 3) of the Armistice of Padua, a whole series of measures were introduced to rapidly demobilize the soldiers returning home from the war. The homecomers were awaited by welcoming committees complete with orchestras and explanatory speeches at the border. On the railway stations hot meals were prepared and the Minister of Food launched a charity campaign. (To support the demobilized soldiers Simon Krausz, the director-general of the Hungarian Bank offered a sum of 300,000 crowns; Leó Lánczy, president of the Commercial Bank, 150,000 crowns; Count Ágoston Zichy, landowner, 50,000 crowns; Adolf Ullmann, director-general of the Credit Bank, 100,000; Manfréd Weisz, owner of the Csepel Ammunitions Factory, 500,000 crowns.)

A decree issued by the Minister of Defence on November 4 prohibited the searching of soldiers' baggage; however it did provide for the confiscation of arms and ammunition. The Budapest police decided to stop the trains carrying returning soldiers outside the capital and to confiscate their arms there. Only those disarmed soldiers were allowed to enter Budapest who could prove that they were local residents.

Simultaneously with the demobilization of the "unauthorized" and the soldiers returning from the war, the authorities in charge of maintaining law and order were organized and strengthened. The government mobilized what had been left of the special police force. On November 2, the Ministry of the Interior ordered the making up through recruitment, of the ranks of the gendarmerie and allocated one million crowns for this purpose. On November 4, the police received a 50% pay rise and provisions were made to raise the police force by 1,500. A recruiting drive was launched for the frontier and military police.

The disintegrated organs of the police force which had belonged to the old order were hated by the people and were thus unsuitable for "restoring law and order". Therefore the Ministry of the Interior and the Ministry of Defence regarded the setting up of new police authorities as a necessary step.

These were: the *people's guard,* which was set up jointly by the SDP and the trade unions and comprised of workers and volunteers who carried out their duties after working hours, without uniform or extra payment. The *national guard* also comprised volunteers; however, its members were paid a high daily allowance. The *defence guard* was recruited from re-enlisted non-commissioned officers and officers and in addition to their wages the members received extra pay. The *railway militia* was organized to protect the railway stations and railway traffic. Not only did the railway militiamen receive provision and high pay, they were also promised land or a job following the cessation of their duties. In addition to those already mentioned several other short-lived guards were formed amid the confusion of the first days: the civic guard, voluntary garrison, student guard, house guard, factory guard, etc.

Wherever they had adequate armed forces at their disposal, the authorities ruthlessly suppressed popular movements, especially in the national minority areas where their activities often turned into bloody reprisals.

In early November the government was reluctant to declare summary jurisdiction. The ministers concerned generally rejected the numerous requests for it and wherever certain local organs ordered it in spite of the situation they made remonstrations. At the same time they not only permitted, but also prescribed drastic measures. The Minister of Defence declared that the national government's fundamental concern was the "patriotic duty" of the soldiers of the Budapest Police Command, "to maintain law and order, personal safety and private property by any means wherever necessary".[61]

There are no exact and nationwide figures as to the total number of victims of the "restoration of law and order" during the first weeks of November. However an idea of the extent of retaliation against the mass movements of November (which primarily affected the peasantry) and indirectly, of the extent and influence of these movements may be formed from reports in the contemporary press and reports compiled by public prosecutors and local authorities.

According to Jenő Hamburger, government commissioner for Nagykanizsa, in the Muraköz Lord Lieutenant Géza Bosnyák ordered the hanging of 173 Croat peasants in a single month. (The cabinet minutes dealing with the case mention 134 cases, while other reports put the number of victims far higher.) In the Bánát region the contingents of the national guard shot dead 68 "looters" on November 7 in the villages of Kula, Melence and Törökbecse. According to the reports of the Bihar County national guard 40–50 people were arrested daily up until November 10. During the suppressing of the popular movement 90 people lost their lives and in some cases even guns were used against the rebels. In Facsád, in Krassó-Szörény County, an aeroplane which took off from Lugos dropped several bombs on the Romanian peasants who had forced their way into the village; 104 people were killed. Transylvanian landowner Nándor Urmánczy, an Independence Party MP, sent armed police from Budapest to protect the family's large estates. According to the report of the deputies of the Hungarian and Romanian National Council in Kolozsvár the national guardsmen arriving at Bánffyhunyad, were accomodated in the Urmánczy castle and shot 40 people dead in Jósikafalva, Kolozs County and other neighbouring villages and burned some of the corpses at the stake. Owing to negotiations then underway with the Romanian National Council, the radicals and the social democrats strongly condemned the incident, Urmánczy published a statement in the press on November 15. In this statement he tried to justify the use of arms and with the incredibly provocative sentence concluded that "law and order cannot be restored by scholarly theories, orations and posters".

In Eperjes the soldiers of the 67th Infantry Regiment mutinied on November 1. Over one hundred rebel soldiers and civilians were condemned to death under summary jurisdiction. According to some sources 34 of them were shot dead by the wall of Eperjes Cathedral. Other sources put their number at 43. In Munkács a special contingent armed with machine guns fought against the peasants who demanded land from Count Schönborn on November 3. The shooting in the market square claimed 7 dead and countless injured. In the village of Galgócz, Nyitra County, 27 people were taken to the military prison in Nyitra because of the

[61] *Schönwald*, p. 348.

pillaging which occurred on November 2. In Látrány, Somogy County, 150 people were—according to a contemporary report—"savagely beaten to death and slapped" for similar reasons. In Adony, Fejér County, a military upholder of order contingent under the command of a lieutenant declared a state of emergency on November 10, undertaking arrests, condemning 6 soldiers to be shot and one woman to be hanged and carried out the sentences. According to a report by the public prosecutor in the town of Miskolc 200 people were escorted to the public prosecutor's jail. Also according to the public prosecutor's report, between 440–460 people were arrested and escorted to Nyíregyháza prison up to November 26. A later report by the president of the Nyíregyháza law-court mentions 1000 arrests and 75 dead in connection with the peasant movements of November.

As early as November 1, a decision was made to shut down the National Council Bureau. Previously, following the victory of the revolution, the Bureau had effected appointments and issued decrees and orders. An agreement between the government and the National Council Executive Committee, which was made public on November 3, announced that the National Council would function only as a monitoring body in the future, that executive and governing power fell to the government, since its members took the oath for the National Council on November 1. Following this decision the National Council Bureau continued its activities for a few days, but only because its customers refused to accept the fact that they had to take their requests and problems once again to the all too familiar organs of public administration.

Following the Austrian example, the SDP leadership was quick to establish a firm grip over the organizing of the workers' councils, as early as October 30, primarily to prevent them being set up without approval from or despite the wishes of the SDP leadership. Following the victory of the revolution the Budapest Workers' Council was officially formed on November 2. The statutory meeting, which was held in the general assembly chamber of the new Town Hall, was attended primarily by party and trade union officials. It was here that the president and vice president of the council were elected. The right wing Mór Preusz was elected president and János Vanczák who was also on the right was elected vice president. Indicative of the fact that the party leadership regarded the Workers' Council as no more than an extended executive committee was that the statutory meeting dealt with among other things, issues and announcements such as who was to be *Népszava*'s new editor. Could Garami and Kunfi accept a ministerial portfolio and if so could such an appointment be reconciled with their membership of the party leadership?

Following the first meeting of the Workers' Council (the next meeting took place on November 13) the organization statute of the Budapest Workers' Council was published in the November 5 issue of *Népszava*. Drawn up by the party leadership, the trade union council and the party executive committee, the organization statute was valid for the rural workers' councils as well. According to the statute 126 members of the Budapest Workers' Council were not elected but delegated. The members of the executive committee, of the Trade Union council aud of the party executive committee automatically became delegated members of the Workers'

Council. A host of party organs and institutions possessed the right to delegate members, as well as the leaders of the free trade unions. Non-delegated members were elected on the basis of the trade union membership, with central trade union supervision; factory workers accounted for at least three-quarters of the members. The Central Executive Committee of the Workers' Council comprised of 126 delegated members.

The Minister of Defence wanted to disband the Soldiers' Council while the Minister of the Interior proposed the arrest of some of its leaders. At the November 4 Cabinet meeting Linder argued that "the enforcement of law and order can be ensured without the Soldiers' Council, by spreading pacifist propaganda amongst the soldiers... The soldiers must be sent home and a national guard must be organized. If there is no army there is no need for a soldiers' council." Neither Kunfi, nor Károlyi accepted this reasoning and rejected the proposal for disbanding the Soldiers' Council. Instead, they suggested its transformation. Kunfi advocated a soldiers' council "composed of honorable elements", involved in "educating, teaching and the democratic organization of work" in the army. Károlyi took the stand that "the soldiers' councils must be given pedagogical, literary and debating-society functions".[62]

At Kunfi's suggestion and due to the ideas he expounded József Pogány was appointed government commissioner to the soldiers' councils on November 1. Pogány, who up to then had handled the affairs of the army in the National Council Bureau, belonged to the SDP's left wing and as such his appointment served to win over the left wing and put its mind at rest. Supported by the Ministry of Defence, Pogány set up a new Soldiers' Council, which was formed as the soldiers' council of the Budapest Garrison on November 3. Its organizational structure followed the trade union pattern. Every military contingent and institution elected stewards: in each battalion the officers elected one, the rank and file four stewards. The statutory meeting, held in the old Lower House was attended by these elected stewards, nearly twelve hundred in all.

After the formation of the Workers' Council and the Soldiers' Council a new agreement was hammered out on the relationship between the government and the councils, which was published in the press on November 5. Under the new agreement it was declared that not only the National Council, but the Workers' Council and the Soldiers' Council as well "were the supervisory and propaganda organs of the government and not governing bodies invested with powers of management".[63]

Under the agreement the SDP leadership strove to separate the workers' councils from the soldiers' councils and the municipal councils from the rural councils. The Budapest Workers' Council declared that the central representative of the councils was none other than the executive committee of the party leadership and the party

---

[62] *OL Cabinet Minutes*, November 4, 1918.
[63] *Népszava*, November 5, 1918. "Executive Power is in the Government's Hand."

committee hindered the establishment of the national organization of the common body of the councils.

The repression of the mass movement and the restriction of the councils was a success. However, the violence which evoked anger and wrangles, which conflicted with the public mood, did not mean that the liberated revolutionary force was totally broken, still less annihilated.

Despite orders, persuasion and surveillance, several soldiers refused to hand back their weapons, but took them home. The temporarily repressed mass movement soon flared anew in the towns and villages. The armed police proved to be weak and unreliable and the people's guard, who wore a red arm band, gradually drifted to the left. In spite of restrictions the councils survived and especially in the provinces, continued to interfere in the activity of the public administration authorities. Despite its composition and subordinated position, the Budapest Workers' Council remained a highly respected institution, withstanding the pressures of a revolutionary atmosphere and its position was one to be reckoned with. Moreover, it soon became clear that the Soldiers' Council considered the fight against counter-revolution as its principal task rather than teaching and educating. The popular organs enjoyed great respect whereas the old apparatus of public administration was inert and unable to keep abreast with contemporary developments.

Nationally, the balance of power revealed the picture of an inconclusive struggle between old and new, between the bourgeois and popular revolutionary forces. Although the bourgeoisie was in power, it could not act as it had wished to. On the other hand, the working class was not in power, but in many instances it was able to assert its demands through the arms it possessed, via the help of the popular organs and the pressure of the masses on the government.

It was merely the effect rather than the cause of this situation which was manifested in the fact that a considerable degree of uncertainty characterized in almost every respect, the policy of the "popular government", which was walking the tightrope of class struggle. It issued orders of coercion against the mass movements, but at the same time condemned violence. It wished to get rid of the popular organs, but also required support from the councils. "Regardless of the problem, it contradicts itself. You never can tell what it could be capable of, for the forces in it tie each other down. Nothing is certain and this is the only thing the government is clearly aware of."[64] This was how contemporary criticism—not unjustifiably—assessed the early activities of the coalition government.

THE PROCLAMATION OF THE REPUBLIC

Regarding the issue of the constitutional form the coalition government claimed a position of legal continuity on October 31. Then very quickly, within twenty-four hours, it abandoned this stand. The release from the oath to the King and the taking

[64] *Szabadgondolat* (Free Thought), December 25, 1918. Z. Rudas, "The Hungarian Revolution".

of the new oath to the National Council legally constituted a complete break with the past and was a revolutionary act. The government had acted the way it did under public pressure. However, it refused, yet again, to draw the necessary conclusions. The decision made on November 1 stated that in regard to the constitutional form the power of final decision lay with the constituent assembly. This delaying decision was also in line with the stand adopted at the SDP's October conference and also with that of the Austrian Council of State which wished to confer the right of final decision upon a national assembly that was to be elected at some later date.

During the days which followed November 1 it appeared that the postponement of decision-making temporarily resolved the problem of the republic. This seemed to be underlined by the fact that as time passed the chances for an early election became more and more remote. A new electoral bill should have been created. Owing to the unclarified frontier question even the place where the election would be held could not be determined. The participation of the nationalities, who were about to break away, seemed doubtful. Finally, some held the view, regardless of the aforementioned, that it would be advisable to hold the elections some time after October 31, amid a "calmer" atmosphere.

Despite the numerous doubts and objections, the delaying of the elections proved to be unfeasible, not least because the international situation made the relaxation of tensions impossible.

On November 9, Kaiser Wilhelm formally abdicated and fled to the Netherlands. The revolution triumphed in Germany. Its very first achievement was the proclamation of the republic, which was announced immediately without any formalities.

As a result of the developments in Germany, a proclamation was issued in Austria on November 11 stating that the Monarch "concedes the handling of the affairs of the state and accepts German Austria's decision regarding the country's future form of government".[65] On November 12, the provisional National Assembly proclaimed German Austria "a democratic republic".

Two days later the Czechoslovak National Assembly, which convened in Prague adopted a similar stand.

The events in Germany and, even more so, in Austria left no doubt that things could no longer be postponed in Hungary either. Citing "international developments", the National Council issued an appeal on November 11 in which it announced that regarding the form of government "the final decision could no longer be postponed, not even until the convening of the constituent assembly". The rural national councils were called upon to state their position: that in the serious decisions of the next few days the Hungarian National Council should feel the united will of the whole country behind it.[66]

---

[65] *Pesti Hírlap*, November 12, 1918. "Emperor Charles Has Abdicated."
[66] *Ibid.*, "The National Council Support the Immediated Declaration of the Republic."

On November 13, a delegation of aristocrats and barons headed by Baron Gyula Wlassics, president of the Upper House, travelled to the King in Austria. At the Eckertsau hunting lodge, to which the Monarch retired following the proclamation of the republic in Austria, King Charles IV, advised by the delegation, signed another declaration expressly concerning Hungary. This in essence, followed the November 11 proclamation drawn up by Prelate Seipel and acknowledged Austria. The declaration allowed for several interpretations. In connection with the manuscript which signified legal reservation rather than abdication, the Cabinet adopted the stand that "it was unnecessary according to the law and under existing conditions". Irrespective of the King's decision the government stated: "Charles of Habsburg is not the ruler of Hungary."[67]

The Cabinet's stand was based on the opinion of university professors, who, on the basis of the Pragmatic Sanction, arrived at the inference that the end of the Habsburg dynasty in Austria also implied a similar fate for the dynasty in Hungary.

The ceremonial declaration of the republic took place on November 16. To help overcome the fact that the pre-revolution Parliament was undesirable in character and that the new constituent assembly had not yet been convened, the representatives of the political parties, the corporate system organs which joined the National Council and the rural national councils were delegated to the National Council, filling its ranks to 500 (some sources put this number at 1,000–1,200). The so-called Great National Council, which was thus created via delegation, was proclaimed a "legal revolutionary organ", which was to serve as a substitute for the national assembly.

On November 16 the Lower House and the Upper House held a brief final session. The Lower House announced its own dissolution and the Upper House, acknowledging the decision "closed its own debates". Afterwards, the Great National Council, which convened in the crowded vaulted hall of Parliament, endorsed the draft resolution proclaiming the set up of the republic.

In addition to the proclamation of the republic, (Plebiscitary Decision, No. 1/1918) the decision also announced the abolition of the Lower House and the Upper House, the transfering of political power to a government presided over by Károlyi, issued an order for the immediate enactment of "popular legislation"; universal suffrage (including women) with secret ballot; freedom of the press; trial by jury; freedom of association and assembly; the distribution of the land among the peasants.

While the National Assembly was in session, a crowd of some 200,000 people marched to the square in front of Parliament. First to arrive were the students, smaller groups and bourgeois associations. Later they were followed by workers who marched under red flags and association banners from Óbuda, Outer Váci Road, Újpest, Kőbánya and Csepel singing revolutionary songs. They wore red rosettes or ribbons on their coats and the customary red paper label on their caps. The square and the neighbouring streets were packed with people, draperies, flags

[67] OL Cabinet Minutes, November 13, 1918.

and inscriptions, many cheering the "socialist republic". The plebiscitary decision was read out in the huge square where the five points and the speeches of the speakers were received with frantic applause.

Although the birth of the republic on November 16 signified an unequivocal decision regarding the constitutional form, to some extent it continued to be provisional.

The filling of the post of president was left open at Károlyi's suggestion. The working out of the fundamental principles of the republican constitution was to be the task of the as yet unelected constituent assembly. (It did not occur to anyone that—as in the neighbouring countries—until the elections were held the national assembly could be convoked on the basis of the corporate principle, or that the Great National Council could also continue to fulfil this function.)

The transference of state power was synonymous with the further strengthening of the role of government and the further restriction of power of the National Council. After the proclamation of the republic all the power the National Council had been left with was the right to debate and the right to advise. Regarding the rural national councils the Cabinet made the decision on the 15th providing—if it was possible—for their abolition.

The republic which was proclaimed on November 16 and to which the Archduke Joseph also took the oath in the afternoon was a bourgeois republic. Although the way it came about and its terms, the "people's republic", "plebiscitary decision", "popular legislation", "people's government", as well as its radical promises indicated the presence of the masses and the ambivalent character of the situation.

3. HUNGARY'S SITUATION IN WORLD AFFAIRS
THE KÁROLYI GOVERNMENT'S FOREIGN POLICY

DIFFICULT SITUATION, UNFOUNDED HOPES

The people's government took over the management of foreign policy amidst grave conditions and in an unfavourable international situation.

Fundamentally, the problem was rooted in the inevitable consequences of a war started and lost by the fallen regime. The country's isolation, the lack of a foreign affairs apparatus which followed from the dismantling of the common ministries, including the common Ministry of Foreign Affairs, compounded difficulties still further. Thus, during the early days the government tried to make decisions on important and complex issues without an adequate organization and even without the basic requirements of information.

Károlyi, who was in control of foreign affairs, and his associates tried everything in their power to change the situation. The new Ministry of Foreign Affairs and an information service were gradually established. On November 4 the Cabinet decided to send a press mission to Switzerland to obtain and pass on information. In the course of November envoys were sent to Zagreb, Vienna, Bern and Prague. On December 15 a people's law was issued on independent foreign affairs administration. At the same time Ferenc Harrer, a professional with considerable experience in public administration, was appointed Foreign Minister. However, no kind of organization could break the negative attitude adopted by the majority of the victorious powers and neutral countries. No kind of apparatus, official or unofficial mission could persuade the victors to recognize Hungary's independent statehood, to establish diplomatic links with a defeated country prior to the conclusion of a peace treaty.

During the days of the take-over of power the public mood was characterized by illusions, despite Hungary's uncertain international position which did not augur well. Even then the view that the Entente, which "stood on the basis of Wilsonian principles" would respond benevolently to the Károlyi government, which professed adherence to the same principles and thus Hungary could expect favourable treatment at the hands of the victors was widespread. "Mihály Károlyi is the only person from whom the population of the country's frontier areas could expect protection from a hostile invasion"—wrote *Magyarország*, the official paper of the Independence Party on October 31. "Hungary wishes to act as a neutral state, indeed it is already doing so"—stressed Károlyi at a press conference on November 3.

Hopes for benevolence from the Entente and fair treatment were based on miscalculations. They did not reckon with the fact that the extent of victory in the aftermath of the war had rendered Wilson's earlier statements and the compliance inherent in them unjustified and outdated.

The Hungarian press carried almost nothing about the elections which took place in the United States on November 5. The brief accounts which surfaced in one or two dailies around November 10 were drowned by the flood of news about the revolution in Germany. Thus the fact had been obscured that in these elections Wilson's Democratic Party had lost its majority in both Congress and Senate. Moreover, no mention was made either of the fact that the Republican Party, who had been in the minority up until then, emerged victorious from the elections and would not hear of negotiations. On the contrary, it demanded unconditional surrender instead of concessions and popularized the principle of revenge and punishment. Even later on there was very little in the papers of the fact that the British general elections, which were held in mid-December, hailed the strengthening of the right, too. In France, Clemenceau in the debate on the budget in the French parliament on December 29, spoke of the Wilsonian programme with challenging scepticism.

THE COMPLICATIONS OF ARMISTICE

The first issue the people's government had to face immediately after the victory of the revolution was the problem of the armistice.

In the course of the aforementioned negotiations for an armistice in Padua the AOK also gave permission to the armistice committee in Újvidék to establish contact with the enemy. (The armistice committee, whose original seat had been in Belgrade and who were now staying in Újvidék, was set up in early October, out of a conviction that an armistice had to be concluded not only on the Italian front, but on the Balkans as well.)

The committee, headed by General Laxa, the former military attaché to Sofia, and its two members, Staff Colonels Dormándy and Kozmovsky received orders to leave for Belgrade during the small hours of November 2. By this time Belgrade was in the hands of the Serb army. The delegates, who arrived at the Serb capital with credentials from Field Marshal Kövess, commander of the Balkan army group, were handed after a short delay on November 4 a list of conditions for a ceasefire sent by Franchet d'Espèrey from Saloniki.

Drawn up in six points, the preliminary conditions of the armistice—the carrying out of which depended on further negotiations—contained the following important demands: troops positioned north of the Rivers Danube, Save and Drina should lay down their arms within a fifteen kilometre zone of the line and evacuate the areas indicated. The ships on the aforementioned rivers and on the Adriatic Sea are to be handed over as prize. Free relations and contact is to be permitted with the Yugoslav National Council operating in the territory of the Monarchy. The deadline for a reply to points one and two was 24 hours. After the reply was handed over a plenipotentiary delegate must be sent immediately, provided with an authorization from which it was clear that he was a plenipotentiary delegate who wished to negotiate in the name of the government.

The Károlyi government approved of and insofar as it could, encouraged the establishment of contact with Franchet, even though the idea of the Balkans armistice negotiations had been the AOK's. The government's stand was based on the actual situation. During the final days of October and the early days of November the Entente's eastern army had reached the line of the Save and the Danube. The chances were that the advancing French and Serb divisions would not stop at the frontiers of the former Austro–Hungarian Monarchy, but would continue their operations and passing through Hungary, would try to deal Germany, still at war, a heavy blow. Moreover, it also seemed likely that under the circumstances the Serb army would attempt to gain possession of the South Slav areas of the former Monarchy.

The nowadays ever increasing number of documents which are made public concerning the Supreme War Council in Paris and the Serb Supreme Command bear witness to the validity of contemporary conjectures. To put the eastern army into action against Germany had been the intention of both the war council in Paris and of Franchet d'Espèrey. Franchet wanted to march against Berlin through Budapest, Prague and Dresden. Under the plan drawn up in Paris the French and British divisions were to be concentrated in the vicinity of Salzburg. The original conception of the Serb Supreme Command had been to ensure rest for his troops upon reaching the Danube who were exhausted by one and a half months of swift advance. When, however the military command received news of the imminent signing of the Armistice of Padua and Italian designs to frustrate the intentions of the Serb government, it immediately shelved all plans for this.

The Supreme Command was informed on the events in Paris by Pašić, the Prime Minister who was staying there, and by Vesnić, the Serb envoy. In a telegramme dated November 2 Pašić suggested that considering the imminent armistice, which was planning to totally disregard the Balkans, they should take into their possession, as soon as possible, the south Slav areas of Austria–Hungary. In a subsequent message Vesnić informed Voivod Misić, the chief of the general staff that whatever his decision concerning expansion to the north should be it would be endorsed here, in Paris. Upon receiving this information from Paris the Serb army continued its thrust forward. The contingents of the first and second Serb army received the order on November 5 to commence the occupation of Syrmia, Slavonia, Croatia, Bosnia-Herzegovina and Dalmatia. After having overtaken the Romanians in the Banat they should proceed towards the Temesvár–Versec–Fehértemplom line. In the north they should press forward up to the River Maros and take possession of the areas of the Bácska region south of Baja and Szabadka.

The Entente forces stationed on the line of the Rivers Drina, Save and Danube represented a significant force in spite of the fact that following the capitulation of Bulgaria part of the so-called Eastern Army (mostly the British and Greek divisions) turned against Turkey. At the beginning of November Franchet disposed over six Serb, three French and one Greek infantry divisions, one Serb cavalry division and one French cavalry brigade on this section of the front. In addition—

5*

had the need arisen—he could have counted on a further nine reserve divisions as well as the support of the Romanian army which comprised of twelve divisions. A further source to strengthen the totally exhausted and thinning Serb army came from volunteers from the liberated areas and from soldiers returning from captivity.

According to a contemporary report by Field Marshall Kövess to the Hungarian Ministry of Defence, the strength of the Monarchy's army along the Rivers Save and Danube consisted on November 2, of half a division with only 10,000 rifles and the artillery accompanying it. On November 1, the German contingents were withdrawn from the subordination of Kövess' army group. Regarding the chances of possible further resistance, Kövess wrote the following in his lengthy report: "Whether or not stopping at the Save would be possible depends solely on the Serbs' behaviour and also on whether or not any serious resistance could be expected on the part of the troops, stationed far away from their country, totally exhausted from earlier combat and retreat and morally weakened by the fleeing of the Croats."[68]

In addition to reckoning with this situation, the Károlyi government advocated negotiations for another reason as well. It believed that if a newly independent Hungary made an independent stand then it could expect more favourable conditions and a separate ceasefire would also signify the recognition of independent statehood.

Károlyi—as his memoires demonstrate—took the stand that it would be advantageous "if those who made and fought the war were to liquidate it and bear the responsibility for the ceasefire".[69] However, Károlyi's undoubtedly correct reasoning, which essentially coincided with the stand adopted by the Austrian Cabinet received no support.

Initially the government's plan had been to send an armistice delegation to Padua. This plan was, however, frustrated by transport difficulties and seemed inexpedient because on November 3 the armistice was signed in Padua, with the approval of the Hungarian government.

(During the afternoon of November 3, Linder sent a telegramme to the supreme command that the government rejected Weber as the common delegate, but to prevent any delay in the conclusion of the armistice he gave his permission for Weber "to represent Hungary's interests too for the time being".)[70]

On November 4 the Cabinet decided to despatch the delegation to General Franchet d'Esperey in Belgrade instead of Padua.

---

[68] Fővárosi Levéltár (Municipal Archives). Budapesti Kir. Törvényszék (Budapest Royal Court of Justice) 36537/1921, p. 35. The documents of the Károlyi Trial. From the Kövess Army Group Command to the Hungarian Ministry of Defence 4/11. 1918–8–5 m. Telegramme copy.

[69] Károlyi 1968, p. 414.

[70] Fővárosi Levéltár, Budapest Royal Court of Justice 36537/1921, p. 35. The Hungarian Government to the Supreme Command. November 3, 6:45 pm. The AOK forwarded the text of the telegramme to Weber at 7:30 pm, the same day. (KA. AOK. Op. Geh. 2110.)

The delegation was to have been headed by Linder. No only because the issues to be negotiated were primarily military in character, but also because Linder was best informed about intricacies and how the armistice talks had progressed up to that point. Since, however, a disagreement had arisen with Linder on November 4 over the issue of the Soldiers' Council, the Cabinet commissioned Dénes Berinkey, the new Minister of Justice, who was sworn into office that day.

When Linder reported at the November 5 Cabinet meeting on his negotiations with the German consul in Budapest and referred to the advantages that would arise out of steps taken against the Germans ("we could provide the final thrust that would ensure the total collapse of German imperialism, we shall force them to capitulate ... which the peace conference will probably appreciate") and to the complications and conflicts involving essential coal shipments which "could only be made up for via Belgrade", the Cabinet changed its mind. "Considering issues of vital importance",[71] the Cabinet decided to send a high-level delegation headed by Károlyi and Jászi to Franchet.

THE BELGRADE MILITARY CONVENTION

The Hungarian delegation left Budapest during the late evening hours of November 5. In addition to the government representatives the delegation comprised of representatives of the National Council, the Workers' Council and the Soldiers' Council (Lajos Hatvany, Dezső Bokányi, Imre Csernyák) as well as delegates from the ministries concerned. Franchet travelled from Saloniki to the scene of the negotiations by car. Breaking the journey in Niš he conducted talks with Regent Alexander and Voivod Misić on the Bulgarian frontier issue and the drawing up of the Hungarian demarcation line. The French general arrived in Belgrade on the afternoon of the 7th and immediately received the Hungarian delegation that awaited him. At the villa which served as the scene of the talks and which only a few days before had been the residence of the Austro–Hungarian vice regent, Károlyi introduced the members of the delegation and immediately inquired whether the commander-in-chief of the Italian or eastern Entente forces was enpowered to negotiate a Hungarian ceasefire. After Franchet declared that he was the person in question, Károlyi read out the Hungarian delegation's memorandum (edited by Jászi) which contained the following important statements:

The war was the product of the old feudal and autocratic Austro–Hungarian Monarchy, which silenced the democratic forces that opposed the war and pursued a policy of national oppression. On November 1 the new government issued orders for an immediate capitulation, which, however, the *Armee-Oberkommando* did not pass on. Since it was impossible to establish contact with General Diaz they came to Belgrade. Their goal was on the one hand, to inform and on the other, to attain an

---

[71] *OL Cabinet Minutes,* November 4, 1918.

arrangement which suited the just and fair wishes of the Hungarian people. They accepted no responsibility for the domestic and foreign policy of the former regime. In domestic politics they wanted democratic reforms and in foreign policy a break with the old imperialist German alliance. They accepted the setting up of an independent Czech and South Slav state, the peace conference should decide the issue of frontiers. On November 1 Hungary ceased to be a hostile country and became a neutral one. Insofar as a wish was expressed to station foreign troops in Hungary they should be French, British, Italian or American troops, not colonial forces. They requested the general's intervention regarding the pressing coal shortage. Requisitioning by hostile forces should be carried out fairly. Objects of art should be preserved in museums. Diplomatic contact should be established between the Entente and Hungary. The general should support the people's government of Hungary in the fulfillment of its difficult task.

Franchet d'Espèrey received the Hungarian delegation with an air of superiority, assuming a Napoleonic pose. He wished to make it clear that these negotiations were not between equal parties. He immediately corrected the point referring to Hungary's neutrality. "Hungary is not a neutral, but a defeated country."

When Károlyi used the expression "hongrois", he interjected: "Dites le pays madjar", which meant that the delegation represented only the areas populated by Hungarians, that is, they should not speak in the name of the national minorities.

The reply given to the memorandum once again stated: Hungary is a defeated country; "in this war the Hungarians fought alongside the Germans and together they would be punished and pay for it". When the delegation quoted Wilson, the general made no comment, only a discouraging gesture with his hand.[72]

After the introductions Franchet invited Károlyi and Jászi into his room and handed over the text proposed by him, which contained 18 points.

The first point indicated the Beszterce–Maros–Szabadka–Baja–Pécs–Dráva line as the demarcation line, which in fact amounted to the evacuation of southern Transylvania, the Banat, Bácska and part of Baranya County. By drawing up this line of demarcation Franchet satisfied the demand of the Serb government, the Serb Supreme Command and partly, the Kingdom of Romania which had entered into an alliance with the Entente once again. (In Romania the pro-Central Powers Marghiloman government was ousted on November 6. On November 10 the King ordered the mobilization of the army. At the same time, the new Prime Minister, General Coanda, issued a 24 hour ultimatum to Mackensen's already retreating army to leave Romania.)

Other points of the agreement called for the demobilization of the army with the exception of six infantry and two cavalry regiments the task of which was to maintain law and order. The passage through and stay in Hungary of the Entente

---

[72] *Pesti Napló*, November 9, 1918. "The Reply of Franchet d'Espèrey". *L'Illustration*, November 5, 1921. P. Azan: L'armistice avec la Hongrie. The *Pesti Napló* also publishes the government's memorandum—in full on November 9.

forces would be guaranteed. The German troops were given fifteen days to leave the country. Point seventeen of the agreement stipulated that should "insurrections erupt on the territory of Hungary the Entente was entitled to draw these areas under its own control".

Considering that some points went beyond what could be expected on the basis of the Diaz Armistice and the preliminary conditions, Károlyi and Jászi said that the cease-fire agreement was unacceptable. Following lengthy negotiations, Franchet made concessions. He agreed to delete the "insurrection and uprising clause" from point seventeen, which the Hungarians strongly objected to. However, he included in the text, as a supplement to point one, that in the evacuated areas "civil administration would remain in the hands of the present government".[73] Finally he even allowed the delegation to send a telegramme to Paris in defence of territorial integrity. The telegramme addressed to Clemenceau contained the stipulation that the government would only sign the treaty if the "Entente guaranteed the present boundaries of the Hungarian state until the peace treaty negotiations (not including Croatia and Slavonia)".[74]

Due to the general's leniency, Károlyi and Jászi were inclined to sign, however, because of pressure from certain members of the delegation, they finally decided to wait for the reply and seek the endorsement of the National Council for their final decision.

Following the delegation's return to Hungary the government, who had received a number of unfavourable reports, submitted the issue of the ceasefire to the National Council on November 10.

Károlyi gave a candid account of the developments and did not conceal the hopelessness of the situation. Clemenceau's reply had arrived, in it he instructed Franchet to confine his "negotiations" to "military issues" only. The Serb troops were already in Novi Sad and had reached the Pancsova–Versec and the Pancsova–Antalfalva line. According to information supplied by Hungary's envoy to Prague, who had just returned to Budapest, the Czechs demanded between seventeen and nineteen counties, their troops had departed and were making rapid progress. The situation in Romania was also serious, "the mood of the Romanians living in Hungary is one of extreme excitement". Taking all of this into account the immediate signing of the treaty would be the best solution "because being aware of the just quality of our cause and our physical weakness we can rely only on the law".[75]

[73] *Document*, pp. 7–9. For the changes and Franchet's concessions *cf.* Károlyi 1968, pp. 422–424. References to the concessions and the omission of the disputed parts of point seventeen were also made by the contemporary press. (*Népszava*, November 9, 1918. "Dispute Over Conditions.")

[74] *Pesti Hírlap*, November 9, 1918. "The Belgrade Talks." For full text of the telegramme, *cf. Acta Historica*, Nos 1–2/1975, pp. 191–192. (Gy. Litván: Documents des relations Franco–Hongroises des années 1917–1918.)

[75] *Pesti Hírlap*, November 12, 1918. "The National Council has Authorized the Government to Sign the Armistice."

The National Council unanimously accepted Károlyi's reasoning that under the circumstances the Belgrade Agreement would provide protection and a legal basis for Hungary against any further demands of the neighbouring countries. Commissioned by the government, Linder went to Belgrade and signed the armistice on November 13. Its original title (Cease-Fire, Military Agreement Between the Eastern Army of the Allies and the Hungarian State) was in the meanwhile modified to "Military Agreement in Regard to the Application of Hungary to the Armistice Concluded Between the Allies and Austria–Hungary". At the signing of the ceasefire agreement the Entente was represented by Voivod Misić and General Henrys, commander of the French Eastern Army (Franchet had meanwhile returned to Saloniki).

At the signing of the ceasefire agreement the plan of the immediate occupation of Budapest was also raised. According to French sources Linder responded to the idea by stating that French troops "could expect an enthusiastic welcome".[76]

THE VIX MISSION. THE ENTENTE'S NEW DEMANDS

Despite the intentions of French military leadership and the approval of the Hungarian government, the immediate occupation did not take place. The press had already carried colourful accounts of the preparations for the imminent arrival of French divisions and British troops. On November 22 the British government decided to oppose the occupation of Budapest. The British, who were primarily interested in the Middle East, did not wish to directly intervene in the complex class and national antagonisms of the former Austro–Hungarian Monarchy and to lend a helping hand to French expansion in Central Europe. Domestic political considerations also made the British reluctant to take part in the endless task of restoring law and order in this region which primarily fell within the French sphere of interest.

As a result of British intervention the French government, left on its own, changed its plans and instead of an occupying force, sent only a military mission to Budapest on November 26. The leader of the mission, Lieutenant Colonel Vix, staff officer of the French Eastern Army received the fundamental order from his superiors (in addition to numerous other tasks—the collecting of economic and military data, surveillance of the activities of foreigners, the establishment of an agent network, etc.) to monitor the execution of and adherence to the Belgrade Military Convention.

This was not an easy task, for it soon turned out that with the exception of the Serbs, no one, not even the French government agreed with the agreement concluded by Franchet d'Espèrey.

---

[76] *Bernachot*, p. 21. "Le ministre de la guerre hongrois assurait d'ailleurs, que nos troupes y seraient reçues avec enthousiasme."

The Czechoslovaks immediately protested against the Belgrade Agreement. Referring to the fact that the Allies had already recognized the Czechoslovak government, Foreign Minister Beneš, who was staying in Paris, demanded the immediate evacuation of Slovakia and paid repeated visits to French political leaders. At the end of November the Italians also demonstrated against Franchet. Sonnino, Italy's Prime Minister branded the Belgrade Agreement as a treaty concluded with an unrecognized and hence legally non-existent state and, moreover, declared it unnecessary on account of the Armistice of Padua.

The French Foreign Ministry accepted the objection of the Italian and Czechoslovak governments and it was only out of practical considerations, "to avoid further complications" that it refrained from the annulment of the Belgrade Agreement. The French Foreign Minister informed in an urgent telegramme on December 1 the Ministry of Defence and Franchet that he had acted incorrectly as he had no right to recognize the new Hungarian state and its government (which at this stage could only be regarded as a local authority). In his telegramme Pichon declared: "Czechoslovakia is entitled to occupy Slovak areas, since the Entente has recognized the Czechoslovak state and regards its army as an allied army."[77]

On December 3 Franchet sent a memorandum to Károlyi via Vix. In this he referred to instructions received from Paris and listing the aforementioned arguments, demanded the immediate evacuation of Slovakia. On the 23rd a follow-up to the memorandum of December 3 also indicated the boundaries of the areas to be evacuated. (Under the memorandum of December 23 the Hungarian troops were supposed to have been withdrawn from the Rivers Danube and Ipoly as well as from south of the Rimaszombat–Ung–Uzsok line.)

The Romanian government did not accept the Belgrade Agreement either, and did not consider itself bound to it as it was concluded without it. After the handing over of the December 3 memorandum the Romanians demanded similar procedure regarding Transylvania, as Vix conceded to the Slovaks. When, in mid-December Romanian troops reached the River Maros, General Prezan, commander-in-chief of the army announced that he intended to press ahead up to the Nagykároly–Nagyvárad–Békéscsaba line. General Berthelot, head of the French mission in Bucharest, accepted and strongly supported the Romanian decision. As commander of the Danube Army, Berthelot informed Vix directly about everything through his liason officer. (The so-called Danube Army, which comprised of French divisions, had been set up in October to help carry out planned anti-Soviet measures.)

Vix was obviously irritated by Berthelot's intervention. When on December 16 he informed the Hungarian cease-fire committee about Presan's instructions he added that he had not received any information regarding the matter from his superior, General Henrys. Notwithstanding, he asked the cease-fire commission to refrain

---

[77] Telegramme chiffré du Ministre des Affaires Etrangères. Paris, le ler Décembre 1918. *Acta Historica*, Nos 1–2/1975. p. 134.

from any act of resistance, in order to avoid possible bloodshed. On December 18 the Hungarian government was informed that Berthelot was demanding the evacuation of Kolozsvár. On December 23 another memorandum arrived. Berthelot had decided to allow the Romanian Supreme Command to cross the demarcation line and occupy several strategical points (nine towns).

The Belgrade Agreement and subsequent events, which were fully reported in the press, aroused excitement and astonishment. For the first time Hungarian public opinion began to realize that Hungary too had lost the war and that this defeat would entail serious consequences.

The position of the government, which insisted on territorial integrity, began to look hopeless. The public mood, which had been extremely enthusiastic when the republic was proclaimed, was changing unfavourably. Reactionary forces immediately surfaced to exploit the situation to their own advantage. Early in December the *Budapesti Hírlap* (Budapest Daily) described the capitulation— which no newspaper had objected to at the time—as "an unusual method" to pursue.[78] Although they did not yet openly attack the Belgrade Agreement Staff Lieutenant Colonel Ferenc Nyékhegyi (appointed as member of the cease-fire committee at the time of the Wekerle government) who had just returned from Padua, drew up a petition on this issue as well. According to the memoires of one Italian participant of the negotiations Nyékhegyi was noted in Padua for the fact that "he did not open his mouth on a single occasion".[79] Yet in his lengthy petition Nyékhegyi tried to prove how advantageous their agreement was as it guaranted Hungary's boundaries. It then went on to stress how unjustified the Belgrade Convention had been leading to the drawing up of a more disadvantageous line of demarcation. The Cabinet dealt with this accusation—later constantly brought up by the counter-revolution—on two occasion at the end of November and the beginning of December. Finally it resolved the issue by arguing that under the circumstances the debate over the Belgrade Agreement was meaningless since the Entente did not intend to adhere to the "less favourable" agreement either.[80]

Whilst the right wing blamed Hungarian leaders for this state of affairs, the public opinion and the pro-government press was inclined to attribute the Entente's unfriendly behaviour, partially or fully, to the malvolence of individuals such as Franchet d'Espèrey or Vix. The truth of the matter is, however, that despite Franchet's offensive behaviour in Belgrade he had put forward an agreement which had in fact been advantageous for Hungary. As far as the behaviour of Vix is concerned the documents now accessible in Paris prove that despite the extremely negative image which existed of him at that time, he was not in fact prejudiced or

[78] *Budapesti Hírlap*, December 11, 1918. "Party Infighting."

[79] *KA AOK Op. 678*. Luigi Barzini: Eine dramatische Szene in der Villa Giusti Gelegentlich der Unterzeichnung des Waffenstillstandsvertrages. Kriegszone, am 10. November 1918. "Neben dem Gen. Weber war Obstl von Seiller, der offene Typus eines alten Soldates... Der Obst v. Nyekhagy, ein gebückter, dicker, rüder Magyare, der nie den Mund aufgetan hat..." p. 2. Uebersetzer: Hptm. Ruggera.

[80] *OL Cabinet Minutes*, November 28, December 1, 1918.

biassed. (In reports to his superiors he dutifully pointed out that the decisions regarding the further claims involving Slovakia and the Romanians contravened the provisions of the Belgrade Agreement. He also expressed the view that he considered the demand for withdrawal of recognition from an already recognized government unjustified. Vix also objected to Berthelot's intervention, pointing out that as a result dual leadership had emerged which was unacceptable.)

The fact that Franchet finally accepted the violation of the agreement concluded with the Hungarian government (as Vix put it: "... the Agreement of November 13 is no more than a scrap of paper"),[81] just as he had submitted to the occupation of Southern Dobruja, which contravened the Bulgarian armistice, should not be regarded as having been motivated by individual sentiment, but by the assertion of a certain policy the logic of which turned out to be ruthless.

The substance of this policy was that in Central Europe the Entente must build its future plans on the countries it recognized as victorious and those who were its allies. In Paris it was believed that in the future these states would be able to fulfil the role for which the Monarchy had been unfit. They could serve—with adequate support—as a buffer against revolutionary aspirations and could be used in an intervention against Soviet Russia. If necessary they would also be suitable to counter-balance German expansionism.

The Entente thus considered it inevitable to fulfil all the promises it had made during the war to the Romanians, Czechs and South Slavs, whom it recognized as its allies. The leading circles of the countries concerned insisted on the maximum fulfilment of these promises.

The pressure on the Entente did not stem solely from expansionist aspirations and from the demand for reparations. It was also rooted in the recognition that the bourgeoisie of the countries concerned believed, not without foundation, that it was only in this way that it could consolidate its own position, which had been shaken owing to the war, to the emergence of violent popular movements and revolutionary aspirations. The Entente—more precisely the French government who, owing to its military presence, had a leading role in Central European affairs—could not evade the fulfilment of these promises as the armies of the aforementioned countries made up the majority of its forces in this region.

Inevitably the Entente adopted a negative attitude to Hungarian claims. Not even antagonisms and growing rivalries in the camp of the victors could change this.

It was clear that inasmuch as the Entente on the one hand promised to fully satisfy the national aspirations and nationalist desires of the states it had recognized as its allies, it could only accomplish these at the expense of the claims coming from the other side, of Hungarian national aspirations and nationalist desires.

---

[81] Peter Pastor: The Vix Mission in Hungary 1918–1919: A Re-examination. *Slavic Review*, 1970. Vol. 29, Nr. 3., p. 489. Vix to Henrys, December 23, 1918.

4. THE DOMESTIC SITUATION

THE ECONOMIC SITUATION

As a result of four years of war and war economy the government inherited an extremely grave economic situation. After the victory of the revolution certain newspapers, referring to the cessation of war expenditure and the possibility of re-establishing commercial links which had been disrupted by the war, promised improvements: low prices, American loans and the imminent arrival of overseas goods. This, however, reflected illusions, unfounded desires and hopes and not the real situation. For the time being the Entente continued its blockade, the question of loan did not even arise, new economic links were not established, moreover the dissolution of the Habsburg Monarchy and foreign occupation destroyed traditional ties.

The shortage of raw materials, which became increasingly oppressive during and owing to the war continued to persist. The coal crisis was particularly serious. Hungary had to import her coal even before the war and these imports served to make up not only for quantity, but for quality as well, as the coal mined in Hungary was of the poorest quality.

Most of Hungary's imported coal, an annual average of four to five million tons which accounted for one third of the domestic consumption, came from Germany, from the Silesian coal field situated near the Czech-Moravian border.[82]

In early November the German government linked any further deliveries of "Prussian coal" to political conditions (the treatment of German forces returning to Germany through Hungary). When an agreement was finally reached with the German consul in Budapest regarding its delivery, the German revolution broke out, then difficulties arose with the Czechoslovak government. The Prague National Committee had originally been willing to allow the Silesian deliveries through, indeed it even offered to deliver coal from its own supply in exchange for food. However, owing to the conflict surrounding Slovakia and the unfolding armed struggle, the original stand changed, negotiations came to a halt and the Czechoslovak government prohibited the delivery of the promised coal and the passage of German shipments through Czechoslovakia.

Early in December there was no foreign coal coming into Hungary. Domestic

---

[82] "Hungary's Coal Production, Imports, Exports and Consumption 1900–1926." Cf. *A Magyar Gyáriparosok Országos Szövetsége XXV. évi jelentése az 1927. évi rendes közgyűléshez* (The 25th Annual Report of the National Federation of Hungarian Industrialists to the 1927 General Assembly), Budapest 1927, p. 140.

coal production was less than half of the previous year's level owing to the loss of production of the mines in Pécs, Nyitra County and later, in the Zsil Valley.[83]

Since transportation, industrial production, the population's supply of coal for heating ultimately depended on the quantity of coal available, a growing shortage of coal entailed far-reaching consequences, though obviously this was not the only cause of the troubles and difficulties.

Regarding transportation by rail, a chaotic situation had already developed earlier. At the last moment—from September 26 onwards—the military leadership despatched enforcements to defend the Balkan front. Consequently the railway network was overcrowded during October with soldiers and supplies posted to the south, which were confused with railway cars heading for Transylvania, arriving back from the Balkans and moving between the various fronts. During the last days of October wagons packed with supplies, goods and equipment jammed the major railway junctions by the thousand and served as targets for suppressed public anger and popular justice after the outbreak of the revolution. (At the outbreak of the revolution the number of railway engines in Hungary was estimated at 5,000, that of open and closed wagons 100,000 and the value of looted goods at several billion by contemporary sources.)[84] After the signing of the ceasefire hundreds of thousands of soldiers returned to Hungary and hundreds of thousands of soldiers departed from Hungary. Between November 7 and December 3, 383,328 Hungarian and 1,128,900 foreign soldiers arrived at Budapest railway stations alone.[85] The transportation of millions of soldiers meant that regular rail traffic came to a halt, everyone travelled free of charge and in any way they could. Normal rail traffic failed to resume fully even following the transportation of the soldiers owing to the exhaustion of personnel, the deterioration of equipment and the stoppage of coal imports. Owing to a lack of black coal the fast trains did not run and at Christmas all traffic halted for a whole week. The President of the Hungarian State Railway (MÁV), Jenő Vázsonyi, estimated passenger and freight traffic in January at seventy-five per cent of the pre-war figure.[86]

After the victory of the revolution industry could not recover. The reason for this should be sought not only in the lack of raw materials, the shortage of coal or transportation difficulties but also in the difficulties of the transition to peace-time production. After the end of the war the industrial plants were unable to make the change from one day to the next, to lay orders from military command aside, to stop production for the army and to switch from producing war materials to consumer goods. Although the government aided the switch-over and helped maintain

[83] Böhm, A háborús korszak bűnei, pp. 13–14. Böhm's figures for daily coal production are 27,000 tonnes in 1918 and 11,900 tonnes in early 1919.

[84] Magyarország, July 7, 1927. Ferenc Julier: Ellenforradalmi lélekkel a Vörös Hadsereg élén (With a Counter-Revolutionary Soul at the Head of the Red Army). After the revolution Julier was director of the military transport command.

[85] Mohácsy, p. 104.

[86] Hajdu, p. 366. Hajdu quotes the President of MÁV, Jenő Vázsonyi's statement. (Világ, January 17, 1919.)

production with among other things loans, the capitalists, who felt that their situation was uncertain adopted-a wait and see stand. Some industrialists tried to withdraw their capital from industrial plants, attempting to take part of their wealth out of the country. The drop and temporary stoppage in production, or the final closing down of certain factories led to unemployment at a time when, owing to the demobilization of soldiers (1.2 million soldiers were demobilized up until the middle of December),[87] many thousands of blue and white collar workers were looking for jobs in their own occupations.

Owing to the neglected state of agriculture and to unfavourable weather, the 1918 harvest was the poorest ever recorded. Whilst over 60 million quintals of grain were produced prior to the war, in 1918—according to figures published in the *Statistical Yearbook*—34,121,000 quintals were harvested. This was just slightly higher than fifty-five per cent of the previous figure. The vast majority of the harvest, when this was possible, went to the army, another part (not a significant amount, slightly less than one million quintals of grain)[88] went to Austria in the summer and autumn months in exchange for consumer goods. After the victory of the revolution large stocks remained in the seceding areas, above all in Voivodina, a major food supplier and from where nothing could be salvaged owing to the swift progress of the Serb army.

Had it been carried out systematically and with adequate preparations, the evacuation of the areas beyond the demarcation line could have improved the situation of the central areas and the remaining parts of the country, not only regarding food supplies, but in other respects as well. However, general chaos, the inadequacy of transportation and the resistance of the local population obstructed the transportation of state assets and other stocks. Moreover, the government considered evacuation unadvisable for political reasons as well. It believed that the official evacuation of these areas would have amounted to an acknowledgement of their loss, whereas in fact under the cease-fire agreement they still belonged to Hungary.

At the very beginning of November the head of the Public Food Supply Office issued an optimistic statement about the population's food supply: "There is no cause for concern", Hungary's surplus produce is sufficient even "for deliveries abroad", soon "it will be possible to obtain food cheaper than the present prices".[89] Subsequent developments failed to verify this optimism and instead of improving, the situation became increasingly more alarming and the winter brought hunger and deprivation yet again. Basic foodstuffs were still rationed and were often unavailable even with ration tickets. Milk supplies dropped to a level where only half the ration for the sick and for infants could be ensured. From mid-December onwards wheat flour was mixed with barley flour so that flour rations could be ensured. In February the lard ration was reduced to one hundred grammes per week

[87] *Böhm*, p. 78.
[88] *Statisztikai Évkönyv, 1918*, p. 46. *Teleszky*, p. 387.
[89] *Népszava*, November 6, 1918. "The Ensuring of the Population's Food Supply."

and two meatless days a week were re-introduced. In March the quantity of food which could be served in restaurants was also restricted.

Speaking about the general situation the Minister for Public Food Supply said the following at the February 20 Cabinet meeting: "Flour consumption up to July 31 is approximately 15,600 wagons; of this 9,200 wagons will be available, the shortage is about 6400 wagons. The sugar shortage could be eliminated when the processing of sugar beet can be resumed. This however depends on a sufficient quantity of coal. The pork requirement up to the end of October is approximately 180,000 pigs, of which about 80,000 will be forthcoming, the shortage is about 100,000. And even the 80,000 can only be ensured if the fattening of pigs is continued. Four thousand wagons of maize are required for this, which is unavailable... Poultry is expensive and there is little up for sale. Egg requirements can barely be met. The demand for potatoes is 12,000 wagons and an extra 5,000 wagons of seed-tuber. Instead of the required 17,000, all we have are 7–8,000 wagons and we do not dispose fully even over this amount as most of the potatoes are out in the clamps. We have enough salt to last us for two months."[90]

In addition to the shortage of food (which, taking into account hidden stocks in the countryside, was probably more favourable than demonstrated by official figures), the shortage of textile articles constituted another serious problem. Since textile imports ceased during the war and the stocks that remained were used for military purposes, it was practically impossible to obtain clothes and underwear. Leather and shoes were also in short supply.

Owing to the shortage of coal domestic heating, the consumption of electricity and gas were curtailed. According to the December 5 decree by the government commissioner for coal, only a single lamp could be switched on in each room, gas consumption was prohibited between 8 a. m. and 4 p. m., the use of gas bathroom stoves and bathroom geysers was confined to a single day, Monday. Using the shortage of coal as a pretext, the Cabinet passed a resolution on December 28 to shut down the theatres and cinemas as of January 1 with the proviso that—until further notice—performances could only be held on Sunday afternoon and evening.

In the aftermath of the victory of the revolution people began to flood to Budapest. At first refugees arrived from the countryside but later, increasingly from the occupied areas. In the first days of December 32,000 refugees were on record in Budapest and the number of unreported refugees was estimated at 10,000.[91] The refugees, most of them public servants, hoped for and demanded aid, jobs, wages and pensions. As all housing had ceased during the war, there were no empty flats in Budapest even prior to the revolution. The shortage of housing was made even more accute and unbearable by the masses of people returning home, moving to the capital and the refugees. The decree for the requisitioning of flats and a housing

---

[90] *OL Cabinet Minutes*, February 20, 1918.

[91] *Pesti Napló*, December 8, 1918. "Budapest Can Take in No More Refugees". Statement by Lieber, government commissioner and by Chief of Police Dietz.

office which was re-organized several times, could not basically change the situation.

This sudden growth of the capital city's population also hampered the systematic distribution of food and other supplies.

The financial situation was characterized by deficit, inflation, chaos and a huge war debt. Actual income—from taxation, levies revenues and state companies—was around 1 1/4 milliard crowns, while expenditure topped the four milliard mark.[92] The government made up the almost three milliard crown deficit with uncovered loans, that is by printing more money. Under the circumstances inflation was gathering momentum and within five months the value of the crown dropped by half. That inflation did not assume greater proportions was due to the hiding of bank notes, that is, the accumulation of banknotes by private individuals. The reason for this must be sought in the confidence, which was totally unjustified—and only psychologically understandable—in the banknotes of the Monarchy. Another factor was the shortage of banknotes in the autumn of 1918 which was due to the fact that the machines of the Austro–Hungarian Bank were unable—owing to the rapid growth of banknote printing—to print a sufficient quantity of smaller denomination notes. The shortage of banknotes continued into the initial phase of the revolution, when not only printing but also delivery to Budapest was highly problematic for the Vienna Bank management.

The government commissioner appointed to the Budapest subsidiary, Lajos Beck, wanted to resolve the problem by issuing new banknotes and printing them in Budapest. As a stopgap measure and to prevent the latter, the directors of the bank in Vienna handed over the plates for the 25 and 200 crown banknotes which were issued in October 1918. Thus began the printing of the so-called white money in Budapest, which, later on, constituted the state's most important "source of income". The population received the new 25 and 200 crown notes with scepticism. The reason for this lack of confidence was rooted not only in the fact that these notes were printed in a series of hundreds of millions, but also that the new banknotes were issued from the beginning as emergency money. "This note is to be replaced by new notes by June 30, 1919."—this was the statement printed on the poor quality paper the milled or plain back of which was blank.

The financial situation was further complicated by the question of national debt. At the end of 1918 the Ministry of Finance estimated the war debt of the Hungarian state at 33–34 milliard; war loans accounted for 16 milliard, loans from the Austro–Hungarian Bank for 10 milliard, credit from private banks foreign lenders (Germany) for 7–8 milliard.[93]

[92] *Számvevőszék jelentése*, pp. 60–61. "Chief Summary of the Real Expenditure and the Real Revenues."

[93] *Pesti Hírlap*, November 16, 1918. "The Financial Situation of the Country. Financial Undersecretary of State Dr. Pál Szende's Statement on the Country's Financial Position."

ECONOMIC-POLITICAL AND SOCIAL WELFARE POLICY MEASURES

The government did not have a comprehensive plan or programme to combat economic difficulties. Instead it tried to alleviate the situation by introducing improvised measures and it also strove to realize the coalition parties' earlier economic policy conceptions.

The government stood on the platform of free trade which was in line with the former stand of some social democrats (Garami) and the more recent stand of certain radicals (Szende). The principle of free trade in foreign policy was in harmony with the plans for federation aiming at rapprochement. In domestic policy free trade signified the end of the war economy and the state intervention which accompanied it; under the circumstances this was indeed the pressing task.

As early as November 4, Garami proposed the gradual demobilization of centres to the Cabinet. The dismantling of the centres had been demanded by commercial capital as well as by small and medium industry. The reason for this was that the various centres—over sixty organizations—which were established during the war because of the war economy, favoured the big companies and served the interests of big capital and the large estate. "The soonest possible abolition of every centre" was at the same time a popular demand as many had blamed the centres themselves, rather than the war situation and the character and the deplorable functioning of the centres, for poverty and economic difficulties.

However, the given situation called for the maintainance rather than dismantling of the centres, for continued state intervention on a new basis rather than its cessation. For reasons which during the war had made controlled economic activity necessary, the shortage of raw materials and goods continued to persist.

Thus, it was not the abolition of the centres, but their transformation and democratization which became a highly important task, the reason being that they should stop profiteering, which had gone on during the war, to serve transition to peace-time production and to enhance the fair distribution of goods.

For different reasons, the National Federation of Hungarian Industrialists and later the Workers' Council opposed the idea of dismantling the centres. The former wished that the centres remain unchanged and continue functioning, while the latter—and here the stance of the left wing was asserted—wanted the centres reorganized to function as "socialized organs".

The Ministry of Commerce had to take this into consideration.

Indicative of the uncertainty and change of mood was that when Garami had proposed the dissolution of the Shoe Centre to the Cabinet on December 14, he also added that the role of the dismantled centre would be taken over simultaneously by another central organ.

Whilst a government commission was being organized "to gradually dismantle the centres"[94] and a separate government commissioner was appointed "to handle

---

[94] *OL Cabinet Minutes*, November 4, 1918.

6 Siklós András

the personnel problems of the centres that were to be dismantled", one of the largest centres, War Produce Ltd., started to build a new head office.[95]

In the March 14 conference the issue of the centres was discussed. At the conference held at the Ministry of Commerce the representatives of trade (Kálmán Balkányi, Ferenc Heinrich) proposed the abolition of the centres, some (Aurél Egry) suggested a compromise, whilst the radicals and social democrats (Szende, Erdélyi, Varga) advocated the dismantling of the old centres and the simultaneous setting up of new state centres. After five month of wrangling all the meeting could accomplish was to set up a committee—at Garami's suggestion—"to investigate the issue".[96]

The government was also planning to intervene in taxation. Tax reform had also been an important part of the programme of the radicals and social democrats. The raising of direct taxation, the reduction, indeed abolition of indirect taxation had been a demand voiced at the October congress of the SDP and the Radical Party.

During the years prior to the revolution the Minister of Finance, Pál Szende, had devoted a whole series of articles and studies to the injustices of the taxation system pointing out the obvious interconnections between taxation and class stratification, tax burden and class oppression.

Proposals advocating a "fair taxation policy" demanded that workers be relieved of their tax burdens and the heavier taxing of the wealthy strata.

After the victory of the revolution Szende's statements left no doubt that he continued to adhere to this programme. He still envisaged financial consolidation through the raising of direct taxes—income tax, property tax and inheritence tax—and by the levying of a single substantial property tax announced in October.

When asked by a Dutch journalist about the size of the property tax Szende replied that "it will be of a scope unprecedented in Hungarian and even in world history".[97] Szende was immediately criticized and attacked by those concerned, claiming that his statement would create panic and spur people on to take their wealth out of the country. Moreover it was bound to prompt wealthy people living in national minority areas to support secession. Unlike his critics, Szende believed that "in Hungary the majority of people wish this issue to be probed, they are in fact put at rest by a resolute statement from the Minister of Finance". Should there be people who turn their back on their country rather than pay a few per cent more tax, they are "dishonourable and traitors". In any case Szende's statement is not radical as world history has not known "a tax rate higher than 20%".[98]

The property tax project made very slow progress. Capitalist circles did everything they could to frustrate it. Their strategy was to play for time. They

---

[95] *Népszava*, January 17, 1919. "The Government Commission of the Employees of the Centres. Statement by Government Commissioner Comrade Aladár Kunfi." *Pesti Hírlap*, November 27, "The Building of the Palace."

[96] *Népszava*, March 15, 1919. "The Dismantling of Centres."

[97] *Pesti Hírlap*, December 1, 1918. "The Financial Situation."

[98] *PI Archives*, 607 f. 6. ő. e. "Minutes of the December 10, 1918 Meeting of the National Council's Financial Conference."

pretended to agree, to support the idea "in principle", meanwhile experts wished to delay concrete measures until after the signing of the peace treaty. The fact that the crown banknotes were in circulation not only in Hungary, but also in the neighbouring countries constituted a serious obstacle. It was questionable whether a large property tax would be able to resolve the problem of foreign exchange and financial consolidation without a simultaneous separation of the banknotes of the newly independent countries. The issue of a property tax became intertwined with the need to stamp banknotes in circulation in Hungary or to replace them with new banknotes. However, the government did not wish to take the initiative in this respect, for at stake here was the promotion of secession rather than rapprochement.

Two people's laws were promulgated in relation to the tax reform. Act II of 1919 prescribed Draconian measures to prevent escape from tax evasion by those leaving the country (triple tax obligation). Act XXIV of 1919 ordered the raising of the war profit tax. The first of these laws, which was published in January, was later toned down; the second (passed in March) was never implemented.

The government had planned to use part of the property tax to repay state debts. Szende stated the following in connection with this: "It is the firm intention of the government to meet every obligation of the Hungarian state." In other words that it would undertake to repay war debts, estimated at 34–35 milliard as well as Hungary's share of other debts.[99]

As regards social welfare policy, the government intended to realize the SDP programme, the demands of the social democrats which were, ultimately, only reiterated in October 1918. To underline this intention, a social democrat, Zsigmond Kunfi was appointed head of the Ministry of Labour and Social Welfare which was established by Act IV of 1918. Following his appointment, Kunfi issued a statement to *Népszava* on December 10 in which he elaborated the task ahead for the ministry: labour safety must be established in agriculture. Act II of 1898 and Act XLV of 1907, "which are the most shameful documents of the servitude and exploitation of the agricultural proletariat", must be abolished. Social security for the disabled and retired had been a joint demand of the agricultural and industrial labour force; "the realization of this must be one of the first honourable tasks of the Hungarian People's Republic". The raising of the minimum age for child work, increased protection for minors and for women is of paramount importance. The switch to the eight-hour working day must be fully supported. The body of trade supervisors must be renewed and complemented with medical, female and labourer superintendents in order to ensure the enforcement of labour safety laws and decrees. A new mining law must be enacted to replace the 1854 mining act. Social security based on the autonomy of workers must be created and it is to be extended to artisans, public servants, housemaids; sick pay must be raised simultaneously. The regulation of the legal status of and the revision of the office regulation of civil servants. The nationalization of the matter of war disabled, widows and orphans, a

---

[99] *Pesti Hírlap,* November 16, 1918. "The Country's Financial Position."

new approach to the problem of disability with the participation of the disabled themselves was to be among the first tasks. The nationalization of public health care and the decentralization of health care administration would be the first step to improve health care in Hungary. Social welfare and health care administration must be established with separate local organs and institutions.

This highly justified programme embodied demands formulated decades earlier. However, hardly any of these far-reaching proposals were realized during the five months of the revolution.

The objectives remained objectives in the majority. The government contributed the idea of the 8 hour working day which in most cases came into force through collective contracts which were drawn up by the trade unions, but its enactment did not come to be.

The legal settlement of social security on a new basis, got stuck at conference level, discussion and debates, at which the social democrats proposed far-reaching plans, while the industrialists, in line with their strategy of procrastination, agreed in principle but wished to delay the final settlement to a "more favourable" time.

The Ministry for Social Welfare, which was to have been formed from the departments of the Prime Minister's office, the Ministry of the Interior, the Ministry of Agriculture, the Ministry of Commerce and the Ministry of Finance, did not in fact function and remained in a stage of preparation and internal organization throughout, that is, up to March 21.

Since large-scale social welfare plans failed for the time being to pass beyond the phase of proposal and promise, the government's social welfare activity amounted to no more than the allocation of aid and benefits.

In exchange for forty days' pay and financial provision for food, the demobilized soldiers received 360 crowns in demobilization extras. (Officers received the multiple of this amount for three months.) The workers of factories which were unable to operate because of the shortage of coal received a raised coal aid, the sum of which equalled that of the workers' wages in the lower brackets and amounted to eighty per cent of wages in the higher brackets. Unemployment benefit was at first, 10 crowns a day, later raised to 15, including Sundays. At the end of November civil servants received an emergency aid of 600 crowns each. War disabled, widows and war orphans were allocated 150 plus 50 crowns paid out to members of their families at Christmas. Pensions were raised, as were wages for certain strata (teachers, nursery school teachers). Refugee civil servants received 20 crowns daily with an additional 10 crowns a day for each family member. Refugees and all those who "suffered damage during the commotion of revolution" were also entitled to reparations. Artisans and retailers who were "hampered in the practice of their trade" during the war, could also apply for aid or loans, as well as lawyers, who were entitled to a maximum of 10,000 crowns "to restore their shaken financial situation". Depending on the deliberation of the Minister of Defence, every "individual who suffered a great deal from the war" could apply for aid.

Financial and direct aid was supplemented with aid in kind and indirect aids. Over 100,000 soldiers (some ten per cent of all demobilized soldiers) were provided with civilian clothes following a clothes requisition decree and the goods were seized from retailers.[100] A cut-price meat sale, a potato sale organized for civil servants, a children's shoe sale, all served to ensure low prices through state support.

Although they temporarily alleviated hardship, they proved inadequate to stem the tide of discontent. This held especially true for certain strata such as demobilized soldiers, the unemployed and the disabled.

From the individual's point view, these benefits meant little, while they cost the government vast sums of money. (The Ministry of Defence alone paid out 423 million crowns in demobilization duty.)[101]

The setting up of labour tribunals constituted an important step forward. The task of these tribunals, which were set up by Act IX of 1918, was the settling of labour disputes. Both employer and employee were represented at the tribunals which in fact began their work from February 6 onwards.

To keep companies running, the state extended massive support not only regarding aids and wages, but also in other respects (such as the payment of advances). This inevitably raised the demand for those companies that could not survive without state support to be nationalized. However, the government rejected the idea of nationalization, though not unanimously or finally. As the competent minister, Garami argued that most of the mines were in the hands of Belgian and French concerns and part of transport in French hands. The nationalization of raw material resources and transport would worsen relations with the Entente and would be opposed by the French. The nationalization of industrial plants which manufactured finished goods, Garami said, would be impossible without the nationalization of the mines and the railway.

Only one important "nationalization" was carried out during the revolution. On October 31, the day of the victory, the National Council issued an order—signed by Béla Szántó in the early morning in the lounge of the Hotel Astoria—for the takeover of the Budapest electric railways "with all property rights remaining intact". The Cabinet endorsed the decision on November 2, adding that "the state takes over and hands over to the capital the management of the public road and electric urban railways..."[102] On November 6, the Budapest United City Railway was officially formed from a merger of two private companies (Public Railway and City Railway). Later developments showed that the nationalized tram service was neglected and could be regarded as an example of the difficulties and dangers of nationalization. Fares were not raised for social welfare reasons and out of political considerations. The capital refused to take over the deficit-making company from the left wing social democrats who ran it. The Ministry of Commerce, which never refused support from capitalist firms—when "higher interests" were at stake—was reluctant to allocate the financial means necessary for maintaining the service. It gave help only when it was forced by a decision of the Workers' Council to extend the highly justified financial support.

[100] Böhm: A háborús korszak bűnei, pp. 24–26.
[101] Számvevőszék jelentése, Appendix No. 18. Ministry of Defence ("Ministry of Warfare"), p. 9.
[102] OL Cabinet Minutes, November 2, 1918.

THE UNRESOLVED LAND ISSUE

The government's behaviour regarding the issue of land reform was also characterized by uncertainty and procrastination, despite the fact that it was obvious that the swift and radical reforms that would satisfy the desires and demands of the peasantry, which accounted for the majority of the population in Hungary, was of decisive significance.

From the very beginning the coalition parties had agreed that the prevailing unhealthy distribution of land had to be changed. (In Hungary over half of the arable land belonged to estates over 100, and almost one-third belonged to estates over 1,000 cadastral yokes). The SDP's October 8 manifesto promised "profound and radical agrarian reform", the bourgeois radicals' October 14 congress promised "the immediate commencement of agrarian reforms", the Independence Party's submission of October 16 promised "radical land policy", the National Council's appeal of October 25 promised "large-scale land reform that would give land to the people and a social welfare reform". Most slogans and demands were very general and none of the parties aspiring to power possessed a detailed programme of land reform.

Following the victory of the revolution it did not even occur to the government for one moment to lead the emerging agrarian revolution. Instead of encouraging the movement of the peasantry, it tried to slow it down and diffuse it wherever possible. The promises of land distribution were designed to mollify public discontent. The government rejected the movement of the peasantry and intended to distribute the land through bureaucratic procedure. "The excitement did not arise out of our promises to distribute land, but we had to promise the distribution of land because it was the only way to quell excitement"[103] stressed **Barna Buza** later, arguing with his opponents.

It seemed in early November that the landowners, fearing a peasant uprising, the possibility of a "new Dózsa-type insurrection", would be willing to support the policy of the coalition to avert revolution. At the November 14 meeting of the OMGE's Board of Directors, the provisional chairman, Ödön Miklós (the previous chairman, the notorious Róbert Zelenski had been ousted) called on the landowners to voluntarily offer any of the land they could do without in order to fully preserve the social order by upholding "the sanctity of property". Following the meeting a delegation called on the Minister of Agriculture. The Hungarian National Agricultural Association (OMGE) leadership was represented by Gyula Rubinek, István Bernát, Barna Buday, Hugó Krolop and many others. The delegation announced: the landowners will "on a voluntary basis offer everything they are able to do without and which will not endanger the livelihood of the landowner". "Touched", Barna Buza replied, displaying his talent as a popular orator: "the spring of '48 has reawakened, the spirit of '48 has inspired you when you decided to adopt a voluntary resolution..."[104]

---

[103] *Buza*, p. 8.
[104] *Pesti Hírlap*, November 15, 1918. "New Land Policy."

The clergy, which owned over 1,600,000 cadastral yokes of land in pre-1918 Hungary,[105] intended to hand over pontifical, prebendal and other ecclesiastical property to a Catholic autonomy which was to be set up as soon as possible. A national and local network of self-government was to be established for this purpose, half of whose members were to be elected by practicing Catholics, the other half were to be appointed by the bishops of both lay counties and dioceses.

Not only the aforementioned vast ecclesiastical estates were to be assigned to this body, but also the major church schools which were run with state subsidy. However, the Cabinet meeting of November 19 rejected the proposal of the Minister for Religion and Public Education on the grounds that it not only forestalled the land reform, but the elections as well. "It is indeed of consequence whether we are confronted with an autonomous body or the prelates of today"— stressed both Károlyi and Jászi. "It would be dangerous to stage elections for the autonomous body prior to parliamentary elections" expounded Szende, Barna Buza and Tivadar Batthyány. The Cabinet opted for autonomy, but adopted a stand against its immediate setting up which would have enhanced the preservation of ecclesiatical estates in this manner.[106]

Despite the reservations expressed by the Cabinet, the conference of the Episcopacy which convened in Esztergom on the following day, pledged its support to the government. The Episcopacy decided to offer, for the purposes of land policy "presupposing the subsequent approval of the Holy See, the ecclesiastical estates under its supervision, in return for fair compensation" and would notify the government of the Hungarian People's Republic to this effect in a joint letter. The letter, which was addressed to Mihály Károlyi was completed and was published within a few days in the press with the signatures of the Primate, two archbishops and twelve bishops.[107]

At the same time the Esztergom conference commissioned Ágoston Fischer Colbrie, Bishop of Kassa, Gyula Glattfelder, Bishop of Csanád and Nándor Rott, Bishop of Veszprém, to enter into negotiations with the Minister of Agriculture and to request and provide information concerning the details of land policy. The bishops, who appeared at the Ministry on November 24, in connection with the "large-scale parcelling action", were primarily interested in the issue of compensation. They requested the following: the forests remain in the hands of the Church; every diocese and parish should have its own household estate; the value of the land should be established on the basis of peace-time prices (with equipment being valued at current prices); small-scale sales and property transfers should be

[105] *Statisztikai Évkönyv 1918*, p. 32. According to figures for late 1916 the area of Roman Catholic estates was 1,450,620 cadastral yokes, those of the Greek Orthodox Church 180,811 cadastral yokes.
[106] *OL Cabinet Minutes*, November 19, 1918.
[107] *Esztergomi Prímási Levéltár* (Esztergom Primatial Archives), Minutes of Episcopal Conferences, 1909–1927. Minute. Taken at the meeting of the Hungarian Episcopacy held on November 20 at the Primatial Palace in Esztergom. *Budapesti Hírlap*, November 26, 1918. "The Episcopacy Offers the Ecclesiastical Estates for the Purpose of Land Reform."

allowed to continue. The Primate should participate at meetings concerning land policy, since "he possesses a sharp vision in economic matters as well". When land was divided up demand should be the sole guiding principle and Church estates should not be the first to be distributed. At the talks, which were characterized by an atmosphere of "cordial politeness", Barna Buza promised everything. The bishops left satisfied. "I do not believe that this project can be executed very soon. According to experts it may take years"—wrote Nándor Rott in his report to the Primate. However, he also voiced his qualms. "Ministerial promises are worth as much as the power and continuity represented by the minister in the Cabinet and the power possessed by the present government."[108]

Meanwhile, a meeting began at the Ministry of Agriculture on November 20 about the land reform which was attended by delegates of the land owners organizations, representatives of the political parties and other professionals. Pro-compromise agrarians (Gyula Rubinek, Ignác Darányi, István Bernát) suggested the expropriation of only the estates over 1,000 cadastral yoke. (At its December 11 meeting OMGE's Board of Directors agreed that the acceptable figure would be estates over 5,000 cadastral yokes.) They allocated several years for the execution of the reform (one contributor suggested 20–80 years!). István Nagyatádi Szabó proposed that lands to be distributed should, above all, serve to supplement existing small holdings. (Later, this conception was incorporated into the smallholders' agrarian programme.) The majority of bourgeois radicals, the so-called georgists (Gyula Pikler, Róbert Braun) did not oppose the distribution of land, though they believed that the key to the land issue was the expropriation of land rent. They proposed that a land value cadastre be compiled on the basis of which land value tax would be apportioned which in turn would serve as a basis for the expropriation of land. They argued that landed property, levied with land value tax (the so-called annuity property) would spur the owners, large and small landowners alike, to cultivate their land intensively. They stressed, furthermore, that "everyone was entitled to land" and, through the land value tax non-agrarians would also benefit from the achievements of the land reform. Some social democrats (Jenő Varga) were inclined to accept this conception. Some (Rezső Ladányi) adopted the stance of small holding based on private property—after the views of the revisionist David Eduard. Another marked trend within the Social Democratic Party was the anti-small property trend which stressed that "through the division of land into small plots, peasants will become conservative, indeed reactionary". The advocates of this view—represented at the meeting by Sándor Csizmadia—wished to link the distribution of the land with the strengthening of public property and cooperative farming.

After the nine-day meeting the issue of land reform was submitted to the Cabinet on December 8. Instead of dealing with the draft people's law, the Cabinet

---

[108] *Esztergomi Prímási Levéltár*, János Csernoch's papers, Cat. D/C 6587. The Bishop of Veszprém, Nándor Rott's Report to the Primate on His Talks with the Minister of Agriculture, Barna Buza. November 27, 1918.

concentrated on the twenty-eight points compiled by the Ministry of Agriculture and already discussed by the conference of experts. In the course of the debate Barna Buza suggested 1,000 yoke as the estate limit and compensation for expropriated land. (Calculated on the average of pre-1913 prices and current prices valid prior to expropriation.) Károlyi expounded that it would be wrong to divide certain large estates which pursued intensive farming, fishing, mining, distilling or sugar beet production. These, he suggested, should be turned into cooperatives, "with part of the shares possessed by the owner of the estate, another part by the state and the rest by the workers". He added that this principle should be extended to industrial firms and to the mines as well, otherwise it will not be acceptable in agriculture either. Kunfi also voiced his objection to land division at any price. "Simultaneously with the land reform steps must be taken to ensure that the majority of large estates, which are important from the viewpoint of production remain, in a changed political structure, in the possession of workers and peasants on a cooperative basis." Jászi also proposed the modification of the expropriation limit, finding the 1,000 yoke limit too high. Regarding the issue of compensation, Kunfi maintained the stand that there should be no compensation for ecclesiastical property, as these constituted the property of the state and, accordingly, "are to be retrieved without any compensation". In response to Barna Buza's evasive answer Kunfi stated that "should the law fail to cover this issue, the socialist members of the government cannot remain in their position another minute". Kunfi also opposed the idea of "giving a constant exchange value" for large estates expropriated by the state.[109]

The Cabinet lowered the 1,000 yoke limit to 500 yokes for lay estates and to 200 yokes for ecclesiastical estates. Regarding the issue of compensation it accepted the proposal that an estimated value must be paid out, which must be retrieved through wealth tax and which, above a certain sum, would be as much as 100 per cent. The Cabinet did not come to a decision on the issue of secularization and, following the discussion of eight points on the agenda, decided to interrupt the debate until the next Cabinet meeting.

The debates at the consultations and at the Cabinet meeting revealed that despite the apparent concensus among the antagonistic classes and strata on the land issue, there existed deep rifts and that "the coming together of the Hungarians", about which Barna Buza talked at the opening of the conference at the ministry, was very unlikely to come about. It also became obvious that there was no concensus as to what should be done even within certain corporate system organs and political parties.

From this it followed that the debate did not, for the time being, continue in the Cabinet. Instead of debate at government level the issue of land reform was handed over to the Workers' Council at the end of December with a view to clarifying the situation first of all in the SDP. On December 20 the Workers' Council passed the draft motion adopted by the SDP and the Federation of Agricultural Workers on

[109] *OL Cabinet Minutes*, December 8, 1918.

land reform. The motion, which was endorsed by the National Conference of Agricultural Workers and Smallholders on December 26, contained the following important demands: a single substantial wealth tax, which, at the highest level, would be as much as 100 per cent. Private individuals may retain estates up to 500, the Church up to 200 yokes. Land transferred to the state either through the wealth tax or expropriation, was to be distributed in the form of redeemable permanent tenure. Applicants may be allocated land up to between half and twelve yokes, but with priority going to the cooperatives of pick and shovel men. The cadastral land tax, which favoured the large estate, was to be abolished and replaced by a new land tax or ground value tax. The state was to pay a price corresponding to the estimated value of the land for property expropriated, in the form of registered unmarketable annuity bonds.

The agrarian programme of the social democrats, which was expounded by Zsigmond Kunfi at the Workers' Council meeting and by Sándor Csizmadia at the Federation of Agricultural Workers and Smallholders (FÉKOSZ) conference constituted a compromise between the various trends within the SDP. It was basically characterized by the georgist views taken over from the radicals (wealth tax, perpetual tenure, land value tax), gave place to the ideas for large-scale farming originating with Kautsky (navvy cooperatives), but it also incorporated the conception of smallholders who demanded private property for the peasants (redeemable perpetual tenure).

While one conference after another was taking place in Budapest (on January 4 the special National Council's financial committee dealt with the issue of land reform), the peasantry, whose illusions had already been shattered by the armed police in the early days of November, was following developments with growing impatience and scepticism.

One sign of unrest was the fact that in many places farmers downed their tools or delayed autumn work. The poor peasantry refused to work for a pittance, it expected the distribution of the land, immediately, without compensation and via its own organs, according to a contemporary report about the Great Plain by Zsigmond Móricz. Landowners did not urge the completion of autumnal agricultural work either, as they could not be sure to whom the harvest would belong. As in industry, some landowners tried to withdraw their capital by selling part of their assets and livestock. Also, they blamed the stoppages and the generally unfavourably situation on the one hand on the government, which promised land reform and, on the other, on the farm hands and agricultural labourers, who in their view demanded unrealistically high wages.

To provide an outlet for the restlessness of the peasantry, the Ministry of Agriculture issued an order on November 7 for the registration of war veterans who were demanding land. On November 15 a decree was issued on "provisional measures to enhance the proliferation of small holdings". (The decree ensured the right of preemption for the Ministry of Agriculture, that from the land thus acquired "wished to allocate land primarily to those veterans who were serving at any of the institutions responsible for maintaining public law and order, or were zealously involved in the upkeep of public order".)[110] Late in November and early in December several confidential circulars and yet another decree called on landowners to cede part of their land voluntarily and "under moderate conditions of lease or for share cultivation" in order to "temporarily stem the tide of public discontent".[111] At the same time a host of appeals called on peasants to take up work, stressing that only "those who work will be given land". The ministry tried to placate the landowners as well. Barna Buza assured them that compensation would be paid not only for the land, but also for equipment so "it is therefore meaningless for anyone to squander agricultural equipment beforehand and thereby make any further cultivation of the land impossible".[112]

There was hardly any response to these appeals. Despite the circulars and statements, maize, carrots and potatoes remained unharvested on many large estates in the autumn of 1918. Some unofficial sources put the quantity of autumnal cultivation and the sowing of the winter corn on the basis of the following year's produce, at 35–40% of the previous figure, while other estimates claim 50%.[113]

STRUGGLE AROUND THE DEMOBILIZATION AND REORGANIZATION OF THE ARMY

From the very beginning the army posed a serious problem to the government. Whilst demobilization was primarily an economic problem, the reorganization of the army was basically a political issue. The struggle over it primarily involved the character of the new army—would it ultimately serve the revolution or the counter-revolution.

Linder's idea that "the old militaristically disciplined army" be temporarily replaced by a national guard and later organized from volunteers, a "republican guard", a new "defence army" be set up, was quickly torpedoed. It was opposed not only by active officers, but also by the Soldiers' Council, since plans to abolish the army threatened the very existence of this revolutionary organization as well.

Regarding demobilization, the Ministry of Defence hammered out new directives at the beginning of November. According to the new instructions connected with

---

[110] *Rendeletek Tára 1918* (Repository of Decrees, 1918), pp. 2244–2245. Decree No. 5300/ME/1918 of the Hungarian Ministry on Provisional Measures to Proliferate Small Holdings.

[111] *Rendeletek Tára 1919*, Vol. I, p. 246. Circular No. 137262/1918 issued by the Hungarian Minister of the Interior to all Lord Lieutenants and Government Commissioners on Placating the People at the Time of the Preparation of the Land Reform.

[112] *Értekezlet* (Conference), p. 68. "Speech by Barna Buza, Minister of Agriculture." November 22, 1918.

[113] *Értekezlet*, p. 67. "Miklós Gara's Contribution." *Népszava*, January 5, 1918. "The Agricultural Situation. Gyula Rubinek's Statement." *Népszava*, January 24, 1918. "The Big Landowners Are Deliberately Adopting Ca'canny Policy." OPB (National Propaganda Committee) data. Miklós Gara estimated the size of sown arable land at 50%, Gyula Rubinek at 40%, the OPB at 35–40%. A similar figure is published by J. Takács in his book *A földmunkásmozgalom története* (The History of the Agricultural Labour Movement), p. 135.

these, the five youngest age-groups (born in 1896 and later) were not to be dismissed and were to remain, for the time being, at the disposal of the Ministry of Defence. The plan to retain the five age-groups ran counter to Linder's idea and came from István Friedrich (who later served as Prime Minister under the counter-revolutionary regime). He had been taken to the Ministry of Defence at Károlyi's recommendation—though without official endorsement—in the turmoil of revolution on October 31.

At the Cabinet meeting of November 5 Linder asked that Friedrich be relieved of his duties and at the same time wanted to find out whether Friedrich, who acted as Undersecretary of State, had been officially appointed to this job in the first place. The Cabinet agreed with Linder and stated that Friedrich "had not been appointed". When, after this incident, the decree on the retention of the five age-groups and another decree concerning the national guard came out although it evaded the Minister, Linder asked to be relieved of his duties on grounds that shadow cabinets were at work in the Ministry. At the same time he criticized the decrees in question, claiming that the age-groups to be retained comprised 300,000 people, which, in theory, was twice the number permitted by the Entente. The younger generations were undisciplined and could easily be used against the government. Lacking police power, the order for their call-up could not be enforced, and if anyone could defy a ministerial order with impunity this would inevitably undermine the authority of the government. The decree on the national guard stipulated a 30 crown daily wage for its members, which was more than the wages of the industrial workers in the highest income bracket.

Following an audience with Undersecretaries Friedrich, Böhm and Fényes (Böhm was responsible for demobilization, Fényes for the national guard), the Cabinet accepted Linder's resignation on November 9, but decided to keep him in the Cabinet as Minister without portfolio (allocating him the task of conducting negotiations abroad for the preparation of the peace treaty). Friedrich was to be removed from the Ministry of Defence and given a post elsewhere. (In reality, however, Linder resigned his new job as well in a few weeks, while Friedrich stayed on for quite some time, retaining his job as Undersecretary, despite the stand adopted by the Cabinet.)

Linder was succeeded as Minister of Defence by Lieutenant Colonel Albert Bartha, who was chief of general staff of the Temesvár Military Command at the end of October and who participated in the setting up of the People's Council in the Banat on October 31. Bartha was suited for the post of Minister of Defence not only because, as military commissioner and later as government commissioner, after the revolution he resolutely set about to restore law and order but also because he was able to cooperate with local SDP leaders. Moreover, through Ottó Róth, who played a leading role in the organization of the Banat, he had established contact with the Budapest leaders of the Social Democratic Party prior to the revolution.

Following his appointment on November 11 Bartha signed a general order on the setting up of an army, national guard and civic guard. In accordance with Friedrich's conception, the order stipulated that the army was "to be formed via the retention and call-up of the five youngest age-groups".[114] A few days later the Ministry also issued a call-up order to this effect.

The decree of November 11 reduced the daily wage of the national guards from 30 crowns to 10 crowns. Obviously, this gave rise to considerable discontent amongst those affected and became the source of as much chaos and trouble as it had generated when it was unjustifiably high previously.

Yielding to the demand of the Soldiers' Council and the SDP, on December 2 Bartha endorsed the publication of new decrees governing new discipline in the Soldiers' Council and the army.

The significance of the decree on the Soldiers' Council lay in the fact that it legalized the operation of the soldiers' councils and defined their organization and sphere of authority. The decree provided for the election of 5 stewards—1 officer and 4 rank and file per subdivision and company. The body of stewards of the higher units comprised the stewards elected by secret ballot. The Soldiers' Council of Budapest comprised of all the stewards of the Budapest Garrison; the soldiers' councils of rural garrisons were established in a similar manner. The goal and task of the soldiers' councils was defined by the decree as follows: "The soldiers' council is a supervising organ which provides officers and rank and file soldiers alike with the social protection to which every citizen of the Hungarian People's Republic is entitled to." "The goal of the soldiers' council is to ensure the achievements of the revolution." The decree concerning army discipline wished to replace "shackles and flogging" by introducing a new democratic discipline. The most important measure of this decree was that it entrusted the execution of disciplinary punitive power to a jury elected by the stewards.[115]

On December 1 the pensioning off of the general corps was published, a measure which was in line with the public mood and intended to strengthen the government's position. Moreover, it also tied in with the aspirations of the younger officers.

Notwithstanding, the activity of the new Minister of Defence was by no means characterized by the aforementioned measures. Bartha was inclined to agree with the active officers. "I live by you, stand by you and fall together with you!"[116]— declared Bartha on November 11 at the rally of officers and re-enlisted officers and he meant it, too. His activity involved the setting up of officer and university battalions, Szekler and Great Plain hussar regiments and other units of similar character. Bartha wished to fill 25 per cent of the effective force with re-enlisted officers. Accordingly, simultaneously with the publication of the decree on the Soldiers' Council, a confidential instruction was prepared at the Ministry of

---

[114] *Rendeletek Tára 1918*, pp. 2231–2234. Circular 5220/ME/1918 Issued by the Hungarian Ministry Concerning the Internal Order of Hungary's Democratic Independence, Personal Safety, the Protection of Property and Generally the Organizations to Be Set Up to Ensure the Maintaining of Law and Order.

[115] *Rendeleti Közlöny* (Decree Bulletin), December 11, 1918. 32204/1981/HM. On the Regulation of the Soldiers' Council and the Military Steward System. 32203/1918/HM. On the Regulation of the New Army Discipline.

[116] *Pesti Hírlap*, November 12, 1918. "Soldiers Organizing Rally."

Defence about the organization of the so-called alert troops. The decree on the alert divisions, which was despatched on December 7 contained, among other things, the following: "one alert infantry battalion per district, one alert cavalry squadron, one alert field battery and one alert mountain gun battery to be set up separately from other military units. Experienced officers are to carry out the organization. Only volunteers may be admitted to the alert divisions but who must, however, be carefully selected". The driving force behind volunteering is "manly Hungarian pride". "Unreliable elements cannot be taken on." Such elements "must be sent on leave for an undisclosed period" even from the five young age-groups. The alert divisions must be supplied with the best equipment and, if there is no other way, this must be carried out "at the expense of the five age-groups which have been called up"[117]

At the time of the revolution Bartha refused to acknowledge that the aim of his army organizing activity was counter-revolutionary. In his memoirs, however—a decade later—he boasted about this fact and gave special emphasis to it: "I decided to set up alert divisions and officers' regiments. I wanted to create the same kind of organization that was later established by Noske in Germany and with which he annihilated the Spartacus movement. I issued orders at my own responsibility . . . and was forced to keep them secret even from the government. Together with my loyal and reliable associate, General Lorx, we decided to negotiate with the Soldiers' Council for appearances' sake, but decided to drag these on until the alert divisions and the officers' regiments had been set up in order to break up the soldiers' councils with them."[118]

Information leaked out of the Ministry of Defence which created unrest among the ranks of soldiers of revolutionary sentiment, all the more so as news of the officers' organization coincided with other alarming phenomena.

At the end of November the police instituted proceedings against certain leaders of the October uprising and attempted to demobilize the marine national guard returning from Slovakia.

Early in December the right wing of the Party of Independence launched an offensive, sharply criticizing the government's activity and radical measures.

The leading article of the December 8 issue of *Népszava* reported that some demanded the setting up of officers' regiments, while others were trying to persuade the government to follow a conservative policy, to conspire with the reactionary elements. Two days later, *Népszava* reiterated: "A number of active officers are going about their business in the most suspicious manner, holding secret conferences and churning out royalist slogans."[119]

Reliable sources reported that the Ministry of Defence was planning to announce summary justice.

---

[117] *OL Cabinet Minutes 40*, Item II. p. 796. The Organizing of Hungarian Alert Troops (32243/pres. 1–1918).

[118] *Neues Wiener Journal*, July 1, 1928. "Wie ich gestürzt wurde."

[119] *Népszava*, December 10, 1918. "White Guard."

According to other sources—and it was this which stirred up the most serious restlessness among the soldiers—the Ministry of Defence had issued a secret decree under which the strength of the Budapest Garrison was to be reduced to one-third its present size.

On the 11th and 12th, excited rallies were held at the barracks, at which the stewards proposed the staging of a demonstration. Following the rallies of the morning of the 12th, the garrison—the 1st Honvéd Regiment, the 32nd Joint Infantry Regiment, two gun batteries and later the marine guard—a total of almost 8,000 people marched onto the streets. Marching in closed ranks and holding red and red-white-and-green flags and wearing red rosettes, the demonstrators headed for Buda Castle, cheering Mihály Károlyi and demanding Bartha's removal (whose resignation had already been decided upon by the Ministers during the previous night). At Buda Castle the soldiers lined up in Dísz Square and Szent György Square in front of the buildings of the Ministry of Defence and the Prime Minister's office. From the balcony of the Ministry of Defence a staff officer (Gyula Gömbös, Prime Minister during the counter-revolution era) tried to make a speech, however, the soldiers wished neither to see nor hear the career officers of the Ministry. Gömbös' appearance stirred up anger and his voice was drowned in the flood of interjections.

In the name of the body of stewards, the memorandum of the garrison was handed over to Károlyi by Lieutenant Pál Moór (later Budapest's military governor). Károlyi promised to fulfill the soldiers' request. The demands, which were summed up in seven points, contained the following: in return for Bartha's resignation, the appointment of a civilian Minister; the re-organization of the Ministry of Defence, the shelving of the general staff; the actual execution of the decree on the Soldiers' Council; the immediate disbanding of the officers' troops; the rank and file be allowed to elect their own officers on the basis of talent and experience; also the rank and file soldiers could be officers, if they have enough talent and knowledge; the barracks must be made fit for living and the rank and file must be ensured impeccable provision. Following the departure of the delegation Mihály Károlyi and Vince Nagy addressed the soldiers in the name of the government. Afterwards, József Pogány spoke from the window of the headquarters of the Soldiers' Council: "By these demands we rise or fall" he announced, amidst endless cheering.[120]

The procession of the Budapest Garrison demonstrated that the action of the democratic forces was able to obstruct counter-revolutionary designs. At the same time, the size of the officers' organization, their sophisticated methods, as well as the fact that Pogány was attacked for having organized the demonstration even by his own party—Garami had criticized and denounced Pogány most sharply—underlined the strength and chances of the counter-revolution, which were, often unjustifiably, underestimated by some. On December 12 the forces of revolution

[120] *Népszava*, December 13, 1918. "The Demonstration of the Budapest Garrison."

scored a victory, the struggle, however, was by no means at an end. The clash of antagonistic forces on the issue of the army—just as in some other areas—had ultimately resulted in deadlock rather than a clear decision. The government denounced counter-revolutionary organization, but then it also denounced the procession as well. After Bartha's departure the post of Minister of Defence was left unfilled and Károlyi himself temporarily took over the affairs of the ministry.

5. THE DISSOLUTION OF THE MULTINATIONAL STATE

It followed from the stand adopted by the Entente that the Károlyi government's conception, namely that a compromise be concluded with the national minorities at the cost of concessions proved to be a futile enterprise. As Minister of the Nationalities, Jászi was well aware that his conception, which arose from different circumstances, "is not favoured by the present balance of power".[121] In spite of this, Jászi remained in his post for the time being. The reason for this was that he had not yet given up hope that at least part of his hopes would be fulfilled. At the beginning of November, scholars, writers, artists, the cream of the Hungarian intelligentsia drafted an appeal advocating a free confederation and demanded that the National Council establish contact with the national councils of the neighbouring countries for the purpose of forming such a confederation. Jászi gave his consent to the publication of the appeal. He felt that the fact that the idea had no chance of realization under the given circumstances, could not justify the shelving of the appeal.

CROATIA-SLAVONIA AND VOIVODINA

When the Károlyi government took over power the nationality issue had been settled in several respects.

The Croat Sabor proclaimed secession from Hungary on October 29. By appointing a chargé d'affaires to Zagreb, Aladár Balla, the government acknowledged secession as fact. Even in the course of the Belgrade talks the Hungarian delegation had stressed that its "present boundaries", to which it wished to adhere until the signing of the peace treaty, should be understood without Croatia-Slavonia.

Under these circumstances the question in early November was not whether any form of legal tie remained between the areas concerned and Hungary, but rather, how the future of Croatia-Slavonia would develop, how the unification of the South Slav peoples would take place within the framework of a new Yugoslav state.

Instead of diminishing, confusion and uncertainty increased in the South Slav territories of the one-time Monarchy following the declaration of secession.

---

[121] O. Jászi, *Visszaemlékezés a román nemzeti komitéval folytatott aradi tárgyalásaimra* (Recollections of My Arad Talks with the Romanian National Committee), Cluj-Kolozsvár 1921.

Social issues continued to dominate protest action by the peasantry, which accounted for four-fifths of the population and by the workers,[122] who accounted for one-eighth. The spontaneous movement of the peasantry aimed primarily at direct economic goals, while on a political level it demanded democratic reforms. The struggles of the working class (the forming of workers' councils, the occupation of factories, attempts to establish "Soviet republics" on a local level) also reflected the desire to take over power.

National aspirations were primarily voiced by a comparatively narrow stratum of intellectuals and white-collar workers, who had expected jobs, promotion and a political career from the realization of nationalist dreams. These strata were supported in their national aspirations by the urban bourgeoisie as well as by governing circles, not least because they wished to channel the mass movements which threatened their wealth and power in other directions. Owing to the different interests of certain groups within the governing circles, ideas in this regard showed considerable diversity ranging from the Greater Croatia concept professing independence through the acceptance of Serbian hegemony to the acceptance of the idea of unification at any cost.

Following several weeks of wrangling, the Greater Serbia movement emerged victorious from the clash of various trends and views. The fundamental reason for this was rooted in the weakness of the Prečan (living beyond the River Save and the borders of Serbia) bourgeoisie of the South Slav state emerging from the ruins of the Monarchy.

Seated in Zagreb, the National Council, which was formed by the representatives of the bourgeois political parties proved incapable with the participation of a few social democrats, to organize a new, successful army from the Monarchy's disintegrated military forces. These attempts of central power were frustrated both in Budapest and Zagreb as well, despite the fact that the South Slav leaders did not profess pacifist principles and had ordered general mobilization as early as November 2. Lacking an army and a reliable armed police force, the *Narodno Vijeće* was unable to take firm action against mass movements that threatened "order and peace". They viewed the progress of the Italian army and the growing demands of the Italian government in Slovenia, Istria and the Dalmatian coastline helplessly. In the new state the machinery of the former public administration was hardly functioning at all, there were hitches in transportation and the economy hit an all-time low. The influence of the central government (the National Council's Executive Committee) was hardly discernible in Bosnia and Herzegovina and Dalmatia and was practically non-existent in Voivodina.

Aware of its own weakness, the National Council turned to the Entente for help as early as the beginning of November, to check anarchy. In order to

---

[122] *Szücsi,* p. 10. In his study József (Bajza) Szücsi publishes noteworthy figures on the national minority distribution of the population as well as on land conditions. According to these, 3.8% of Croatia's population was Hungarian and 5.6% was German in 1900. At the same time 36.9% and 54.8% of estates over 100 yokes and 28.5% and 31.7% of estates over 1,000 yokes were owned by Hungarian and German landowners, respectively (pp. 27–28).

counterbalance Italian expansionist aspirations it invited Serbian troops—which had been coming in anyway. According to the Hungarian chargé d'affaires in Zagreb the Serb regular army had been enforcing law and order in Croatia by the middle of November. The strength of the Serb army in Croatia was estimated at 40,000, in Bosnia and Herzegovina it was put at 30,000.[123] Indicative of the weakness of central government was the fact that for the time being the new South Slav state did not press for the occupation of the predominantly Croat Muraköz, leaving the suppression of the local peasant uprising to the Hungarian authorities. (The Narodno Vijeće did not in principle object to the occupation of Dalmatia, the only request it made was that as many British and American troops also be sent there as possible.)

The difficult situation of the Southern Slav state which was emerging from the ruins of the Monarchy was further complicated by the fact that the Allies, accepting the reservations of the Italian and Serbian government, refused to recognize the new state. In addition to Hungary, only Austria and Czechoslovakia established diplomatic links with Zagreb.

The unfavourable domestic and international situation, as well as fear of the revolution and the Italians, strengthened the Serbo-Croatian trend. Due to the joining of Serbia the bourgeoisie expected on the one hand, the restoration of law and order, and on the other, that it would emerge from the war on the side of the victors, despite the fact that for four years it had fought on the side of the Central Powers. The presence of the Serbian army was another weighty argument, as was the possibility that the Serbian population and the areas under the greatest threat from the Italians would, in the case of further wrangling, arbitrarily declare union, sidestepping the National Council.

Subsequently, the Executive Committee of the National Council disregarded earlier negotiations and adopted a proposal submitted by the representatives of Dalmatia and Bosnia. On November 24, it declared its support for immediate union with Serbia. Only Radić, the president of the Peasant Party voted against the Executive Committee's resolution at the meeting which continued into the small hours. Demanding the declaration of a republic and greater independence for Croatia, Radić declared the National Council decision null and void at the Peasant Party meeting the following day. Certain nationalist groups of the Croatian bourgeoisie, among them the reorganized Law Party, a faction of the clericals and intellectuals around the journal *Obzor* and even a few democrats held a similar stand. These groups placed the emphasis on the demand for independence or for a republic, depending on their conservative, democratic or "popular" political outlook. The representatives of the pro-Serb majority in the National Council, among them Svĕtozar Pribičević, the vice president of the Council, accused the opposition of having enhanced Habsburg domination and the restoration of the old order through its move. They also argued that the move against Serbia played into

---

[123] *Pesti Hírlap*, November 22, 1918. "The South Slav Complications. The Hungarian Chargé d'affaires in Belgrade on the South Slav Situation." *Bajza*, p. 111.

7*

the hands of Italian expansionist aspirations. In connection with a conspiracy disclosed at the end of November, the Hungarian government was suspected of complicity, which Budapest officially denied.

On November 27 a committee was despatched to Belgrade to implement the resolution and effect unification. Full of anxiety because of inadequate public safety and fearing the appearance of the Green Cadre, the 28 member delegation arrived safely after a long train journey. Acting on behalf of the ailing King, the proclamation of the Kingdom of Serbia, Croatia and Slavonia, which was also joined by Montenegro, was carried out by the Regent Alexander Karageorgević on December 1.

Following the announcement of the unification a demonstration and an armed uprising erupted in Zagreb. The pro-Serbian trend quickly put down the Croatian officers' coup d'état attempt with the help of the Serbian army and responded to the opposition's action with arrests and the introduction of censorship. The National Council did not consider it its task to endorse the decision adopted by the committee sent to the Regent; it regarded the proclamation of unification as the fulfilment of its role.

In Belgrade a central government was formed on December 20—"with the participation of the representatives of the three religions and every province".

The Károlyi government acknowledged the secession of Croatia-Slavonia. However, this did not mean that it agreed with the secession of Voivodina which, at the time, denoted Bácska, the Banat and part of Baranya County.

In Voivodina lived an almost equal proportion of Hungarians, Germans, Romanians, Serbians and other Slav ethnic groups. (According to the 1910 census the distribution according to mother tongue in Bács-Bodrog, Torontál, Temes and Krassó-Szörény Counties was the following: Hungarian: 605,670; German: 578,242; Romanian: 592,435; Serbian and Croatian: 435,543; other Slav ethnic groups: 182,628.)[124] Notwithstanding, the mass and poor peasant movements which flared up at the beginning of November were primarily motivated by economic and social grievances. It was only in a few places that anger against the oppressors was tinged with national sentiment and even then it was directed against public administration–Hungarian public administration in particular. During the confusion of the first few days, even the conflicts between the various nationalist elements of the bourgeoisie lost their significance. Whenever revolutionary movements had to be suppressed the Hungarian, Serbian and German national councils joined forces and made every effort to restore "public security and the protection of property". The reliable officers of the former police force, and the demobilized army, the well-paid national guardsmen regardless of nationality, were well-suited to this purpose. During the "most critical days" units organized from Serbian prisoners of war maintained law and order, at Nagybecskerek German officers carried out "guard duty".

[124]*1910 évi népszámlálás,* Vol. VI., pp. 114–117.

Following the marching in of the Serbian army (November 7–19) the task of restoring law and order fell to the newly arrived soldiers. For this reason the non-Serbian bourgeoisie as well as the civil service looked forward to the arrival of the Serbian army. When it became obvious that the soldiers of the "White Eagle" had arrived not only to collect arms and to restore law and order, but also to immediately dismantle Hungarian public administration, this engendered new conflicts. This was further aggravated by the fact that the Serbian army backed the Serbian bourgeoisie with all its might, which, in the changed situation aspired to hegemony and tried to act as the sole heir to local authority.

Pointing out that the removal of Hungarian public administration and the stoppage of transportation had violated the Belgrade Agreement, on November 21 the Károlyi government turned to Franchet d'Espèrey and tried to lodge a protest. There was no response to the telegramme sent to Saloniki.

On November 25 the Skupstina convened in Novi Sad. The Slav National Assembly, which comprised of 757 deputies, adopted two resolutions. One resolution declared adjoinment to the Kingdom of Serbia, the other declared secession from Hungary. The latter also announced that the Skupstina would form a fifty-member People's Council (*Narodni Svet*) to administer the annexed territory and would set up a provisional government under the name Popular Directorate (*Narodna Uprava*).

The joining of Serbia signified victory for the Greater Serbia movement. At the same time it also meant defeat and decline for those democrats who had wished a unification led by Zagreb—like Vasa Stajić who was later shunned—and had fought for greater independence for Voivodina and the peaceful co-existence of the peoples living there.

The joining up of the Serbian army and the Novi Sad decision made the secession of the southern region an accomplished fact. The only controversial issue that remained to be solved was the exact definition of the northern and eastern boundaries of the area. (The latter, the eastern frontier presented an extremely difficult problem for the peace conference. Not only the new South Slav state, but the Kingdom of Romania had also put in a claim for the Banat, claiming that the secret agreement signed in Bucharest in the summer of 1916 had awarded this region, which was inhabited partly by Romanians, to Romania.)

In the disputed areas owing to the weakness or the lack of local Serbian bourgeoisie, the old body of public administrators remained in its place for a while. The law-enforcement organs brought to life by the October revolution, the various councils, the government-commissioners, and Lord Lieutenants appointed by the Károlyi government also continued their work. When the Serbian army made an attempt to take over public administration in these areas, this, as well as the increasingly explosive political and economic situation, led to the eruption in February 1919 of a militant strike movement in Pécs and Temesvár, which was also joined by other towns, among them Szabadka and Nagykikinda. The railway workers and miners formed the backbone of this movement which was supported by various strata of the population, primarily by civil servants afraid of losing their jobs. The action taken by the organized workforce—not only the Hungarian but workers of other nationalities as well in towns of mixed ethnic population—was a manifestation of protest against the reactionary Greater Serbia trend, against the disfranchising measures of the Serbian bourgeoisie, which had replaced the Hungarian bourgeoisie. According to a *Népszava* report the Serbian socialists supported the strike movement as well and "expressed their solidarity for their oppressed fellow workers" at some twenty public rallies.[125]

SLOVAKIA

On October 30—a day after the Croation Sabor decided upon secession from Hungary—the Slovak politicians also convened in Turócszentmárton. Convened by Matúš Dula, president of the Slovak National Council, the conference was attended by the representatives of every Slovak political party and faction. Among those present were the Turócszentmárton conservatives who were inclined to separatism, pro-Czech Hlassists (who were the followers of Masaryk and Beneš), some members of the People's Party, of clerical orientation and of the social democrats. Held on the premises of the Bank of Tátra, the meeting adopted a resolution in the name of the Slovak National Council, which was published on the following day, in *Národné Noviny,* the paper of the Slovak National Party. In its original form the declaration stressed secession from Hungary, "total independence" and the "unrestricted right to self-determination". It was in the course of the drafting of the final version that adjoinment to the Czechoslovak state was unequivocally expressed. This was done at the suggestion of Milan Hodža, who had contacts with Czech politicians and who had arrived at the scene of the meeting in the evening of the 30th. Referring to the latest developments (Andrássy's telegramme and the events of the 28th in Prague) Hodža corrected the original text and complemented it with the following interpolation: "We agree with the newly emerged international legal situation, which was formulated by President Wilson on October 18, 1918 and which was recognized by the Austro–Hungarian Foreign Minister on October 27, 1918."[126] The improvements aimed at the emphasizing of Czechoslovak unity and deleted passages about independent Slovak representation.

The declaration was signed by 103 people. Their distribution according to occupation: 13 industrialists, artisans and shopkeepers, 5 bank managers, 14 Lutheran and Roman Catholic priests, 4 landowners, 3 free-lancers, 15 lawyers, 4 medical doctors, 3 architects, 3 teachers, 7 college students, 13 white-collar workers employed by private firms, 5 workers and 7 agricultural workers.[127]

[125] *Népszava*, March 8, 1919. "Against the Aggressiveness of the Occupiers."
[126] *Steier*, p. 571., *Opočenský*, pp. 173–175.
[127] *OL K 40–1918–VII.* t. 275. Deklarácia Slovenskeho Národa.

On October 30 Mihály Károlyi sent a telegramme to Turócszentmárton in the name of the Hungarian National Council. "The Slovak National Council will come to a decision", said the telegramme, "as befits the best interests of the Slovak people . . . the Slovak and the Hungarian people are mutually dependent on each other . . . we must seek a more attractive future and a better life for ourselves through peaceful agreement and fraternal cooperation." The reply which came from the Slovak National Council, which was worded by Hodža and signed by Matúš Dula courteously declined the offer of cooperation and stressed that "the free Czechoslovak nation wishes to be a good neighbour and brother to the Hungarian nation".[128]

Unlike the similar resolutions adopted in Prague and Zagreb, the Turócszentmárton declaration did not signify the immediate, the de facto takeover of power. Hungarian public administration continued to function in the Slovak-populated areas and disappeared only in certain regions, primarily in villages, where hated public administrators and the local law enforcement organs fled, as in other parts of the country, from powerful mass movements.

The Hungarian–German and Slovak bourgeoisie joined forces to suppress the revolutionary mass movement of the returning soldiers and the peasants, which did not spare even the property of the Slovak landowners and merchants, regarding its distribution rightful and justified as the appropriation and taking away of the assets of exploiters of other nationalities. The various national councils cooperated and supported the public administration organs, insofar as the maintaining of law and order and the protection of private property were involved. On orders from the Slovak National Council, Slovaks, too, applied in large numbers to be taken on by the newly organized national guard. (Under an agreement signed with the Hungarian Ministry of Defence, Slovak national guard was to maintain law and order in towns and villages with a Slovak majority and Hungarian national guard in those with a Hungarian majority.)

Aware that civil war could erupt at any moment, the Slovak bourgeoisie did not wish to sharpen antagonisms. Aware of its own weakness, it made only very few attempts to seize power by force. The activity of the Slovak National Council was aimed at calming down public anger and, simultaneously, at popularizing the idea of union with Bohemia. The latter was opposed by some, primarily in Eastern Slovakia, who advocated the idea of an independent Slovakia and the proclamation of the Slovak People's Republic with support from the Hungarian authorities.

On November 2 a Czech military division arrived from the Moravian small town of Hodonin to Szakolca to restore law and order. Fears were widespread at the Hodonin Town Hall that the armed insurrection would spread to Moravian territory from the other side. Having accomplished its task, the special detachment was preparing to leave when the representative of the Turócszentmárton National

[128] *Pesti Hírlap,* October 31, 1918. "Mihály Károlyi's Telegramme to the Slovak National Council." *OL K. 40–1918–VII.* t. 44. Matús Dula, President of the Slovak National Council to Count Mihály Károlyi, November 4, 1918.

Council arrived at Szakolca and called on the detachment, which comprised of volunteers, to stay.

At the same time members of the Slovak National Council in Prague turned to the Prague National Committee with the request that, considering the state of anarchy, the "looting" and the "total collapse of law and order", it should send in the army and occupy the Slovak-populated areas. The *Narodni Vybor* fully agreed with this request for it felt that without the occupation of Slovakia, which had also been urged by the political exiles, the fate of the Czechoslovak state, which existed only on paper at that point, could be considered uncertain. The first volunteer units comprised of Sokolists and deserters from the old army and other applicants, were complemented with gendarmes and directed to Slovakia. At the same time the reorganizing of the one-time Czech and Moravian regiments of the former common army began.

On November 5 a provisional Slovak government was formed in Szakolca, headed by Vavro Šrobar. This remained in office until November 14, the setting up of the first Czechoslovak government. At this point Šrobar joined Kramář's government in which a ministry was organized for him.

Citing the orders of the provisional Slovak Government, the volunteers arriving at Szakolca occupied Malacka, Szenic, Nagyszombat and pressed forward, in the south, as far as the vicinity of Pozsony to the railway station of Dévénytó. On November 8 further volunteer divisions crossed the border at the Vlara Pass and the Jablonka Pass. Those arriving from the Vlara Pass occupied Trencsén and Vágújhely on November 10 and those arriving across the Jablonka Pass reached as far as Kralovan along the Kassa–Ödenburg railway line and occupied Zsolna, Ruttka and Turócszentmárton on November 12.

The representative of the Hungarian government, Géza Supka, was told in Prague by the Czechs that the invasion of Slovakia by the volunteers had been necessitated because of looting and the disintegration of law and order. The representatives of the Czech National Committee argued that "the Hungarian authorities and gendarmerie had left the areas in question unprotected". The Czechoslovak army was party of the Entente forces, the reasoning continued, and their soldiers were confronted with two main tasks under the given circumstances: first, "protection against the threat of Bolshevism from Galicia", and second, preparing for the prevention of a possible aggressive breakthrough attempt by Mackensen's army. In principle Supka agreed with the need to restore law and order, but suggested that "if possible, British troops occupy Upper Hungary if occupation was vital".[129]

At the beginning of November the government's official stand was that "it would not resort to armed resistance against the law-enforcing forces".[130] For a while there were no clashes between Czech and Hungarian armed units in Western

[129] *Népszava*, November 12. "Why are the Czechs Coming to Hungary?" *Pesti Hírlap*, November 12, 1918. "The Czechs are Using Strategic Reasons to Justify the Occupation of Upper Hungary."

[130] *Népszava*, November 20, 1918. "The Events Leading up to the Clashes."

Slovakia, the various military and police units strove to delimit the areas under their surveillance.

When it became obvious that more was involved on the part of the Czechs than just the restoration of law and order, that the Hungarian authorities were to be replaced before the final decision of the peace conference, the government, referring to the Belgrade Agreement, lodged a protest. On November 11, a proclamation signed by Károlyi and the new Minister of Defence Albert Bartha, was released, which announced that the government "would defend the country's boundaries against any attack that violated international law with armed force".[131]

Following the release of the proclamation the Ministry of Defence despatched several infantry and machine gun companies and police detatchments from Budapest, Nagykanizsa, Zólyom and Kassa, as well as artillery and an armoured train to Western Slovakia. The 400 strong marine national guard under the command of Viktor Heltai was also directed to Pozsony. The latter was despatched with the undeclared purpose of removing sailors who were thought to be too revolutionary and consequently unreliable from Budapest.

Weak in strength, but superior in numbers, the armed forces directed to the Slovak areas re-occupied the majority of the occupied towns and villages in a matter of days. The Czech units (which numbered only a little over a thousand at the beginning of November and less than five thousand at the end of November and the beginning of December)[132] retreated to border villages in the north, to Moravia.

The Czechs protested against these latest developments. On November 19 Kramář stated in a memorandum that the Entente had recognized the Czecho-slovak state and from this it followed that the territory inhabited by the Slovaks formed part of the Czechoslovak state. He stated that they would accept the decision of the peace conference, however, it would only be able to draw the exact boundaries as the Entente had already made the final judgement in regard to the national status of Slovakia. The Belgrade Agreement was not binding for Czechoslovakia as the Hungarian government could not conclude a cease-fire in the name of a territory which, following the Entente decision, already formed part of the Czechoslovak state and could not conclude a cease-fire in the name of the Slovaks either, since the new order had been proclaimed in Hungary without Slovak representation. Kramář once again pointed out the role played by Czechoslovak forces in the maintaining of law and order and added: "our law enforcement guards also protected the Hungarian minority". In conclusion Kramář quoted Wilson's November 5 message: "Law and order must be maintained and there must not be any bloodshed."[133]

---

[131] *Népszava*, November 12, 1918. "The Hungarian Government Protests Against the Czech Attack."

[132] M. Hodža: *Slovenský rozchod*, p. 25. According to Hodža the strength of the troops was 1,150 on November 15 and 4,700 on December 2. A similar figure for initial strength is quoted by *Opočensky*, p. 213.

[133] *Népszava*, November 21, 1918. Kramář's memorandum: "The Slovak Territories Are Parts of the Czechslovak State."

At the end of November Milan Hodža arrived in Budapest as the Czechoslovak government's new envoy, where he was later joined by several representatives of the Slovak National Council. Hodža's commission was to negotiate the dismantling of Hungarian public administration in Slovakia and the withdrawal of the Hungarian army. It soon became clear that Hodža was also willing to discuss other issues: a provisional arrangement whereby the situation of the Slovak-populated areas could be consolidated until the signing of the peace treaty. The substance of the concept that emerged in talks with Jászi was that the areas in question would be given extensive autonomy: power would rest with the Slovak National Council which would be responsible for public administration and would maintain law and order with the help of the national guard subordinated to it. The autonomous area would elect its own national assembly, and common affairs would be discussed by the Slovak and Hungarian National Assembly via delegations.

The Slovak leaders' willingness to negotiate—although Hodža later tried to suggest that this had only been a tactical move—arose from the uncertain state of the situation. The Slovak leaders were aware of domestic unrest and the military weakness of the Prague government and were also sceptical about imminent help from the Entente, as Vix had told Hodža on November 28 that he "disapproved of the presence of the Czech army in Slovakia and regarded it as the violation of the Belgrade Agreement".[134]

The Károlyi government discussed plans for a possible agreement on several occasions. The Cabinet meeting of December 1 finally voted for the agreement, despite reservations expressed by some of the Ministers in regard to concessions. The government felt that an agreement with the Slovak National Council, rather than with the Czechoslovak government, could possibly drive a wedge between the Czechs and the Slovaks. This, however, was not the only or the most important reason. A more important argument was that through common affairs Hungary could, ultimately, retain Slovakia and this example would be followed by the other nationalities as well. Moreover, the preliminary agreement would be advantageous from the viewpoint of the peace talks. Those who proposed that the draft be accepted pointed to the consequences as the ultimate argument. "If some sort of agreement does not come about, anarchy and in its wake, Bolshevism will follow."[135]

The talks, which were nearing completion, reached a deadlock at the last moment. On November 30 the Czechoslovak government disowned Hodža. An official statement announced that he had not been empowered to conduct negotiations of this nature. Behind the Prague statement lay not only the indignation of the Czech and Slovak leaders who had been staying in Prague and who regarded the one-sided action of the Slovak National Council as treason, but also far more serious developments than this, namely that at the end of November

[134]Opočensky, p. 216. J. Sebestyén: *Dr. Hodza Milán útja* (Dr. Milan Hodža's Road), Bratislava 1938, p. 94.

[135]OL Cabinet Minutes, December 1, 1918.

Foch and the French government totally accepted Czech reasoning. (Mention of this has already been made in the previous chapter.) On December 3 Vix made Franchet's message known which said that "the Hungarian government should immediately withdraw its troops from Slovakia".[136]

The Károlyi government did not dare, indeed did not wish to oppose the Entente's stance. Open disagreement would have amounted to a break with a foreign policy that was declared to be pro-Entente and would carry the risk of a new war, a risk which the government, aware of the dreadful state of the army, wanted to avoid at all costs. At the Cabinet meeting of November 29 the question was put to Albert Bartha, Minister of Defence, "could we possibly conduct a proper war from the occupied area against a Czecho-Slovak state in alliance with the Entente?" The minister replied that he considered such an event impossible. On December 3, upon giving an account of Vix's letter, Minister of the Interior Tivadar Batthyány, Party of Independence MP, was of the view that "there can be no opposition, this must be carried out".[137]

Vix's letter and the government's answer was published in the press on December 5. At the same time a proclamation bearing Károlyi's signature was also published. Drafted by Jászi, the proclamation spoke about having to act under the pressure of necessity and pointed out once again: "We wish to create a free democratic Switzerland of the East from old Hungary. We seek friendship and peaceful agreement with the peoples living beyond our frontiers and we hope that we shall find this . . . the time will also come for the heartfelt reconciliation of nations. We should face the world as a nation who has done everything in its power to help bring this about as soon as possible."[138]

Since the letter of December 3 did not state the boundaries of the areas to be evacuated, Hodža and Bartha agreed upon a provisional line of demarcation on December 6. The provisional agreement gave rise to further complications after having been declared null and void by the government in Prague. Finally, on December 22, the Supreme War Council in Versailles decided upon a line of demarcation slightly further south than this. (The decision, which has already been discussed in the previous chapter, placed Slovakia's provisional boundaries north of the Rivers Danube and the Ipoly, south of Rimaszombat and west of the River Ung.)

The evacuation of the areas adjoined to Czechoslovakia was completed at the end of January. Fighting erupted only in places where certain units put up resistance despite government orders or where the Czechoslovak army attempted to move beyond the December 6, and later, the December 22 line.

The distribution according to nationality of the population living in the area, stated by a Hungarian statistical survey carried out in 1910, delimited by the

---

[136] *Document*, p. 95. Le Chef de la Mission Militaire Alliée au Président de la République Hongroise. 3. decembre 1918.

[137] *OL Cabinet Minutes*, November 29, 1918; December 3, 1918.

[138] *Népszava*, December 5, 1918. "The Government's Proclamation to the People."

demarcation line of December 22 was as follow: 58.2% of the population was Slovak (the Czechoslovak census of 1919 put this figure at 63.3%). The proportion of Hungarians was 28.9% and 27%, respectively, that of German-speakers 6.8% and 4.7%, respectively and Ukrainians accounted for 3.8% and 4.5%, respectively.[139]

Simultaneously with the occupation of Slovakia, the Czech army also occupied the German-populated areas of Bohemia and Moravia and removed the local German–Austrian provincial governments. The Austrian State Council, which regarded these areas as part of German Austria suggested a referendum, however, this proposal was rejected by the French and later also by the British and Italian governments, in the same way as they had rejected a similar proposition submitted by the Hungarian government.

In the course of December and January legionaries arriving from Italy joined the volunteer units—complete with Slovaks—in the occupation of Slovakia. Equipped in Italy and commanded by Italian officers, the 20,000 strong legionary corps was the finest and most disciplined part of the Czechoslovak army.[140]

Simultaneously with the arrival of the Czechoslovak army the setting up of civilian public administration began. From December 10 a Slovak Ministry headed by Šrobar, began to operate in Zsolna, which later, on February 4, moved its headquearters to Pozsony (Bratislava). The social democrats (Emanuel Lehoczky) also participated in the work of the ministry, which was invested with full powers; one of Šrobar's first measures was to dismantle the councils and national committees.

Since owing to the uncertainty and chaos that accompanied the evacuation, the mass movement flared up with renewed strength in December. The non-Slovak landowners as well as the Hungarian and German bourgeoisie eargerly awaited the appearance of the Czechoslovak army, particularly the Italian officers and the legionaries arriving in Italian uniforms. In Kassa the frightened government commissioner asked the Czechoslovak units to enter the town on December 29 instead of January 1—as had originally been planned —in order to restore law and order. A similar move was made in Érsekújvár, where "the town sent a delegation to the Czechs to call them into the town to prevent looting".[141] In Pozsony, the German bourgeoisie made a firm protest against the possible defence of the town and on December 20 sent a petition to the Hungarian government with the request that "it should use its influence to prevent an attempt of this kind that would

---

[139] *A magyar béketárgyalások*, pp. 446–447. According to the 1910 Hungarian census the percentage figures stand for the following absolute numbers: Total population: 2,909.160, Slovak: 1,693,546, Hungarian: 841,198, German: 197,875, Ruthenian: 110,935, other: 65,606.

[140] *Truppendienst*, 6/1969, p. 534., Die Kämpfe in der Slowakei und in Teschen in den Jahren 1918–1919. *Jezek*, p. 34 and Appendix 2.

[141] HL *Tanácsköztársasági gyűjtemény* (Republic of Councils Collection), 771/A. p. 99. J. Breit: *A csehek hadműveletei Magyarországon 1918/19 évben* (Czech Hostilities in Hungary in 1918/19), manuscript.

endanger the life and property of the citizens".[142] After a workers' council took
over power in the town at the end of December, the Hungarian bourgeoisie adopted
a similar stand. Following the marching in of the legionaries (January 1), the retired
Lord Lieutenant Count József Zichy appeared before the bailiff and declared the
divine origin of the new power. "All power descends from God", he said in his
welcoming address and "he would support the new power with all his might".[143]

In spite of the army which marched in under the pretext of restoring law and
order and despite the measures of a public administration that made arrangements
to combat Bolshevism, the organized workers, the railway workers and the white-
collar stratum who stood to lose their jobs protested in the areas awarded to
Czechoslovakia just as forcefully as they had done in Voivodina. A host of strikes
erupted at the beginning of February. The workers fought for economic demands
(the elimination of unemployment, a ban on reducing salaries and wages, the
payment of benefits, the provision of food) and for the restoration of political
rights. In some towns the nationalist elements tried to impart an anti-Czech slant to
these movements, in which not only Hungarian and German, but Slovak workers
also participated and an anti-Hungarian slant to the retaliation following them.

TRANSYLVANIA AND ROMANIANS LIVING IN HUNGARY

The Romanian National Council was formed in Budapest on October 31 at the
Vadászkürt Hotel. Its forming marked the beginnings of an alliance between the
SDP's Romanian section and the Romanian National Party. It will be remembered
that at the October 13 emergency meeting of the Social Democratic Party Flueras,
the spokesman for the Romanian section spoke out against the bourgeois
politicians and the Romanian nationalists ("Aurel Vlad and his associates do not
want genuine social order... We cannot and will not associate with them"). It is
thus obvious that the forming of the Romanian National Council signified the
Romanian section's previous stance which had rejected cooperation. The forming
of the Hungarian National Council obviously also played a part in the fact that at
the end of October the trend advocating alliance with the bourgeois parties
triumphed amongst the Romanian social democrats who later split up into two
factions. Following October 25 the advocates of the alliance could point out that if
the Hungarian social democrats had acted in such a way they were able to do so as
well.

The principle of parity was asserted in the Romanian National Council. Of the
Council's 12 members 6 belonged to the Romanian National Party, 6 to the social
democrats.[144] This was a favourable ratio for the social democrats if account is

---

[142] *OL K 40–1919–VI*. t. 38. Der "Deutsche Volksrat" an die Ungarische Volksregierung, 20
Dezember 1918.

[143] Gy. Panajoth-Fejér: "Pozsony sorsdöntő órái" (Pozsony's Decisive Hours). In: *Váci Könyv* (Vác
Book), Vác 1938, p. 222.

[144] *Korunk* (Our Time), 12/1957. p. 1661. Gheorgiu–Nuţu, p. 102.

made for the fact that in the South Slav and Slovak national councils the social democrats constituted a weak minority from the very beginning. This only appeared to be a favourable position, however, since the National Party filled key posts with its own people from the beginning and also laid down as the condition of cooperation that only those social democrats should participate in the Council's activity who "do not impede decision-making".[145] After moving its headquarters to Arad in the early days of November, the Romanian National Council was expanded by the representatives of other organizations and associations. This entailed a change in the original ratio and later developments increasingly followed this tendency.

One of the first acts of the Romanian National Council was to issue, on November 1, a joint appeal with the Hungarian National Council and the representatives of the Saxons. Signed by Teodor Mihali, János Hock and Vilmos Melzer on behalf of the two national councils and the Saxon MPs, the proclamation called upon "the sons of the Hungarian, Romanian and Saxon nations" to join forces and defend domestic law and order and "the safety of people and property".[146] Jászi announced the agreement at the Cabinet meeting on November 2 as a significant event and, with the endorsement of the Cabinet, immediately called upon the Lord Lieutenants as well as the local municipal authorities to support "the spontaneous social campaign".[147]

In spite of the revolutionary movements cooperation between the Hungarian and the Romanian bourgeoisie became actual in the early days of November. According to the account of the president of the Kolozsvár National Council the activity of the Hungarian, Romanian, and Saxon national councils was characterized at the beginning of November by "fraternal cooperation".[148] Those members and staff of the Romanian National Council who had previously been public employees continued to receive their wages. The Romanian national guard with a few exceptions, organized independently, but maintained law and order with the Hungarian national guard and the military commands with the approval of the Ministry of Defence, supplied it with arms and money.

Cooperation was based on the fact that the revolutionary movement had spread to purely Romanian villages as well, posing a threat to Romanian landowners, farmers, officials and shop-keepers. Romanian peasants attacked Teodor Mihali's Nagyilonda estate and the wealthy landowner leaders of the Romanian National Party—Alexandru Vajda, Aurel Vlad and György Illyésfalvi Papp also suffered a similar fate. Not only the Gyulafehérvár estate of the Roman Catholic Church fell

[145] *Albani*, p. 159; Z. Szász; Az erdélyi román polgárság szerepéről 1918 őszén (Concerning the Role of the Romanian Bourgeoisie in the Autumn of 1918), *Századok* (Centuries), 2/1972, p. 314.

[146] *OL K 401 1918. IX.* t. 1. Circular Telegramme to the Lord Lieutenants and the Municipal Authorities. The original copy of the proclamation is enclosed in the file.

[147] *Ibid.*

[148] *Új Magyar Szemle*, Nos. 2–3/1920, p. 158.

victim to the anger of the peasantry, but also the Greek Orthodox archiepiscopal estate in Balázsfalva and the Greek Orthodox episcopal estates in Nagyvárad.

The cooperation which emerged at the beginning of November did not, however, mean that the antagonism between the Romanian and Hungarian bourgeoisie had disappeared. This remained despite a common interest to suppress the revolutionary movements and as time went by increased. The Romanian bourgeoisie wished to give a nationalist direction to the revolutionary movement and felt that the use of force to restore law and order was inadequate in itself. The kindling of nationalist sentiment promised to bear fruit as the main targets of the popular movement were the following: public administration which became particularly hated during the war, the law enforcement organization which was overwhelmingly Hungarian and the majority of the landed estates, which were also the property of Hungarian landowners.

In areas later awarded to Romania 60.1% of the over 100 yoke estates, 85.7% of the over 1,000 yoke estates were in the hands of Hungarian landowners.[149] The distribution according to mother tongue in the same area was, according to the 1910 census the following: 53,2% Romanian, 32,4% Hungarian and 10.6% German.[150]

The central and local Romanian national councils strove, on the one hand—and not unsuccessfully—to take over local public administration and, on the other, to pursue more far-reaching goals.

On November 9 the Romanian National Council, which had its headquarters in Arad, sent a letter to Budapest, "to the government of the Hungarian National Council" in which it demanded the handing over of "full governmental power" of the Romanian-populated areas to protect "law and order, public security and property". The Romanian National Council wished to extend Romanian domination over 23 counties and a part of 3 counties (Békés, Csanád, Ugocsa), adding that it would respect the Wilsonian principles in regard to the other peoples living in the area in question. The letter warned the Hungarian government that if it rejected Romania's demands, Romania would discontinue any further cooperation.[151]

Since the Romanian bourgeoisie considered itself too weak to carry out the double task of restoring law and order and taking over power on its own, it pressed for the intervention of the Romanian royal army.

[149] *Az erdélyi föld sorsa*, p. 208.
[150] *A magyar béketárgyalások*, Vol. I., p. 145; *1910. évi népszámlálás*, Vol. VI., p. 116; *Jakabffy*, p. 4. In his statistical proclamation Elemér Jakabffy published and criticized Romania's 1920 official figures. (C. Martinovici–N. Istrati: "Dictionarul Transilvaniei"). His principal objection was that the Romanian statistics listed the Jews, 76–89% of whom declared themselves Hungarians in 1910, as a separate nationality—putting their number at 181,340. According to the 1920 Romanian census the percentage ratio in the areas annexed to Romania was as follows: 57.9% Romanian, 25.8% Hungarian and 10.5% German. The percentage distribution in absolute terms, according to the data of the 1910 Hungarian census, is the following: total population: 5,265,444; Romanian: 2,800,073; Hungarian: 1,704,851; German: 559,824; Serbian: 54,874; Croatian: 2,141; Slovak: 30,932; Ruthenian: 16,318; other: 96,431.
[151] *OL K 40–1918–IX.* t. 240. The letter of István C. Pop, president of the Romanian National Council, to the government of the Hungarian National Council. November 9, 1918.

On November 10 and the days following it several delegations set off for Iasi. Using the "Bolshevik threat" and the retaliatory measures of Hungarian reactionaries as a pretext they asked for the help of the Romanian army.

Since the letter of the Romanian National Council had set a deadline for reply (6 p.m. on November 12), the government urgently set about to discuss what was to be done in the matter. In the afternoon and evening hours of November 10, first the National Council and then a meeting held with the participation of experts dealt with the issue. At the series of talks participants accepted the bourgeois radical stance which advocated negotiations. A delegation, led by Jászi, was set up, in which Jászi represented the government and Dezső Ábrahám and Dezső Bokányi represented the National Council. Accompanied by experts and journalists, the delegation set off for Arad on the 13th, where two days of talks commenced.

Jászi submitted two proposals to the representatives of the Romanian National Council. The substance of the first proposal was that if possible in Transylvania homogeneous national blocks should be formed rather than the artificial county framework. Following the Swiss canton pattern, these blocks would possess cultural and administrative autonomy, joint organs would be established to handle common affairs, and they would have representatives in the national central government. As a temporary solution, the second proposal suggested that the Romanian National Council take over public administration in all districts and towns with Romanian majorities and that it represent itself in the Hungarian government through a representative. This second proposal comprised of 11 points and, among other things, stipulated that in the areas in questions, the old body of civil servants, with the exception of the Lord Lieutenants and government commissioners, would remain in their place and the Romanian National Council would guarantee the protection of people and property and would not avail itself of help from the Romanian royal army.

The Romanian leaders rejected both proposals. The greatly renowned Iuliu Maniu, who had arrived in Arad on the 14th, demanded full sovereignity. Jászi's argument that taking "the spirit of inhumanity and injustice" too far would lead to the dictatorship of the workers' and soldiers' councils, was ineffective.

The Romanian National Council's reply stated that the Hungarian government "does not recognize the right of the Romanian nation to exercise executive power itself over the areas populated by the Romanian nation". The Hungarian proposals submitted "prospects for only partial and limited administrative activity for the Romanian nation". They cannot accept the offer as it does not provide an adequate basis for the guarantee of "the full maintenance of public order".[152]

Despite the failure of the Arad talks, contact was not broken with the Romanian National Council. Despite what had been stated in the ultimatum ("we shall cease all further cooperation with the authorities") of the 9th, the Romanian leaders continued to be willing to cooperate "for the protection of public order, of personal

---

[152] *Pesti Hírlap,* November 15, 1918. "The Romanians Request Arms for the Romanian National Guards. The Resolution Submitted by Dr. Aurel Lazár, Member of the Romanian National Council."

safety and of property". For this reason the government continued to extend financial support to the Romanian national guards, though the Cabinet meeting of November 18 refused to supply arms.

On November 20 the Romanian National Council published a proclamation, which was also translated into French. Addressed to the peoples of the world, the proclamation announced the intention to secede in unequivocally clear terms: "the Romanian nation in Transylvania and in Hungary does not, under any circumstances, wish to live in any kind of state community with the Hungarian nation, and it is determined to create a free and independent state in the areas inhabited by it". "The government of the former oppressors has refused to endorse this decision of the Romanian Nation"—the proclamation stated, adding, however, that "in spite of this we shall not resort to force, but will await international arbitration, that will replace crude force with justice".[153]

In response to the proclamation, which, while listing the Romanian grievances in detail, disregarded the difference between the government of the former oppressors and the national minorities policy of the new Hungarian government, a proclamation signed by Mihály Károlyi was published in Budapest on November 24. The call, which was addressed to "all non-Hungarian speaking peoples of the people's republic", promised democratic reforms, land, local administrative and cultural autonomy for the national minorities, stressing that the people's government, too, wished to realize the Wilsonian principles.[154]

The Romanian National Council rejected Jászi's proposals not only on the grounds of their inadequacy. In the background of the rejection stood the developments of the international situation. The Romanian leaders had been familiar with the secret Bucharest Agreement of August 1916 as well as with Lansing's Iasi telegramme of November 5, 1918. ("The Government of the United States is not unmindful of the aspirations of the Romanian people without as well as within the boundaries of the Kingdom.")[155] They knew about the turn of the tide in Romania, the change of government, about the ultimatum handed over to Mackensen's army and they also knew that the Entente once again regarded Romania as an ally. It was obvious that under the circumstances it was only a matter of time before the Romanian royal army would march into Transylvania, which the Belgrade Agreement had also made possible.

The first reports of the appearance of the Romanian army reached Budapest on November 13 and Arad at probably the same time, or perhaps even earlier. According to the report of the Brassó frontier police and the gendarmerie Romanian troops appeared at the frontier gates of Tölgyes and Gyimes and on November 12 marched into Gyimesbükk and Gyergyó. The Romanian soldiers

---

[153] *Pesti Hírlap*, November 21, 1918. "The Proclamation of the Romanian National Council."

[154] *Pesti Hírlap*, November 24, 1918. "Government Proclamation to the Nationalities."

[155] *Documents Relating to the Foreign Relations of the United States, 1918*, Suppl. 1. Vol. I., p. 785. The Hungarian translation of the message is published by *Pesti Hírlap*, November 8, 1918. "Lansing's Message to Romania. He Endorses the Wishes of the Romanian People Concerning the Areas Beyond the Kingdom."

who appeared at the passes of the Eastern Carpathians were the sentries of those two divisions which the Romanian Military Command had set up from the mobilized units of the army (for the time being eight age-groups were being called up) to occupy Transylvania. By early December the troops (7th Division) which were pressing forward from the direction of Tölgyes and Borszék, had occupied the upper valley of the Maros, and the units arriving from the direction of Gyimesbükk and Csíkszereda (1st Fighter Division) occupied the upper valley of the Olt. On December 2 the Romanian royal army marched into Marosvásárhely, reaching Beszterce on 4 and Brassó on December 7.

The two divisions pressing forward from the east were later joined by a third (2nd Fighter Division). Following the retreating German (Mackensen) army, this division drove forward from a southern direction with the target of occupying Fogaras, Szeben and Hunyad Counties. Its most pressing task was to occupy the Zsilvölgy mining district and the restoration of law and order so as to "to curb anarchist agitation". First a battalion arrived in the neighbourhood of Lupény, Anina and Petrozsény (December 4 and 5) and this was followed by the occupation of Nagyszeben, Szászváros, Piski and Déva. The Romanian army reached the demarcation line laid down in the Belgrade Agreement by the middle of December.

Romanian commanders on the occupied territories referred to the Entente commission and justified the occupation as help that had to be extended to the Romanian population and as the need to restore "law and order endangered by the Bolshevik spirit".[156] A proclamation addressed by the Romanian King, Ferdinand to the Romanian soldiers and bourgeoisie at the time of the volte-face of November 10—which was distributed in leaflets by the occupying army—stated that Romania "sees its century-old desire, the unification of all Romanians in a free and great state fulfilled".[157] The appeal of the Chief of General Staff, General Prezan, which also "passed through many hands", spoke about a Romania "extending from the Danube to the Tisza" and ensured every citizen of this area that the Romanian army would protect "the population's personal safety and property regardless of nationality or religion".[158] The official proclamations left no doubt that the Romanian army was following even more far-reaching goals and it was unlikely that it would respect the demarcation line laid down without it in Belgrade.

It was under these circumstances that the "National Assembly" of the Romanians living in Transylvania and Hungary convened in Gyulafehérvár on December 1. Out of the 1,228 members of the national assembly, 600 were elected and 628 were delegated. The right to delegate was possessed by the churches, cultural associations, various societies, schools and artisans. The Social Democratic Party was entitled to delegate 18 members in the name of organized workers.[159]

The leaders disagreed over the issue of the proposal to be submitted to the national assembly. Supported by clerical circles, the right wing (Mihali, Vajda

---

[156] *Mărdărescu*, p. 15.
[157] *OL K 40–1918–IX*. t. 367. King Ferdinand of Romania's Proclamation.
[158] *OL K 40–1918–IX*. t. 367. Prezan's Call. *Bernachot*, p. 238—239.
[159] *Erdély története*, Vol. II., p. 444.

[Voivod] and Maniu who was with them in this matter) advocated unconditional union. Some leaders—such as, for example, Stefan C. Pop—who feared the rivalry of the Romanian bourgeoisie, proposed autonomy (because "otherwise it may easily happen that the soldiers of fortune from Regat invade the new territory to the Romanians' disadvantage").[160] The social democrats wished to make union subject to certain conditions, to democratic reform, Romania's democratic transformation. ("We want to unite with Romania, but only on the condition that Romania trasforms into a truly democratic country, too. We want to unite with the Romania of the workers, but under no condition with the country of exploitation or of the Hohenzollern.")[161] The representatives of the democratic line, Vasile Goldis, Ioan Suciu, Emil Isac also spoke out for autonomy and reforms. At the conference of the Romanian National Council and the Romanian Social Democratic Party, which had convened on November 30, a day earlier than the opening of the national assembly, the social democratic leaders, Joan Flueras and Iosif Jumanca, relinquished their original stance. Following a lengthy debate which stretched into the small hours, the meeting held at the Hungaria Hotel in Gyulafehérvár adopted the stand of an unconditional union.

The final text of the resolution submitted to the Romanian National Assembly represented this stance, though as a concession it did not refer to the dynasty by name and ensured provisional autonomy for the territories in question, until the legislative assembly was convened. The resolution put a host of democratic demands, "as the basic principle of the new Romanian state", into writing: full national freedom for the peoples living together, universal, direct suffrage with secret ballot, total freedom of the press, the right of organization and assembly, the free propagation of all human ideas, radical land reform, all rights and advantages for the industrial workforce which their counterparts in the most advanced industrialized nations already possess.

The stressing of democratic demands reflected the public mood and the presence of the left wing.

At the National Assembly, which convened in the banquet hall of the officers' club of Gyulafehérvár Castle, the draft resolution was read out by Vasile Goldis, accompanied by the approval of those present. At the same time, some one hundred thousand enthusiastic people gathered at the military drill ground outside the castle (where Horia, Cloşca and Crişan had been executed in 1785) and in the town's streets which were now adorned with Romanian and Entente flags. After the session was adjourned, appointed speakers gave an account of what had happened in front of a crowd singing ecclesiastical and national songs (a few thousand workers marched under red flags).

Instead of the existing Central National Council, the Romanian National Assembly elected, on the basis of Alexandru Vajda's proposal, a Great Romanian National Council. The distribution according to occupation of the 200 strong

---

[160] *Mikes*, Vol. II., p. 27.
[161] *Erdély története*, Vol. II. p. 445, and *Századok*, 2/1972. p. 239.

central organ, which fulfilled the role of parliament was the following: 95 lawyers, 44 ecclesiastical persons (bishop, dean, priest), 13 teachers, 9 landowners, 8 journalists, 6 bank managers, 4 primary school teachers, 3 judges, 3 doctors of medicine, 1 factory manager, 1 engineer, 1 merchant, 16 social democrats and 1 (!) farmer.[162]

A cabinet council was formed at the first meeting of the Great Romanian National Council on December 2. Iuliu Maniu became president of the Cabinet Council (consiliul dirigent), which after this moved its seat to Nagyszeben. Willing to cooperate, the social democrats once again obtained a ministerial portfolio—just as they had done in the provisional governments formed in Zagreb, Belgrade, Voivodina and Slovakia. In the 15 member Nagyszeben government Flueras became Social Welfare Minister, while Jumanca was appointed Minister of Industry.

The text of the Gyulafehérvár resolution, which was written on parchment paper, was taken to Bucharest on December 11 by a five-member delegation (2 bishops and 3 members of the National Party) and ceremoniously handed over to the King. On December 26 a decree was published about the union in the official paper *Monitorul Oficial*; at the same time the first measures regulating the union were also published. The King appointed the Nagyszeben Cabinet Council to supervise the public administration of the areas in question until the final organization of united Romania. At the same time three MPs of the Romanian National Party (Alexandru Vajda, Vasile Goldis, Stefan C. Pop) became ministers without portfolio of the central government, which was re-shuffled in mid-December under the leadership of Ioan Brătianu, an advocat of pro-Entente financial capital.

The majority of the Romanian population welcomed the takeover and the union. It felt—and not without reason—that these developments would bring about an improvement of its situation and bring to an end a century of oppression. However, a certain amount of reservation was expressed by the working class and the representatives of the democratic movement, and rightly so, for the union favoured Romanian financial capital and the Romanian bourgeoisie of Transylvania. The coming to power of the Romanian National Party held promising prospects in store primarily for the emerging and aspiring Romanian bourgeoisie and the Romanian white-collar professional strata. The party's paper, *Patria,* which was first published on December 1 in Nagyszeben, carried leading articles openly advocating the desires of these strata and conveying their mood: "Our time has finally arrived—being Romanian no longer means sacrifice. The items of the state budget are open to us. We can fill important positions. There is nothing to prevent us from attaining affluence, to rise socially, indeed from procuring a life of luxury for ourselves."[163]

Following a certain amount of vacillation, the Saxons of Transylvania also proclaimed union with Romania. On January 8 the Saxon Central Committee also

[162] *Cherestesiu,* p. 63.
[163] *Patria,* Cluj, 43/1918. In: *Cherestesiu,* p. 65.

arrived at a similar decision at the Saxon National Assembly which was formed at Medgyes from the local committee and the representatives of the Saxon National Council. The Medgyes Assembly adopted a declaration which emphasized the statements concerning national freedom and religious equality from the Gyulafehérvár resolutions: "The education, public administration and jurisdiction for all peoples in their own mother tongue, by individuals from the people in question. All people are entitled to proportional representation in the country's legislative and governing body. Full religious and educational autonomy."[164]

The Hungarian government rejected the Gyulafehérvár decision. When János Erdélyi, the Budapest representative of the Nagyszebén government handed over the authentic text of the resolution, Jászi proposed remonstration at the Cabinet meeting of December 8. He pointed out—in line with the stand of the Ministry of Defence—that "the Romanian act conflicted with the ceasefire agreements", the resolving of the issue must be left to peace negotiations. On the same day the government set up a chief government commission with Kolozsvár as its seat "in defence of the Hungarians in Eastern Hungary", appointing István Apáthy, a Kolozsvár university professor as chief government commissioner of the 26 counties in question, despite the fact that owing to his earlier chauvinistic statements and behaviour his person was like a red rag to the Romanian National Party.

Meanwhile the organization of the army began in Transylvania. At the end of November the Kolozsvár National Council despatched recruiting officers to the Sekler counties and tried to effect the calling up of the previously withheld five age-groups.

The effort, however, bore little fruit. The Transylvanian Military Commander Károly Kratochvil (formerly the tutor of the Archduke Joseph's sons) had arrived from the Italian front as a colonel and was appointed Kolozsvár's district commander on November 23. According to him on December 1 the armed units (soldiers, national guard, gendarmerie) numbered 545. Kratochvil estimated the number of Seklers gathering at Kolozsvár at the beginning of December at 1,700, adding that only 600 had rifles.[165] During the ensuing weeks the situation remained essentially unchanged. According to Apáthy's account the armed forces in the unoccupied parts of Transylvania numbered 3–4,000 at the end of December. At the same time he estimated the strength of the Romanian army in Transylvania at 15,000.[166] According to recently published documents of the French Ministry of Defence the total strength of the Rumanian army was 180,000 on January 1, of which 39,000 were stationed in Transylvania.[167]

To counterbalance Gyulafehérvár, the Hungarian and Sekler National Council in Kolozsvár convened a rally on December 22. Whereas only 2,000 people had

[164] *Teutsch*, p. 263.
[165] *Kratochvil*, pp. 13., 18.
[166] *Új Magyar Szemle*, Nos. 2–3., December 1920. pp. 168, 170.
[167] *Bernachot*, p. 53.

attended a similar rally earlier at Marosvásárhely, this time tens of thousands of people turned up. Among them were the Swabians of the Banat and the representatives of the Romanian social democrats. Száva Stengar Demian spoke out in the name of the latter, more precisely in the name of the social democrats who disagreed with Flueras and Jumanca. Demian, who later fought under the Republic of Councils as battalion commander in the Red Army, stated: "the Romanian socialists do not identify themselves with the Gyulafehérvár resolution, do not wish to be subjected to Romanian imperialist oppression". Speaking for the social democrats of Romania, Gheorge Avramescu said that there had been great oppression not only in Hungary and Transylvania, but in Romania as well, "in 1907, when the peasantry asked for bread and received bullets, fifteen thousand Romanians perished on orders from the King". Avramescu came up with the following proposal "for resolving the present situation": Transylvania should be made an independent republic along the lines of the Swiss cantons. The rally did not go as far as this. Although there had been previous talk of an independent republic, the proposal submitted—which took Budapest's legal worries into consideration—demanded, within the framework of a united and democratic Hungary, "full equality for every nation, liberty and self-determination".[168]

When it became clear that the Romanian army was preparing to cross the demarcation line and official notice arrived that Berthelot had authorized the occupation of Kolozsvár and subsequently nine other Transylvanian towns (as these were strategic points)—this was possible under the Belgrade Agreement—the government, following several meetings in which it contemplated the possibility of resignation, finally declared the situation hopeless and spoke out against armed struggle and bloodshed.

Under the command of Colonel Gherescu, the Romanian troops marched into Kolozsvár on December 24, after the Hungarian armed units stationed there had been withdrawn.

At the same time the chief government commission remained as did, at least symbolically, the district military command, since the Belgrade Agreement did not stipulate military evacuation in the case of occupied strategic points.

On December 31 General Berthelot, commander of the Entente's so-called Danube Army, arrived at Kolozsvár. Trying to mediate in an increasingly sensitive situation, he proposed the establishment of a neutral zone which was to have extended fifteen kilometres east of the Dés–Kolozsvár–Nagybánya line. According to Apáthy's account Berthelot stressed "our common goal, the struggle against Bolshevism". "Wherever there are Bolsheviks, they must be hanged on the outskirts of the village or town"—this was the French commander's advice.[169]

The agreement about a neutral zone was not recognized either in Budapest, or by the Romanian High Command. The Hungarian government refused official recognition on grounds that it violated the Belgrade Agreement. Romania

[168] *Népszava*, December 24, 1918. "The Kolozsvár Protest Rally."
[169] *Új Magyar Szemle*, Nos. 2–3/1920. p. 174. *Kratochvil*, p. 28.

considered the agreement inadequate compared with her goals ("to press forward to the Szatmárnémeti–Nagykároly, Nagyvárad–Békéscsaba line").

Ignoring the neutral zone, the Romanian army marched into Nagybánya in mid-January and subsequently to Zsibó, Bánffyhunyad, Zilah and Máramarossziget. However, east of this line progress ground to a halt and the subsequent Máramarossziget–Zám front line remained unchanged for a considerable period of time. This was partly due to the growing resistance on the part of Hungarian army units, and partly to the fact that at the end of January the French Ministry of Defence curbed Berthelot's authority to Franchet d'Espèrey's advantage and took a firm stand against further arbitrary violations of the status quo.

As in Voivodina and Slovakia, the reaction of the Hungarian population to the takeover of power and the presence of the Romanian army differed, depending on social position. Owing to the revolutionary situation, the majority of capitalists and landowners regarded the appearance of the Romanian royal army as the lesser of two evils. They were joined by certain conservative politicians who hated the Kolozsvár National Council, and generally speaking all those—among them a good many aristocrats—who opposed the idea of revolution.[170] Convinced that the new system posed a serious threat to their livelihood, the civil servants embarked upon the path of resistance. Encouraged by the chief government commission and hoping for financial support from the Budapest government, the majority of civil servants refused to take the oath of allegiance demanded by the Romanian authorities. The workers, too, turned against the new system. At the end of January the social democrat railway workers and postmen, the workers of the Kolozsvár industrial plants and the Nagyszeben printers called for the restoration of democratic rights, the safe-guarding of existing achievements and for economic demands. Miners of different nationalities fought side by side in the Zsil Valley. Here the January strike developed into an armed uprising and the artillery was called in against the miners who were demanding the setting up of a republic (a socialist republic!). The peasantry adopted a wait and see position and received news of land distribution—which was reported by the Gyulafehérvár Romanian delegations—with reservation.

[170] The attitude of this stratum is reflected by the following diary excerpt from the already quoted I. Mikes' book, *Erdély útja,* pp. 48–49. The diary entry for December 16, 1918 of Samu Barabás, a Protestant dean from Kolozsvár: "We held a church meeting which was also attended by general superintendent Károly Zeyk—István Tisza's brother-in-law. Shaken in soul and painful in heart I explained that Transylvania's fate was sealed, that within a few days Kolozsvár would be occupied by the Romanians. The darkest future and indescribable suffering was in store for us. Zeyk interrupted me: And I say that I wish the Romanians were already here! Horrendous emotional blindness! And most people do not perceive the impending fate precisely in this manner. I feel they hate the Kolozsvár National Council and are looking forward to the arrival of the Romanians—an awful mistake."

CARPATHO-UKRAINE

It was only in regard to the Ukrainians (Ruthenians) and Germans living in Hungary that the Károlyi government's national minority policy could boast certain achievements. The secret of success as far as the Ukrainians were concerned lay in the fact that the emerging Western Ukrainian state in Galicia, which, among the neighbouring countries, had the principal claim to Ukrainian-populated areas, was too weak to realize its aspirations.

The Western Ukrainian republic was at war not only with Poland, but also with Romania and later with Soviet Ukraine. Under the circumstances it was important for it to maintain good relations with Hungary. The Ukrainian leaders wanted to conduct trade and hoped that in exchange for the appropriate services, the Hungarian government would supply them with whatever they needed for the war. Both Czechoslovakia and Romania put in claims for the north-eastern counties, in their case, however, the division, in part or in whole, of this peripheral area signified a long-term goal.

Under these circumstances, in the territory in question, which was perhaps Hungary's most backward area, the pro-Hungarian faction of the Ukrainian leading stratum—priests, lawyers, teachers, civil servants—gained the upper hand. The domestic situation also played its part in this: the revolutionary acts of the Ukrainian soldiers returning from the war, the movement of the poor peasantry and the savage retaliation on the part of the Hungarian law-enforcement detachments.

The pro-Hungarian trend was primarily represented by the 35 member "Hungarian-Ruthenian People's Council" in Ungvár, which was formed on November 9. The government readily accepted the demands put forth on November 19 by the Ungvár Council whose president was Simon Szabó and its secretary Avhustyn Voloshyn, both new Lord Lieutenants, who had contact with the Ruthenian people in the Counties of Máramaros, Bereg, Ung and Ugocsa, with the Ruthenian department at the Ministry of Culture and the Ruthenian department at the university. To perform further tasks, the government appointed Orest Szabó, previously the government commissioner for Ung County, as Central Government Commissioner.

On the initiative of the government commission the Ukrainian leaders convened in Budapest on December 10. Since at the meeting, for which the invited participants were transported to the capital by a special train, an agreement, though not a unanimous one, was finally reached, the government promulgated the law "on the autonomy of the Ruthenian nation living in Hungary" on December 25.

Act X of 1918 ensured the right of self-determination for the Ruthenians in the spheres of internal affairs, jurisdiction, public education, culture, religion and language. It also stipulated that an autonomous government sphere under the name of *Ruszka-Krajna* was to be established in the Ruthenian-populated parts of Máramaros, Ugocsa, Bereg and Ung Counties.

(According to the 1910 census the population of the four counties was 848,428, of which 356,067 were Ruthenian, 267,091 Hungarian, 94,273 Romanian, 93,047 German and 37,950 Slovak. These figures do not, however, provide an accurate picture of the distribution according to national minority as the statistical survey listed the Jews living in this area—the so-called Khazars who numbered 128,791— partly with the Hungarians and partly with the Germans. It is likely, and the large number of Greek Catholics underlines this, that the statistical survey put the Ukrainians who spoke Hungarian as well in the category of people whose mother tongue was Hungarian.)[171]

The law made no provision for Ukrainians living in the neighbouring counties— according to contemporary statistics they numbered almost 100,000—and left the issue of other "Ruthenian-populated areas" unresolved until the negotiating of the peace treaty.

Under § 4 and § 5 of the law the Ruthenian National Assembly was to act as the legislative organ of the autonomous area in autonomous affairs, whilst a common parliament, to be set up in Hungary, was to handle common affairs—foreign affairs, defence, finance, citizenship, civil law and penal law legislation, economic, transport and social welfare issues. The Ruszka-Krajna ministry and the Ruszka-Krajna governorship were to be the main government organs. The non-Ukrainian population living in Ruszka-Krajna were entitled to local administrative and cultural autonomy. The state treasury lands, mines and forests in the autonomous areas passed into the hands of the "legal representatives of the Ruthenian nation".

The Ruszka-Krajna Ministry, with its chief seat in Budapest and the governorship with Munkács as its seat, were formed shortly. The former Government Commissioner, Orest Szabó, was appointed to head the Ruthenian Ministry, while the Rahó lawyer Avhustyn Stefan was appointed as governor of Ruszka-Krajna.

Its creators intended the Ruthenian act—immediately criticized by the right as being too lenient—to serve as an example and model for the drafting of similar legislation. They hoped that the creation of the first "Hungarian canton" could serve as tangible proof of the government's good intentions at the peace negotiations, making the situation more favourable and at the same time calming down the Ukrainians, thereby toning down and defusing separatist tendencies which were becoming increasingly powerful.

In addition to the "Hungarian–Ruthenian People's Council" in Ungvár, a "Ukrainian People's Council" functioned in Eperjes and Máramarossziget. The Eperjes council was dominated by the pro-Czech trend (Antonii Beskid), the Máramarossziget council (the Brashchaiko brothers, Iulii and Mykhailo) by the pro-Ukrainian trend. On January 7 the Eperjes council announced joining of Czechoslovakia; on January 21 the national assembly convened by the people of Máramaros to Huszt—420 delegates representing 175 towns and villages—decided upon reunion with the Ukraine. By Ukraine the leaders, the nationalists, meant the

---

[171] *1910. évi népszámlálás*, Vol. VI., pp. 11., 116.

state of Western Ukraine and Petlyura. To the workers and poor peasantry the Ukraine had also meant Soviet Ukraine; they yearned for union with it.

On December 26 the Ungvár council expressed "its gratitude and loyalty on the occasion of the enactment of the people's law of the Ruthenians".[172] A few days later, however, the delegation, led by Voloshyn, arrived in Budapest and conducted negotiations with Hodža about the possibilities of coming to an agreement with Czechoslovakia.

The appearance of the Romanian and Czechoslovak armies played an important role in subsequent developments. Following the occupation of Nagybánya the Romanian royal troops headed for Máramarossziget, while the Czechoslovak army marched into Ungvár on January 12. Upon receiving news of this, the Ukrainian nationalists also sent troops to the north-eastern counties. By January 16, the divisions arriving from the direction of Kőrösmező pressed ahead as far as Máramarossziget, while those arriving from Lawoczne got as far as Munkács and later as far as Csap. The Ukrainian envoy informed Károlyi well in advance, at the same time outlining the relative advantages of the planned occupation. At the Cabinet meeting of December 29 Jászi expressed his belief that were the northern parts occupied not only by the Czechs and Romanians, but also by the Poles and the Ukrainians, "this would be of strategic advantage to us".[173]

The Hungarian army put up no resistance against the Ukrainian forces. Their orders were that should the Ukrainians clash with the Czechs or the Romanians, they should "adopt a neutral position".[174] In spite of this, the Ukrainian units remained in the occupied settlements for a few days only. Having clashed with the Romanians at Máramarossziget, their main forces were defeated and it was necessary for them to quickly withdraw from this minor theatre of war. Since Czech and Romanian progress had also ground to a halt by the end of January Hungarian public administration continued to function for the time being in most of Ruszka-Krajna—while the establishment of autonomy also continued, though at a slow pace.

WESTERN HUNGARY (BURGENLAND) AND THE GERMANS
LIVING IN HUNGARY

Austria which was to be formed from German–Austrian provinces put in a claim for the German-populated areas of Western Hungary and the Austrian right wing also demanded the partial or total annexation of Pressburg (Pozsony), Wieselburg (Moson), Ödenburg (Sopron) and Eisenburg (Vasvár), or more precisely the Moson, Sopron and Vas Counties.

---

[172] *OL K 40–1918–X*. 1084. President Dr. Simon Szabó's Telegramme to Mihály Károlyi. Ungvár, December 26, 1918.
[173] *OL Cabinet Minutes*, December 29, 1918.
[174] *Breit*, p. 230. The response of the 39th Divisional Headquarters to the Ukrainian move, on January 16, 1919.

In official Austrian policy, however, the moderate stand of the social democrats prevailed over the extremist stand of German nationalists. The reason for this lay not only in the moves taken by the Hungarian government—the Hungarian envoy to Vienna threatened to halt food supplies and to abandon talks on the subject— but also in the weakness of the new German Austrian state. Defeated in war and struggling with domestic problems, Austria, lacking an army and adequate diplomatic support, could hardly have contemplated the use of force of military intervention to back up its claims.

On November 21, the Austrian State Council and on November 22 the provisional National Assembly decided to refer the issue of the areas in question to the peace conference—let the population concerned decide which country they wished to belong to.

The resolution, with which the Károlyi government, too, agreed in principle, meant that for the time being German Austria recognized the authority of the Hungarian state over the "disputed areas".

The Austrian government adhered to the principles adopted in the resolutions of November 21 and 22. It isolated itself from the subversive activities and coup d'état attempts of the German nationalists. It gave no—at least no official—support to separatist aspirations which were primarily motivated by economic considerations: the fear that the frontiers would be totally closed, as Vienna had been the principal market where the peasantry of the border region had sold its agricultural produce and the Viennese industrial district had given employment to many workers.

Under these circumstances Hungarian public administration continued to function in western Hungarian counties. Its work was obstructed not by the Austrians but by the fact that here too the mass movements of early November had forced the local organs of administration to flee.

From the very beginning the Károlyi government tried to reach an agreement with the German leaders living in Hungary, who were organizing in the name of all Germans, i.e. not only in the name of Germans living in Western Hungary.

According to the 1910 census the number of people in pre-1918 Hungary, including Croatia and Slavonia, whose mother tongue was German, was around 2 million. Major German settlements included: Voivodina 565,000, Transylvania 186,000, Northern Hungary 106,000, Tolna-Baranya County 180,000, Pest County (Budapest) 160,000, Veszprém and Fejér Counties 53,000.

According to the statistics figures there were 332,148 Germans in Western Hungary (Pozsony, Moson, Sopron and Vas Counties), of whom 52,600 lived in Pozsony County—which soon fell under Czechoslovak occupation.[175]

The German leaders presented comparatively moderate demands. Their stance was influenced in part by links with the Hungarian leading stratum—German bourgeoisie strongly assimilated during the period of the dual Monarchy—and in part by the fact that the German population, mostly peasants, though many

---

[175] *1910. évi népszámlálás*, Vol. VI., 63*, pp. 114, 116.

workers as well, represented less power than their actual ratio, since they lived scattered all over the country instead of being concentrated in one area.

Two German people's councils were formed in Budapest at the beginning of November. The Ministry of Nationalities communicated primarily with the Hungarian German People's Council which also embraced Transylvanian Saxons and social democrats, but it also negotiated with the people's council of the so-called "patriotic Germans"—the German–Hungarian People's Council—despite the fact that its leader, Jakab Bleyer, maintained contact primarily with Hungarian reactionary circles rather than the government.

At the end of November the government repealed the discriminatory provisions of Apponyi's educational bill, with respect to German schools, as well.

After this the question of German autonomy arose. It was the German People's Council of Western Hungary, whose seat was in Sopron, who pressed for autonomy most. Around the Sopron People's Council—which was led by Géza Zsombor, (who was a newspaper editor) and which joined the German People's Council on November 19—rallied the urban artisan-shopkeeper strata to whom secession was less important. The demanding of autonomy on the part of these strata was aimed not least to diffuse secessionist movements—and to this extent the Sopron Hungarian National Council supported autonomy too. By stressing this demand the leading German stratum at the same time also strove, by giving prominence to the nationality issue, to weaken the movement of revolutionary workers and on the pretext of common interests to subordinate it.

After lengthy negotiations and repeated consultation, the law on German autonomy was passed at the end of January. Act VI of 1919 ("Concerning the Exercising of the Right to Self-Determination of the German People in Hungary") defined autonomous affairs and common affairs along the lines laid down in the law governing the Ukrainians. The organizational structure of German autonomy was also identical, the only difference being that in their case the law stipulated the setting up of not only a single, but several governing bodies without giving any explicit specification as to their number and area.

Through the law on German autonomy the Hungarian government wished to counter-balance secessionist aspirations and to win over the Germans living in Hungary. The law was meant to prove to the German population of the seceded sections of the country that they could expect better treatment in Hungary than in the new emerging successor states.

Hungarian reactionary circles—the same nationalist trend which had considered the concessions made to the Ukrainians excessive—opposed the law on German autonomy as well on the grounds that it was unfeasible and not only would it be unable to prevent secession, but it would ensure more extensive rights to the Germans than they had actually demanded. Joining the attack by the Hungarian counter-revolution, Bleyer also rejected autonomy. In this, however, he found no support and became isolated even within his inner circle.

At the beginning of February the Szeged Judge of the Court of Appeal, János Junker, was appointed as German Nationality Minister. At the same time

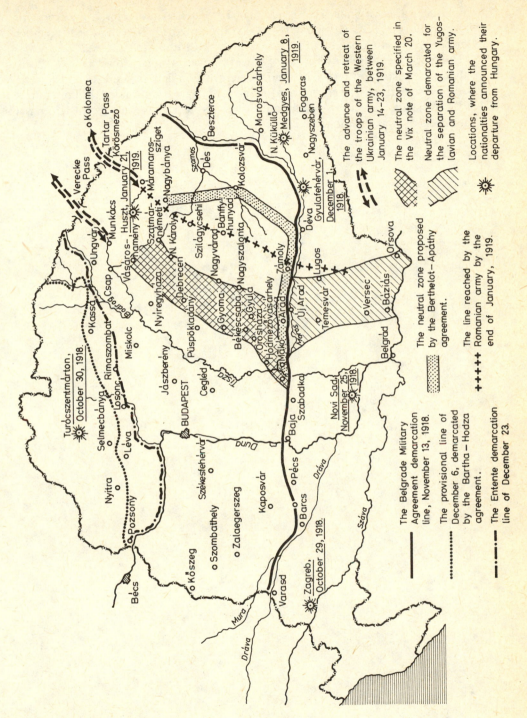

The dissolution of the multinational state

The advance and retreat of the troops of the Western Ukrainian army, between January 14–23, 1919.

The neutral zone specified in the Vix note of March 20.

Neutral zone demarcated for the separation of the Yugoslavian and Romanian army.

Locations, where the nationalities announced their departure from Hungary.

The neutral zone proposed by the Berthelot–Apáthy agreement.

The line reached by the Romanian army by the end of January, 1919.

The Belgrade Military Agreement demarcation line, November 13, 1918.

The provisional line of December 6, demarcated by the Bartha–Hodza agreement.

The Entente demarcation line of December 23.

Undersecretaries of State (Henrik Kalmár, Péter Jekel) and, later, a governor for Eastern Hungary (Géza Zsombor) were also appointed. On March 7 the 36 member German Cabinet Council was formed, which substituted the national assembly.

The implementation of the law, however, was a very slow process. Local public administration resisted it and numerous conflicting interests and criteria asserted themselves. The government did not even dare to determine the boundaries of the Western Hungarian autonomous area. As in the case of Ruszka-Krajna, a final decision was postponed.

6. THE COMMUNIST PARTY OF HUNGARY
AND THE COMMUNIST
GROUPS OF NON-HUNGARIAN WORKERS

THE SOVIET GOVERNMENT'S APPEAL

The news of the revolutions in Austria and Hungary first reached Moscow at the end of October and the beginning of November. Upon receiving news of the favourable turn of events, the Council of Commissars, the All Russian Central Executive Committee and the Moscow Soviet turned to "the working people of the Austro–Hungarian state" with a joint appeal. It was drafted with Lenin's efficient help and he also submitted it to the Council of Commissars. Forwarding the fraternal greetings of the workers, peasants and soldiers of Russia, the appeal called on the workers of the former Austro–Hungarian Monarchy not to be satisfied with their liberation from imperial and royal bureaucracy, but to settle their accounts with their own oppressors, with the domination of Hungarian "landowners, bankers and capitalists", "German and Czech bourgeoisie", "the Romanian Boyars, lawyers and popes". The appeal called on the workers fighting for their own liberation to join forces: "We are deeply convinced that if German, Czech, Croat, Hungarian and Romanian workers, soldiers and peasants take power into their own hands and carry the work of national liberation to fruition, then they will have established the fraternal alliance of free peoples and overthrow the capitalists with joint forces ...the key to success lies not in alliance with its own national bourgeoisie, but in the alliance of the proletariat of every nationality living in Austria." To ensure that victory was final, "the workers of every country must unite for a joint struggle against international capital". Workers should not believe the Entente promises and Wilson's democratic slogans—the people's councils of Austria–Hungary should strike an alliance with each other and enter into alliance with Russia's soviets.[176]

Contemporary articles in the Soviet press also expounded the substance of the appeal. At the end of October *Izvestia* expounded that the Austrian revolution was only in its initial phase, characterized by violent national struggle, the national revolution would, however, transform into the revolution of the workers and peasantry, the way it had done in Russia.

The disintegration of Austria, the forming of small states served the interests of the victors because a situation similar to that on the Balkans would emerge in the heart of Europe, accompanied by bitter struggles and squabbling which would enable Entente capitalists to pit the small nations against each other, to continue the policy of "divide and rule". The fuelling of nationalism and the falling apart of the

---

[176] *Lenin Magyarországról*, p. 49.

Austrian state would be of advantage to the bourgeois hawks, who wish to change the struggle of the Austrian working class against the Austrian capitalists into the struggle of the nationalities living in Austria.

The interests of the proletariat did not lie in the breaking up of the areas connected by the River Danube but in linking them together, not in order to save Austria, but in order to safeguard those economic advantages which arise from maintaining the unity of economic areas dependent on each other and which constitute the foundation of a new and better life of the people living there.

New centres would emerge in Europe as a result of social revolution. In the course of further development these would increasingly interlink because the joint struggle against the bourgeoisie and the bonds of trade bind them together. "The Balkan Federation, the Danube Federation and Poland act as a bridge between the Russian workers' state and the German workers' state; owing to economic and geographical conditions these links are becoming increasingly visible."[177]

On November 3 hundreds of thousands of workers marched in the streets of Moscow, celebrating the victory of the Austro–Hungarian revolution. From the balcony of the municipal council Lenin delivered a brief speech: "We are struggling against capitalism in every country, against international capitalism—for the freedom of every worker. Although the struggle against hunger was a difficult one— we have realized that we have many millions of allies."[178]

THE FORMATION OF THE COMMUNIST PARTY OF HUNGARY

On November 4 "communists from the area of the former Hungarian state" convened for a meeting in Moscow.

Influenced by the latest news, the conference of November 4 made several important decisions. It decided to form the Communist Party of Hungary (KMP) and called on every Hungarian member of the Russian Communist Party to return to Hungary as soon as possible.

The conference also decided to send internationalist Red Army soldiers fighting in Soviet Russia back to Hungary and turned to the federation cf communist groups with the request that it make every affort to achieve this.

The new organization was formed on November 4 as the joint organization of every Hungarian and non-Hungarian speaking worker in Hungary. The provisional Central Committee elected by the meeting comprised of three Hungarians (Béla Kun, Ernő Pór, Károly Vántus), two Romanians (Ariton Pescariu and Emil Bozdogh), two Slovaks (Matej Kovač and Matej Krsak) and two South Slav communists (Ivan Matuzović and Franjo Drobnik).

The return home of the communist prisoners of war began in the first half of

---

[177] *Izvestia,* October 18, 20, 1918. K. Radek: "Revolutsia v Austro–Vengrii, I. v kotle vedmi, II. Proletariat i razdelenie Austrii."

[178] *Lenin Magyarországról,* p. 49.

November. According to the figures of an official report 80 trained activists and 100–200 "rank and file" communists had returned to Hungary by mid-November. In groups of four or five the communist prisoners of war returned along the German lines, through those parts of the Ukraine, Poland and Galicia which were under Ukrainian and Polish counter-revolutionary control. The extremely difficult and dangerous journey lasted at least a week, often much longer. Béla Kun left Moscow together with three other communists on November 6 and assuming the name of the regimental surgeon Emil Sebestyén, arrived on the 17th to witness an agitated Budapest (the group travelled through Harkov, Kiev, Lemberg and continued its journey by car from Brody to the Hungarian border).

As a result of revolution, left wing organization was intensifying in Hungary. On November 1 the left wing opposition organized pro-republic actions and it was partly owing to left wing pressure that the government was forced to retreat on the issue of the constitutional form.

The Soviet government forwarded the text of the November 2 appeal to Budapest via wireless telegraph with the request that the revolutionary government of Hungary should publish it and forward it to Zagreb and Prague. The government did not comply with the request and tried to conceal the appeal. However, the revolutionary socialists procured the text of the telegramme with the help of the workers of the Csepel wireless station, had its substance printed on leaflets and on November 16, the day the republic was proclaimed, scattered them among the celebrating crowd in Parliament Square from an aeroplane. The red leaflets picked out the idea of the "world republic" from the message to the "liberated peoples", as well as the warning that the revolution "could only be said to have been successful if it ended with the victory of the working people".[179] The opposition move was successful. After the appearance of the leaflets the whole city was discussing Soviet Russia's appeal. The Workers' Council was also forced to deal with the telegramme and the government's behaviour. As a result, a few days later, the appeal was published in the November 20 issue of *Népszava*.

Prior to and immediately after the revolution closer cooperation developed between left wing groups. However, conceptions as to what was to be done next differed. An open break with the Social Democratic Party was on the agenda, but the idea of a new independent workers' party was opposed by many. The majority of the old left wing opposition was afraid of breaking with the social democrats because it felt that owing to the strong links between the party and the trade unions the forming of a separate party would not be feasible. They thought, although earlier experience denied this, that a closed left wing grouping within the party could press the Social Democratic Party to the left and this could serve their goals more effectively. Members of the underground organization of the revolutionary socialists were less bound by social democratic traditions; notwithstanding they, too, were not very keen on the idea of forming a new party because they did not

---

[179] *MMTVD 5*, p. 245. The leaflet is published in facsimile in A. Siklós: *Magyarország 1918/1919. Események—Képek—Dokumentumok* (Hungary 1918/1919. Events—Pictures—Documents), p. 190.

understand and therefore assess the importance of the role of such a party. One segment of the opposition suggested that for the coordination of the left wing within the Social Democratic Party a Marx circle or an Ervin Szabó circle should be formed. One group wished to create the "Association of Independent Hungarian Socialists".

The leaders of the left were discussing precisely this issue at MIMOSZ (Workers' Literary and Art Federation) headquarters, when news arrived (from Ernő Seidler who had returned from Russia earlier) that Béla Kun, leader of the group of communist prisoners of war, had arrived in Budapest.

On the following day, the 18th, Béla Kun met with left wing leaders on several occasions: László Rudas, Béla Vágó, Béla Szántó, Jenő László, Ottó Korvin and János Hirossik attended the first talks. On the 19th Kun went to Vienna to establish contact with the Austrian left and to forward Lenin's greetings to Friedrich Adler who had just come out of prison. He was back in Budapest on the 20th, where talks about forming a party were soon crowned with success. In his recollections Béla Kun wrote the following about the events of these days: "I talked with between twenty and thirty people daily, trying to convince them individually that the forming of a party is indispensable to the further development of the revolution and consequently to the dictatorship of the proletariat. The receptiveness to the necessity of the dictatorship of the proletariat and Soviet rule was wonderful. Everyone quickly understood that only the factory can be the basis of the movement. These were wonderful days filled with fruitful discussions, it was only the idea of the necessity of forming a new party that people found hard to grasp."[180]

Resistance was finally successfully overcome. On November 24 the Communist Party of Hungary (KMP) was formed at a conference held at the Városmajor Street flat of József Kelen, Ottó Korvin's brother.

The members of the party's first central leadership were the following: former communist prisoners of war in Russia Ferenc Jancsik, Béla Kun, Ernő Pór, József Rabinovits, Ernő Seidler, Károly Vántus; left wing social democrats Ede Chlepkó, Rezső Fiedler, János Hirossik, László Rudas, Dezső Somló, Béla Szántó and Béla Vágó; and Ottó Korvin and József Mikulik of the revolutionary socialists.

Tibor Szamuely, who arrived in Hungary only at the beginning of January via Berlin, (where he had held talks with Karl Liebknecht and Rosa Luxemburg) was also elected a member of the central leadership. Later, the so-called engineers' group (the one-time leaders of the Inter-Factory Organizing Committee: Gyula Hevesi, Ármin Helfgott, József Kelen) and a smaller group of intellectuals also joined the Communist Party. The latter, the so-called "ethicals", as they were later known, were led by Georg Lukács.

---

[180] Béla Kun: "Hogy alakult meg a kommunisták Magyarországi Pártja". (How the Hungarian Communist Party was Formed). In: *Új Előre 25 éves jubileumi albuma* ("New Advances" 25th Jubilee Album), New York 1927, pp. 10–15. Also published by *Társadalmi Szemle* (Social Review), 11/1958, pp. 96–98, under the title "Összehívjuk az alakuló ülést" (We Convene the Statutory Meeting).

THE PARTY'S PROGRAMME AND ITS GOALS

The Communist Party's programme was fundamentally determined by those principles and goals which had been expounded in the publications of the Russian Communist Party's Hungarian group, in articles published in *Szociális Forradalom* and finally—in detail—in the declaration adopted at the conference held on October 24-25. The programme drew primarily upon Bolshevik teachings and the experiences of the Russian Revolution.

The KMP took as its point of departure the fact—which the Social Democratic Party tried to conceal and deny—that under the given circumstances socialist revolution became the order of the day. The opportunity of grasping power had emerged.

"Capitalism is ready for defeat" . . . "The time has arrived for the realization of socialism" . . . "the dictatorship of the proletariat is now on the agenda"—stated the programme-outlining article of *Vörös Újság* (Red News), the main paper in Hungary of the Communist Party.

Characteristic of the Hungarian situation was that the ruling class did not possess the armed forces or a solid system of public administration which could have been mobilized against the urban and rural proletariat, the working class. Under the circumstances the rule of the wealthy rested "on the lack of consciousness and the awkwardness of the working class" . . . "the bourgeoisie is in power because the Social Democratic Party voluntarily relinquished power".

The workers should avail themselves of the opportunity which had arisen, they should take the handling of their fate into their own hands, they should destroy the bourgeois state and they should realize the dictatorship of the proletariat in the interests of "a common socialized mode of production". Accordingly, effort should be concentrated on the mass struggle of the proletariat rather than on parliamentary work: mass strikes, the armed insurrection of the peasantry—"these are the communists' means to win political power through the proletariat". The constitutional form is not the bourgeois republic in which the bourgeoisie retains possession of all of its rights and is able at any moment to prepare a counter-revolution. "The form of government under the dictatorship of the proletariat is the republic of councils (soviets), in which the bourgeoisie is excluded from governing power and in which proletarian state power rests on the mass organizations of the workers, the trade unions, the party organizations, factory workers' committees and other organizations of a similar character..."[181]

In accordance with the principles outlined above, the Communist Party took steps to dissipate people's illusions about parliamentary politics. The constituent assembly—explained *Vörös Újság*—signified the consolidation of bourgeois power, the maintaining of private property and exploitation, "the renouncing of revolution". The "workers', soldiers' and poor peasants' councils" are the organs of procuring and taking over power. Since the Budapest Workers' Council was only

---

[181] *Vörös Újság,* December 7, 1918. "Why Are We Communists?"

a distorted image "of a system created by the Russian Revolution", it was in reality not more than "the expanded body of shop stewards belonging to the Social Democratic Party and the trade union committees" and every effort must be made to turn the workers' councils into genuine organizations of struggle and power (the organs of revolutionary struggle and later of the dictatorship of the proletariat, of the proletarian state), that is, into genuine workers' councils.

The Workers' Council should be more than a consulting body convened from time to time, a continuously guiding organ that possesses its own executive committee. The Budapest Workers' Council should convene the National Congress of Councils. At the highest level, the National Committee of Councils should be formed as a national executive body.

Vörös Újság repeatedly called attention to the organization of counter-revolution. In order to safeguard private property, the reactionary bourgeoisie were "recruiting mercenaries" and "organizing White Guards". In the face of counter-revolution, which intends to use armed force, there is no choice but to arm the workers, to form Red Guards and to prevent the army from becoming a tool in the hands of the bourgeoisie or the Social Democratic Party's army against the proletariat.

The Communist Party advocated the introduction of worker supervision in the factories, as a temporary provision until "the working class conquers political power", until "the appropriation without compensation of the means of production and the taking over of banks by the workers' state" can take place.

At the beginning of December, the communist faction of the Federation of Iron and Metal Workers submitted a draft resolution to the body of chief trade union stewards. The proposal pointed out that the partial or total stoppages in production in the industrial plants were only partly due to the shortages in raw materials as a consequence of the war. The real reason was the sabotage and machinations on the part of the financial oligarchy, who wanted to crush the working class by starving them. To prevent further impoverishment the communist faction came up with a draft resolution: "Worker supervision councils should be set up in every major industrial plant and these should monitor, as the workers' organs of power, the whole process of production and distribution of goods, the acquisition of raw materials and the financing of the industrial plants. The worker supervision councils should be organized as a one-sided embodiment of power and not as joint institutions. Moreover, they should definitely not serve to resolve controversial issues between worker and employer, but, rather, the monitoring of production, etc."[182]

This was also a response to the planned decree issued by the Ministry of Commerce, which wished to create a "factory constitution" and "factory committees" with a view to restricting the rights of factory committees to that of an arbitration councillor.

---

[182] *Vörös Újság*, December 11, 1918. "The Communists' Draft Resolution."

The Communist Party's stand on the agrarian question may be summed up in two fundamental demands, namely that all land not cultivated by its owner and his family must be occupied by revolutionary means by the peasants' councils, and moreover, that compensation was not to be paid.

Although the Communist Party of Hungary denounced the propagation of land distribution which would have "strengthened private property", it accepted the fact that this slogan had, for the time being, "left an ineradicable impression on public opinion". The proposal for land reform which was submitted to the December 13 meeting of the Workers' Council, regarded that the substance of the issue was to ensure the provision of the agricultural working-class and semi-working-class elements, as well as of the urban proletariat. Taking this as its point of departure the proposal, correctly, called for a national congress of agricultural cooperatives' representatives, where the poorest segment of the agricultural workforce should be made to choose between two alternatives: "large-scale agricultural production based on collective production, or small production based on individual labour".[183]

In regard to the nationality issue the Communist Party of Hungary took steps to counter the irredentist agitation and expansionist chauvinism of the bourgeoisie. It denounced the slogan that called for territorial integrity and believed that under the given circumstances the constant reference to the right to self-determination was also a cover-up for nationalist goals.

Under those circumstances "national war" meant the war between bourgeoisies of clashing interests, for plunderous goals and capitalist concerns in defence of market and profit. "It is the historical task of the Hungarian workers to be the first to transform 'national war', that is, the war of the bourgeoisie, into a civil war, in order to replace the war between the bourgeoisies with the collective front of the workers of various nationalities against their common oppressors."[184]

A sharp struggle was waged to place social democratic views that had made concessions to bourgeois nationalism in a true light. *Vörös Újság* ridiculed the social democrat leaders who participated in the "Territory Protection League" and even accepted co-presidential posts. It denounced the stand which did not wish to distinguish between the concept of a bourgeois and that of a proletarian homeland and which refused to accept the fact that the working class could only be mobilized in defence of the latter.

In one of its earliest articles on KMP policy *Vörös Újság* defined as one of its most important tasks that "the consistently erased sentiment of international solidarity" must be rekindled in the Hungarian proletariat. "The fate of Hungary's proletariat is inseparably linked with international revolution"—stated a draft resolution submitted by the communist faction of the Workers' Council. "The next task will be to join the revolutionary class struggle which is at the moment headed by the proletariat in Russia and Germany."[185]

[183] *Vörös Újság*, December 18, 1918. "Communist Agrarian Proposal Before the Workers' Council."
[184] *Vörös Újság*, March 20, 1919. "Romanian Imperialism—Hungarian Imperialism."
[185] *Vörös Újság*, January 11, 1919. "Communists on the Situation."

On January 30 *Vörös Újság* published the full text of the appeal announcing the convening of the Communist International. This famous document was signed by eight; one of the initiators was the Communist Party of Hungary.

In the realm of foreign policy the KMP sharply criticized the government's pro-Entente policy. "The Entente represents victorious imperialism. It regards the defeated countries as plunder with which it wishes to help its bourgeoisie recover, even at the cost of preparing an even more horrific war in the immediate future than the present one. Only one thing can thwart the Entente's plunderous plans: victorious Bolshevism. If the socialist revolution emerges victorious and an alliance will come into being with Soviet Russia, the whole world will open up for us . . . the red revolution will eradicate demarcation lines. . . ."[186]

THE ENLIGHTENMENT AND ORGANIZATION OF THE MASSES

The Communist Party launched an extensive and excellent propaganda back-up to make its demands and goals widely known. One after the other, pamphlets and brochures were published, among them Béla Kun's propaganda booklets, which had first been published in Soviet Russia: „Kié a föld?" (To Whom Does the Land Belong?); „Mi a Tanácsköztársaság?" (What Is the Republic of Councils?); „Ki fizet a háborúért?" (Who Pays the Price of War?); „Mit akarnak a kommunisták?" (What Do the Communists Want?). For the first time, the writings of the leaders of the Russian Revolution were published in Hungarian; of Lenin's works the *April Theses* and the speech delivered at the Third Soviet Congress appeared (under the collective title „A harc útja"—*The Path of Struggle,* with a foreword by Béla Kun assessing Lenin's work) and later, *State and Revolution,* translated by László Rudas.

The main paper, *Vörös Újság,* the first issue of which had been published on December 7, successfully eliminated the obstacles posed by the bourgeois democratic government. It was a brave, well-edited, highly popular paper which was, at first, published twice and later three times a week. The publishers provided no means for its distribution, the workers themselves organized this on a voluntary basis. Later the party published a separate paper entitled *Vörös Katona* (Red Army Soldier) for the army and another, *Szegény Ember* (Impoverished Man) for the peasantry. The *Internacionálé* (International), a scientific and literary journal run by Gyula Hevesi and Aladár Komját, appeared as the party's scholarly journal from February 1919 onwards.

This period was without doubt the Communist Party's heroic epoch. Working day and night, the party's leaders agitated and organized. They lived together with the masses, were familiar with the workers' way of thinking, desires and everyday problems. At meetings, rallies and conferences they took every opportunity to advocate the immediate demands of the workers and it was with revolutionary

---

[186] *Ibid.,* March 11, "Moscow and Paris."

fervour and passion that they advocated the justice of socialist revolution. There can be no doubt that it was constant close contact with the masses which made the party's newspapers and leaflets lively and interesting, imparting a powerful thrust to their whole agitational work.

The Communist Party—correctly—supported trade union unity. They launched a struggle to make it possible for workers to belong not only to the Social Democratic Party, but to the Communist Party as well. Following several days of heated debate over worker supervision the communist iron turners succeeded in convincing the biggest and most important trade union, the Federation of Iron and Metal Workers, to accept a proposal to this effect. This made it possible for the Communist Party to build its organizations into the trade unions, with the unity of the latter remaining intact. During December communist factions were formed by the printers, tailors, state railway employees, timber workers and miners.

In Budapest and in the vicinity of Pest communist organizations were primarily set up in big industrial plants with a significant tradition of left wing influence. (The aeroplane factory at Aszód and Mátyásföld, the Lipták and Teudloff-Dietrich Factory at Kispest (now district 19), the United Electric Bulb and Lamp Factory, Újpest (now district 4), the Ganz Danubius Ship Factory, Ganz-Fiat, Magyar Fiat, Ganz Wagon Factory, MÁV Northern Main Workshop. etc.). The shop stewards and workers of these large industrial plants formed the backbone of the Communist Party. Communist organizations were formed in Budapest, according to districts, as well as in some provincial towns (Salgótarján, Tata, Győr, Miskolc, Diósgyőr, Szeged, Debrecen, Sároraljaújhely, Sopron, Kaposvár, Nagyvárad). Communist factions operated in the army and in the people's guard.

From the very beginning the Communist Party exerted substantial influence over the unemployed, the demobilized rank and file soldiers and junior officers.

In the countryside former prisoner of war peasant soldiers who had returned from Russia advocated communist ideas.

According to the recollections of József Rabinovits, the Party's organizing secretary, "hundreds of barely legible letters arrived addressed to Vörös Újság and the party secretariat, in which prisoners of war arriving from Russia (farmhands, peasants) who had been members of the prisoners of war's revolutionary organization, were red guards, etc.—requested orders, work and posts".[187]

According to the estimates of the Budapest Public Prosecutor's Office party membership at the beginning of March 1919 was between 10—15,000 in Budapest, and between 20—25,000 in the provinces.[188]

Communist influence was significant from the very beginning in the National Federation of Young Workers (IOSZ), which was formed on November 30 in the crowded hall of the former Lower House. The majority of the 11 member leadership and the 20 member committee came from the ranks of the communists. János

---

[187] Új Előre naptár (New Advances' Diary), 1929, p. 88. J Rabinovits: Négy párthelység (Four Party Premises).
[188] PI Archives, 653. f. 4/1919/9977.

Lékai, who was immensely popular among young workers, was the new organization's first secretary. On December 30 the IOSZ's all-union meeting broke with the Social Democratic Party and organized itself into an independent youth organization. Although the youth organization did not openly call itself communist, IOSZ and its weekly, *Az Ifjú Proletár* (The Young Proletarian) in fact followed the guidance of the Communist Party.

After the publication of *Vörös Újság* commenced, the Social Democratic Party decided to take action against the communist movement. A whole series of articles appeared in *Népszava* to counter-balance communist ideas, to slow down the progress of the Communist Party. In the middle of December a group of agitators was set up and this was later followed by the publication of brochures. *Népszava* charged the communists with "undermining party unity", "demagogy" and "adventurism". In defense of social democratic policy the social democrat publications stressed that they, too, advocated communism, that is, there was no difference between them as regards the ultimate goal, but the social democrats' realistic strategy, which took into account the balance of power, was the correct strategy, whilst even "the fundamental preconditions" were lacking for the realization of communist demands. "The proletariat in Hungary is not strong enough to procure and exercise dictatorship", and this is not disproved by the Russian Revolution either, "since the latter has so far only existed in a world war", and "it is more than doubtful whether it will survive the restoration of freedom of movement".[189]

Whether written or spoken, agitation was not even deterred from defaming and denigrating communist leaders.

Those tested methods, however, which the leaders of the Social Democratic Party had previously applied so successfully to repress left wing opposition, misfired at the end of 1918, when the flame of revolution was burning in Hungary. Despite the attacks, the popularity of the communists grew and the social democrat leaders looked on helplessly as the Communist Party forged ahead in both the ideological and the organization spheres. Communist ideas began to penetrate the social democrat circles as well.

THE COMMUNIST GROUPS OF ROMANIAN, SOUTH SLAV
AND OTHER NON-HUNGARIAN WORKERS

An important element was that in addition to the Communist Party, which, in accordance with the changed situation, was formed in Budapest as the party of Hungarian workers, the national minority sections, the communist organizations of non-Hungarian workers were also emerging.

---

[189] *Népszava,* December 15, 1918. "Party Unity Must be Preserved." *Népszava,* December 19, 1919. "Ideological Struggle or Demagogy." "An Open Letter to Hungarian Social Democratic Workers!", Budapest, January 7, 1919, p. 7.

These organizations were formed, on the one hand, by those non-Hungarian communist subjects who lived in Hungary and had returned from Soviet Russia, and, on the other, by the left wing members of the Social Democratic Party's national minority committees, those social democrats who did not wish to join the right wing of their party in cooperating with the bourgeois political parties, a process which implied concessions to bourgeois nationalism and submission to the bourgeoisie.

The Romanian communist group was formed in Budapest on December 26. Its president, Henri Kagan, had fought in Soviet Russia as commander of a battalion of Romanians in the Red Guard.

Only a few days later, on December 31 and January 1, the communist group was fully represented at the congress of Romanian socialists and by that time the first issue of the group's Romanian language paper, *Steagul Rosu* (Red Flag) was already on sale.

The congress, which was held in Budapest, had been convened by the leaders of the "Romanian internationalist faction" (Jacob Cretulescu, Gheorge Avramescu, Száva Demján Strengar) with support from the Hungarian Social Democratic Party, with the aim of giving an opportunity for members of the Romanian faction who had been forced into opposition, to expound their objections to the Gyulafehérvár resolution. Two draft resolutions were submitted to the congress, one of which stated that "it regarded Flueras', Jumanca's and their associates' stance at Gyulafehérvár as treason, a violation of internationalist principles... Flueras, Jumanca and their associates tried to rise with the help of the workers and then sold themselves to the ruling nationalist class". The resolution had rejected a state community with contemporary Romania, and justified the rejection with the argument that Boyars ruled there, that "contemporary Romania did not ensure those political, cultural, economic and social welfare rights which the Hungarian republic is ensuring at present". Parts of Transylvania, Banat and Hungary populated by Romanians should be made into an "independent republic", in a way that "the form of government of these areas be provisionally determined by a congress of every nationality living in the area in question".[190]

The congress unanimously adopted the first draft resolution, but rejected the proposal concerning the tasks which lay ahead against which the Communist Party came up with a counter-proposal. Both communist speakers and the communist draft proposal wished not only to denounce the tactics of the right wing Romanian social democrats (Flueras and Jumanca), but the tactics of the social democrats in general, that is, the behaviour of the Hungarian social democrats as well! "Flueras and Jumanca are not burdened for their sins by individual responsibility, every social democratic party is responsible which united with the capitalists of their nations and are working against the interests of the proletariat..." "They should

---

[190] *Népszava*, January 2, 1919. "The Romanian Internationalist Socialists Want a Separate Republic."

assess the deeds of these social democrats not as Romanians, but as socialists, as Flueras and Jumanca worked in accordance with social democracy."[191]

The majority of the congress (36 votes against 27) accepted the communists' aforementioned proposal.

Following the congress, this communist group continued its activity under the name of "the Federation of Romanian Communists Living in Hungary, the Banat, Transylvania, Romania and Austria". The centre of the groups' activity gradually shifted to Nagyvárad, Arad and Bihar Counties. Ariton Pescariu, a member of the provisional leadership set up in Moscow on November 4, worked in Nagyvárad, among other things editing the weekly *Foaia Taranului,* which had earlier been published in Soviet Russia. (At the end of April Pescariu was arrested by the intelligence corps of the Romanian royal army and died soon after his release from prison where he was severely tortured.)

It was not only in name that the Romanian communist federation maintained contact with the left wing socialists, the eventual founders of the Romanian Communist Party, in Romania. At the end of November the Romanian Socialist Party denounced mobilization and the intervention of the "Romanian oligarchy" in Transylvania, Bukovina and Bessarabia. "The salvation of the Romanian people does not rest with the struggle between nations and peoples, but only in the struggle between classes, which we must continue under the red flag"—stated an appeal published in the November 27, 1918 issue of *Lupta.*

The South Slav members of the provisional leadership formed in Moscow, Ivan Matuzović and Franjo Drobnik, arrived in Budapest at the beginning of December. Drobnik went on to Zagreb, Matuzović, however, remained in Budapest and formed the legal South Slav communist group on January 6. At the beginning of February Lazar Vukicević, president of the communist group organized alongside the Russian Communist Party, accompanied by Nikola Grulović, a member of the group's executive, arrived in Budapest. Following talks in Budapest they set up (on March 2 according to contemporary accounts) with the participation of other Serbian and Hungarian communists, the Pelagić Federation of Voivodina, the first communist organization in Yugoslavia which began its activity with support from the Hungarian Communist Party, with which later it cooperated.

At the same time, those South Slav social democrats who disagreed with the activity of the South Slav nationality section, the Serb-Catholic-Serbian Agitation Committee, which had embarked upon the path of cooperation with the Serbian bourgeoisie, formed the South Slav Social Democratic Party of Hungary with the leadership of Svetozar Mosorinski, who was a well-known figure of the movement in Voivodina. At the meeting convened on March 9 to elect the executive, Mosorinski denounced the "renegades", "the Novi Sad comrades", who, for well-paid jobs, betrayed and misled the workers in order to play into the hands of the Yugoslav bourgeoisie. "We have not yet reached genuine freedom"—he explained

---

[191] *Vörös Újság,* January 4, 1919. "The Communists Formed the Majority at the Congress of Romanian Workers."

in relation to the situation in Hungary—"as the October revolution was not yet the workers' revolution but that of the bourgeoisie. But the revolution of the workers will arrive and the South Slavs, too, stand prepared."[192]

The communists, of whom only a few appeared at the meeting owing to police persecution (the public prosecutor charged Matuzović at the end of February), did not present such a show of strength as they had done at the Romanian congress; however, here the difference between the two trends was not as sharp. The South Slav groups of the Social Democratic Party and the Hungarian Communist Party united, and under the Republic of Councils this entailed not only formal, but real cooperation.

KMP had links with the Czechoslovak communists and left wing social democrats as well, who were also working toward the uniting of revolutionary forces. One of the most prominent was Alois Muna, who at this time together with Antonin Zapotoczky worked among miners in agitated Kladno. Muna had taken part in the revolution in Russia, he was president of the Czechoslovak group of the Russian Communist Party in Moscow and left for Czechoslovakia roughly at the same time as Béla Kun returned to Hungary. Before his return he wrote an article entitled "On the Ruins of Austria", which was published in Hungarian in *Szociális Forradalom* on October 30. Muna expressed his belief that "the German and Hungarian army will not fight against the Czech proletariat" and "similarly, the Czech soldiers will not fight against the German and Hungarian workers". Independent bourgeois states will not emerge from the ruins of Austria, but, rather, the socialist republican federation of the proletariat will be formed.

At the invitation of Béla Kun, Czech left wing leaders sent Antonin Janoušek to Hungary to supervise revolutionary work among the Czechs and Slovaks in Hungary and to publish a Slovak newspaper. (Janoušek worked at the Wagon Factory in Győr at the beginning of the century and later became a newspaper editor; he moved to Kladno at the beginning of the war.) The unfavourable turn of events in February, the police measures taken against the KMP did not make the legal forming of the Czechoslovak communist group possible. Consequently the first issue of the planned paper *(Cervené Noviny)* could appear only following the proclamation of the Republic of Councils (March 21), as was the case with *Cervena Zastava*, the newspaper of the South Slav group.

A Ruszka-Krajna and a German communist group were also formed alongside the KMP. Ruszka-Krajna communist organizations functioned in Munkács, Beregszász, Szolyva, Perecsény. The German groups was comparatively weak and found it difficult to overcome the resistance of the traditional and firmly established organizations of the Social Democratic Party.

In addition to communist groups of national minorities, the communist organizations of foreigners were also emerging. Among them the Russian group was the most important. Russian Bolsheviks living in Hungary who were taken to the country as prisoners of war, had been organizing from 1914 onwards and their

---

[192] *Népszava*, March 16, 1919. "The Organizing of South Slav Workers."

large numbers ensured favourable work conditions. (There were almost 300,000 Russian prisoners of war in Hungary.)

Among the leaders of the Russian group of communists were Vladimir Justus, Vladimir Urasov and the Serbian Filip Filipović. All three took part in the Russian Revolution of 1905. Justus was staying in Budapest as an emigré, while Urasov was brought here as a prisoner of war. Prior to the war, Filipović was one of the leaders of the Serbian working class movement. He was arrested by the Monarchy authorities in 1916 in Belgrade and interned to Austria. In the autumn of 1918 he worked toward the establishment of the German–Austrian Communist Party in Vienna. It was after this that he came to Budapest, where he participated in the organization of the South Slav and Russian communist groups. In a letter dated December 18 to the Committee of the Russian Communist Bolshevik Party, he maintained close contact with the KMP as well; he spoke admiringly about the work of the Hungarian communists. "Our Hungarian comrades... have attained enormous successes within the shortest possible time . . . the Hungarian communist movement has now almost overtaken the Austrian; the movement here cannot even be compared with the movement in Vienna."[193]

Filipović continued his work in Yugoslavia. Urasov acted as courier between Moscow and Budapest. He handed over Béla Kun's messages to Lenin, Justus remained in Budapest throughout. Under the dictatorship of the proletariat he organized international divisions, fought at the helm of a Russian battalion and took part in the defence of the Republic of Councils to the very end.

---

[193] *Voprosi Istorii KPSZSZ,* 7/1966, pp. 67–69. "Dokumenti i materiali. O russkih komunisticheskih gruppah v Avstrii i Vengrii v 1917–1919. gg."

7. THE CHARACTERISTIC TRAITS
OF DISSOLUTION—OUTLOOK

In historiography and specialist literature Oszkár Jászi, the Károlyi government's Minister of Nationalities and particularly his activity in 1918—1919, is repeatedly described as being a pedant, his plans for a federation naive and anachronistic, his ideas belonging to the realm of utopia. Both nationalist, counter-revolutionary publications and contemporary historiography agree on this, the only difference being that while the former describe Jászi's ideas in terms of negative epithets ("obsession", "dangerous aspirations", "ludicrous", "serving the Hungarians' enemies"), more recent literature describes these utopian conceptions as a "noble and honorable attempt".

Although he admitted in his book on revolutions that his policy "held prospects of only very meagre achievement for the present", Jászi tried to refuse this assessment of his conception. "I was not the kind of naive professor or a dry as dust scholar, who was not taken seriously by the Romanian and other national minority gentlemen"—he wrote and at the same time expounded its realistic character, its *real-politik* substance.[194]

What was the essence of Jászi's *real-politik* as regards his concept of a federation? The obvious answer is to look in his book, *A Monarchia jövője,* which was published in October 1918—and to which reference has already been made in the chapter on the bourgeois radicals. According to Jászi, "only the internal link between the peoples living in the Monarchy and the Balkans" could ensure "free cultural development between the German and Russian millstone". In his view "the Danubian United Nations" must be the cooperation of peoples "who would be able to hold their own ground under the double pressure of the German and Eastern Slav threat".[195]

This conception, the fear of the German threat (German imperialism which was not a topical issue just then) and of the Russian threat, that is, of revolution, socialist revolution (which was very much a topical issue just then), occupied a common ground in spite of the differences and offered a realistic opportunity for reaching an agreement with the national bourgeoisie, the reasoning of which was later often repeated by Jászi as the ultimate argument. "We would not go too far because if the Entente continues with its ruthlessly imperialist and selfishly nationalist policy, then the peace of the world will not, ultimately, be decided by

---

[194] Jászi: *Magyar kálvária*, p. 64.
[195] Jászi: *A Monarchia jövője*, pp. 76—77.

generals and diplomats, but Europe's soldiers' and workers' councils"—came the warning after talks at Arad with the Romanian National Council.[196] Jászi believed that the threat of revolution, "Central Europe's appalling social and economic situation", would not only encourage the national bourgeoisie to try and reach an agreement rather than sharpening conflicts, but would also force the Entente powers to defend themselves against the threat of revolution by restructuring the Monarchy, or if this is not possible by creating a federation to replace it. A number of historians are correct in pointing out that plans for a confederation did in fact exist during the final phase of the war and these were apparent among Entente circles later, even after the opposing conceptions carried the day.[197]

The popular character of the October revolution, the mass movement which spread throughout the whole country, the storm of passions it inspired, created a favourable opportunity for an agreement with the national bourgeoisie, for the realization of Jászi's conception.

The Hungarian–Romanian joint communiqué on Transylvania, signed on November 1, which took a stand against "the destruction of property" and called for the protection of "internal order" and the "safety of individuals and property", clearly reflects this tendency.

It was not without reason that Jászi described this appeal as a success at the Cabinet meeting of November 2, requesting authorization to call upon "the municipal authorities to support this spontaneous social action".[198] Further concessions made to the national minorities (amnesty, the release of the interned, the

---

[196] Jászi: *Magyar kálvária,* p. 64. In his recollections about the Arad talks, Jászi wrote the following: "... I warned the Romanian leaders that they should not go too far ... I referred to the appalling social and economic situation in Central Europe and warned those present that the spirit of inhumanity and injustice would only strengthen those currents which, overturning the present framework of the state, would place Europe at the mercy of the dictatorship of soldiers and workers' councils." Polemicizing with Masaryk, Jászi also stressed that "in the face of a possible Pan-German threat it is not the right mode of defence... to make permanent in this area the spirit of national unrest, irredentism and revenge. What we would thereby achieve would only be a chaotic situation which any imperialism could exploit at will". *Világ,* January 5, 1919., p. 8.

[197] Zsuzsa L. Nagy: "Összeomlás és kiútkeresés 1918–1919-ben. Jászi Oszkár és a forradalmak." (Collapse and Search for a Way Out in 1918–1919. Oszkár Jászi and the Revolutions). *Kritika* (Criticism), 5/1978. Zsuzsa L. Nagy describes the views, the stance of British diplomats and the conceptions of French conservative and royalist French circles that surfaced within *Inquiry,* which was involved in making preparations for peace.

In a study on the problems of the Monarchy (*Acta Historica,* 1–2/1971, pp. 46–47.) "Ungarische politische Bestrebungen und die Probleme der Monarchie im Zeitalter des Dualismus", Domokos Kosáry correctly points out that these Entente conceptions formed the background to Jászi's plans. It was for this reason that Jászi referred in his book among other things to a study by the French scholar Joseph Reinach (*La Revue politique internationale,* Jan–Feb. 1918. "Le problème des Etats-Unis d'Orient"), who represented the anti-revolution aspirations of French policy.

In the official American explanation to point 14. (October 1918), the commentary to point 10. was concluded with the following remark: "The United States is clearly committed to the programme of national unity and independence. It must stipulate, however, for the protection of national minorities, for freedom of access to the Adriatic and the Black Sea, and it supports a programme aiming at a Confederation of South-Eastern Europe." *House, IV.,* p. 207.

[198] *OL K. 27. Cabinet Minutes,* November 2, 1918.

abolition of property sequestration, the prevention of police abuses, the lifting of bans on various newspapers) interlinked with this appeal. The most important concession was that national guards were permitted and the Romanian national guard were supported with arms and money.[199]

Although there was no such written agreement with the South Slavs, initially there had been cooperation in both Voivodina and areas with a Slovak population. Here, too, the oppressors of various nationalities—the Hungarian, South Slav and Slovak political leadership—rallied to a common front and tried to take joint action against popular, worker–peasant movements. (These movements lacked national character and if they had any at all they were directed against Hungarian landowners or Jewish shopkeepers.)[200]

[199] According to a letter, dated January 14, 1919, by László Fényes, government commissioner of the national guard, the Ministry of Defence allocated 450,000 crowns even in December 1918 for the stipend of the Romanian national guard in Arad and Arad County. (*OL K. 40. 1919–II.* t. p. 202. Magyar Nemzetőri Kormánybiztosság. Hadügyminisztérium Arad szab. város és Arad vármegye kormánybiztosának. (Hungarian National Guard Government Commission. Ministry of Defence to the Government Commissioner of Arad Free Town and Arad County, January 14, 1919.)

Lajos Varjassy, the government commissioner for Arad, wrote in his recollections the following about the functioning of the Romanian national guard: "The Hungarian society looked upon the setting up of the Romanian guards with great disapproval as it was convinced that they served not only the maintanance of law and order, but were secretly preparing for the takeover of the Empire. It must be objectively acknowledged that the Romanian national guards did some outstanding work in maintaining law and order. There was hardly any looting and robbery in Arad County following the revolution and credit for this must go to the leaders of the guard." (*Varjassy*, p. 23.)

The opinion of István Apáthy, president of the Kolozsvár National Council (the activity of the Hungarian, Romanian and Saxon national councils could be described as "fraternal cooperation" at the beginning of November) has already been described in the chapter on Transylvania. According to Apáthy, during November the Kolozsvár quartermasters' corps "paid out, to Captain Kotucz, one and a half million and later, another 800,000 crowns for the Romanian national guard". (*Új Magyar Szemle*, December, 1920, p. 157.)

[200] Regarding the background to the "anti-Hungarian" mood, Professor Rezső Szegedy said the following at the debate at the Public Education Association (February 23, 1919): "The district administrators were cruel, they were hated everywhere and the Hungarian people will also always hate power that demands the execution of the law from the people. Only, things in the national minority regions were not quite the same as in the Hungarian areas because the Hungarian person hated the district administrators in his capacity as such, whilst in national minority areas they hated them for being Hungarian because most of them did not even speak the language of the people." (*Vitaülés*, p. 29.)

For a more detailed and more concrete account of the events of early November 1918, see Márton Wladimir Fajnor's memorandum of November 16, 1918. Fajnor, who, as representative of the Slovak National Council, took part in the talks with Hodža, wrote the following about the movements of early November in a report to the Kassa District Command (Fajnor had been requested to take steps against current threats to the Hungarians' personal safety and their property): "In my experience the looting, disturbances and irregularities in general were not so much of a nationality but rather, of a social character. For it was primarily against the village notaries, the manorial stewards, publicans and shopkeepers against whom the people turned—seeing them as the immediate cause of their troubles. Undoubtedly, there had been numerous abuses, especially in connection with the distribution and handling of food as well as around the payment of war relief. And since in our region all of the aforementioned consider themselves Hungarian, to those who are unfamiliar with the situation it appears as though the movement had an anti-Hungarian slant". (*OL K. 40. 1918–II. t. 370.* "Dr. Fajnor

It was not without justification that in his recollections Jászi described negotiations conducted with Hodža at the end of November as promising which were also joined by Slovak leaders, among them Matúš Dula, president of the Slovak National Council. "...I could have come to an agreement with the Slovak leaders—at least until the peace talks—had not Milan Hodža received such a resolute pushing down from Prague at the last moment."[201]

The people's law which codified Ruthenian autonomy could also be regarded as an achievement, which was enthusiastically welcomed by the Ruthenian National Council in Ungvár ("In the name of the Ruthenian people the National Council of Ruthenians in Hungary expresses its greetings and thanks to the Hungarian nation—expresses its thanks and affection to the Prime Minister and his government..."[202]). Another achievement was the German people's law which was of a similar character, which the majority of German subjects in Hungary warmly welcomed.

Márton Wladimir ügyvéd népf. élelm. tiszt—Kassai Kerületi Parancsnokságnak." (Dr. Márton Wladimir Fajnor, lawyer, mess officer to the Kassa District Command. Kassa, November 16, 1918.))

According to the account of the *Trencsényi Lapok* (Trencsén Papers), a conference convened in Trencsén on November 6 pointed out that owing to a lack of armed forces they were unable to stop "robbery and looting" in the county. The Lord Lieutenant announced that "it requested armed assistance from the government on several occasions, however it received none", instead they were recommended to organize civic guard. "The district administrators, notaries and military persons present came to the conclusion that this was impossible in this region." In this situation Károly Stur, a Trencsén lawyer, said that he was willing to form a Slovak national council to ensure personal safety and property and to seek the necessary armed force on the council's behalf from the Czech Sokolists... "Those present welcomed Károly Stur's offer with enthusiasm and asked him to take the necessary steps immediately." The Slovak National Council was formed on the very same day and the committee set up to seek armed assistance headed by Antal Bulla, a judge of the Court of Appeal, immediately departed for Brno where they had already sent a telegramme. The Czech army (600, according to the paper) soon appeared and marched into Trencsén at 3 p.m. of the 10th. (*Trencséni Lapok*, November 10, 1918. "Slovak National Council.") Among the documents of the Ministry of the Nationalities is Lord Lieutenant László Mednyánszky's telegramme which he sent to the Minister of the Interior on November 5. According to the telegramme: "... the public are increasingly demanding that the Czech and Slovak National Council be requested to help protect law and order, the safety of property and people... we ask for orders." (*OL K 40.1918–VII*. t. 163.)

A study, in manuscript form and compiled with the help of original sources, said the following about the initial situation in Pécs that emerged in the aftermath of the occupation: "As early as November 23 the Pécs National Council lodged a protest with the Serbian Military Command against illegal requisitioning. Notwithstanding this, the mayor pressed for cooperation even in December. A feeling of sympathy with the Serbians which developed in a number of local leaders was rooted in the fact that the occupying troops provided protection and assistance to the suppression of political and economic movements. At the meeting on December 10 of the county administrative committee, it was noted with satisfaction that "law and order had been restored in the wake of the occupation..." (B. Kéri Nagy: *Párt és osztályharcok Pécsett* (1918–1922) (Party and Class Struggles in Pécs, 1918–1922). Doctoral dissertation, Budapest 1980, pp. 22–23. Manuscript.)

[201] Jászi, *Magyar kálvária*, p. 65.

[202] *OL K. 40. 1918–X. t. 1084.* President Dr. Simon Szabó's Telegramme to Prime Minister Károlyi. Ungvár, December 26, 1918.

Although in his talks with the national minority leaders Jászi made more and more concessions (administrative and cultural autonomy, the canton system, territorial autonomy and, finally—though with strong reservations—the recognition in principle of the right to secession),[203] it soon became clear that an agreement with the national bourgeoisie, the leading stratum of the national minorities was hardly possible. The reasons for this attitude of rejection may be sought in the following factors:

1. It became clear to the national bourgeoisie that coercion on its own could not overcome the enflamed passions, quell the discontent of the people, to restore law and order. An emotional approach would also have to be considered and it was "the national idea which could be used to diffuse anarchist forces".[204] A compromise with the Hungarian leadership, the former oppressors regarding the national idea would have signified appeasement, the renouncing of and turning against nationalism. On the other hand, allocating priority to nationalism as national ideology not only provided a remedy to social demands, but also an opportunity for broadening the mass base, for winning over the peasantry and the workers, to fuel antagonism, to disrupt the unity among workers of differing nationality.

2. It was also obvious that the Budapest government was weak, its public administration organs were falling apart and it did not possess a disciplined army, a reliable armed force. As regards the police force the main problem was that on its own, it was unable to resolve the problems raised by the revolutionary situation, "for the protection of the safety of individuals and property". Things were made even worse by the fact that even where it existed at all it operated inefficiently.

3. By contrast with the weak and powerless central power, the Serbian and Romanian royal army—later, after the arrival of the legionaries, the army of the Czech republic as well—appeared to be strong, disciplined and capable of "restoring law and order". It was for this reason that, despite their reservations, the national bourgeoisie and that segment of the Hungarian leadership who opposed revolution also eagerly welcomed the appearance of these troops—though later they became disenchanted for a number of reasons. The appearance of the armies of the neighbouring countries made it possible for the national bourgeoisie to wage a struggle on two fronts, to take simultaneous action against both the former oppressed and the former oppressors. This was class struggle against the demands of the workers and peasants, for the maintaining of exploitation and a struggle for the repression and denigration of the leading Hungarian stratum. It should be noted that although it had been the national bourgeoisie who called in and

---

[203] Regarding the issue of secession, Jászi, going beyond his former stand, wrote the following: If the proposal "for extensive home rule" is "rejected by one or more all of the Hungarian peoples, the government does not intend to obstruct their secession, provided that the rejection takes place in a form that is recognized by some international forum as a manifestation of the will of the people in question..." (*Politika* [Politics], December 1918. "The Foundations of our National Minorities Policy", p. 12.)

[204] *OL K. 40. 1918–IX. t. 677.* "Anonymous Report on the Situation in Transylvania", December 6, 1918.

welcomed the armies of the neighbouring countries, they would, no doubt, have appeared uninvited. It was vital for Bohemia that the new state be a Czechoslovak state formation rather than just a Czech one. In Romania the serious domestic situation, the movements of the workers, the threatening spectre of a new peasant uprising made the realization of Greater Romania an indispensable demand. Without the appearance of the Serbian army Southern Slav unity could hardly have come about under Serbian hegemony.

4. In the autumn of 1918 and later too, the course of events was greatly influenced by the stand taken by the Entente. Lansing's telegramme of November 5, the Belgrade Agreement, then particularly Franchet's memorandum of December 3 and Berthelot's decision received on December 23 (these two decisions made possible, by going beyond the provisions of the Belgrade Agreement, on the one hand the occupation of Slovak areas, and on the other, the crossing of the demarcation line in Transylvania) made it obvious whom the Entente sided with regarding the fulfilment of national aspirations and nationalist desires. It became obvious that the national bourgeoisie, the leading stratum of the emerging new states could expect the greatest possible support on their part. Unity with Serbia, Bohemia and Romania meant that those who joined would, in the future, belong to a victorious power recognized as an ally, rather than as a defeated country held responsible for the war and burdened with compensation.

5. The stand of the national bourgeoisie was ultimately determined by the appearance on the political scene of Hungarian counter-revolutionary forces, the flaring up of Hungarian nationalism. Jászi and the Károlyi government tried to reach an agreement in the name of democracy; the old representatives of the former public administration who had remained in their places, the officers, the refugees, the one-time leading stratum once cast aside but never eliminated, would not even hear of all this. The nationalists "put the Károlyi government in an impossible situation with their blind and uncouth agitation"—stated Jászi later, recalling the events of these months.[205] While Jászi was negotiating in Arad, Urmánczy had Romanian peasants shot dead by the dozen at Jósikafalva. While Varjassy was trying to reach an agreement with Maniu at Nagyszeben, the Hungarian army staged a blood bath at Arad. The flaring up of Hungarian nationalism appeared to confirm the national minority leaders' opinion of Hungary: "The names have changed, but the system will remain the same."[206]

It became obvious in the course of December that the policy of trying to come to a compromise agreement regarding the national minorities had reached a deadlock.

---

[205] *Bécsi Magyar Újság* (Viennese Hungarian Daily), May 14, 1922. O. Jászi: "The Foreign Policy of the Károlyi Government."

[206] *Varjassy*, p. 19. According to Varjassy the Romanian leaders made a statement to this effect at Arad, on the occasion of the negotiations held there in November. Varjassy also gives an account of the events which took place in Arad at the end of December, which were linked with Berthelot's visit there. (p. 37.) The Budapest dailies also carried accounts of Berthelot's visit to Arad and the clash following it. *Pesti Hírlap*, December 31, 1918. "Clash Between Romanians and Hungarians at Arad. Four Dead and Fifteen Injured."

At the Cabinet meeting of December 25 Jászi openly announced: "It is impossible to reach an agreement with the Slovaks and the Romanians."[207] The new situation demanded a new policy. At several Cabinet meetings Jászi referred in unmistakeable terms to resistance, the possibility of new methods, though he obviously regarded himself as unsuitable to represent the new methods which he had proposed and thought feasible. At the beginning of January he tendered his resignation, the Ministry of the Nationalities ceased its activity and after the forming of the Berinkey government (January 15) Jászi was no longer a member of the Cabinet.

At the December 18 Cabinet meeting Kunfi expressed the view that the government's policy should be based on the ethnographic principle, that "the government govern in a Hungary which will emerge within the boundaries of ethnographic unity ... this is the consequence of losing the war".[208] However, Kunfi remained isolated with his *real-politik* stand which relinquished territorial integrity.

What were the new methods approved of by the majority? Ideas covered a wide spectrum. The possibility of "active resistance" also arose, that is, armed resistance against aspirations judged unjustified. A "new war" for which there was, for the time being, no army, primarily for the reason that the character of the army that was to emerge from the ruins of the common Austro–Hungarian army had not yet been clarified. Was it to serve revolution or counter-revolution? The removal of Festetich, who supported counter-revolutionary plans, and the appointment of the social democrat Böhm (January 19) appeared to decide the issue; however, the recruiting for a new "trade union army" was a rather slow process.[209]

The opportunity arose to exploit the antagonism between the nationalities, in the form of support to the "partial national movements". The government unofficially supported the movement of the eastern Slovaks—the "Council of the Eastern Slovaks", the *Vichodnoslovenska Rada* and the Slovak People's Republic set up by it at the beginning of December *(Slovenska Ludova Republika)*—though it was rather doubtful how strong and influential this organization and the new state organization, which more or less existed only on paper, actually was. The Seklers could also count on extensive support (on December 17 the Cabinet allocated

---

[207] *OL K. 27. Cabinet Minutes*, December 28, 1918.

[208] *Ibid.*, December 18, 1918.

[209] At the Cabinet meeting on February 18 Böhm put forth his conception regarding the reorganizing of the army: the disbanding of the existing army, the organizing of a mercenary army via recruiting, primarily from among the ranks of the urban proletariat between the ages of 24 and 42 on the basis of references from and recommendation by the unions. Accepting the proposal, Károlyi spoke about the possibility of "a liberation campaign": "If we are unable, on the basis of law and justice, we are ready to use arms to retrieve the conditions of our livelihood." (He repeated this on March 2 during a visit in Szatmár to the Szekler Division: "as a final resort we will use even arms to liberate this country".) Böhm later recalled (*Két forradalom tüzében*, pp. 210–211) in connection with the army that "every effort proved futile..." "After five weeks of recruiting only 5,000 people had volunteered in the whole of the country—whereas we would have needed 70,000."

10*

100,000 crowns for the Seklers). In addition to the exploitation of the antagonism between the Czechs and the Slovaks, with support given to Slovak aspirations to independence, the antagonism between the Romanians from Transylvania and Regát could also be exploited, via the propagation of the idea of an independent Transylvania. The antagonism between the Croats and the Serbs, Serbia and the Serbs in Voivodina were also possibilities.

The international situation also offered opportunities. The fact that almost three million German-speaking people came under the authority of the new Czecho-slovak state served as a pretext for a joint action against the Czechoslovaks. It seemed that the Poles too could perhaps be involved in this as there had been a conflict between Czechoslovakia and Poland over the issue of the eastern Silesian mining region. Fighting erupted at the end of January over the possession of Teschen. (The seven-day Teschen war, January 24—31, 1918.)

On February 24, Count Imre Csáky, head of the Foreign Ministry's political department, spoke openly about attacking Czechoslovakia in front of the Austrian envoy. He expounded that a concentrated offensive against Moravia, in which Hungary and German Austria would both take part on the basis of mutual interests, would force the Czechs to evacuate Slovakia. (In a ciphered telegramme sent to the envoy dated March 6 the reply was that "they were not contemplating armed military action for the moment". The Austrian Foreign Ministry was reluctant to accept the proposal which it considered adventurist. However, Vienna was willing to discuss the issue and supported the idea of a secret meeting, on the one hand, between Renner and Bauer, and, on the other, between Károlyi and Garami.)[210]

The antagonism between Romania and the Western Ukrainian state also seemed to provide a good opportunity. When at the end of December the Ukrainian envoy informed Károlyi that the Romanian army was preparing for the occupation of the north-eastern countries, which were inhabited by the Ruthenians, and that the Ukrainians intended to do something about it, Jászi said at the Cabinet meeting on December 29 that he would "not think it was a bad thing if the Ukrainians occupied this region instead of the Romanians. If the northern areas were to come into the hands not only of the Czechs and Romanians, but also the Poles and the Ukrainians, that would be of a tactical advantage to us".[211] At the Cabinet meeting of February 28 Garami, in his account of his meeting with Ukrainian delegates, said that what the Ukrainians were after most was ammunition and that they would be willing "to enter into joint action with us against the Romanians".[212]

There was antagonism between the new South Slav state over the question of the Banat. There was an armed struggle with Austria for Kärnthen, armed and unarmed

---

[210] *HHSt. NPA. Fasz. 880.* Liasse Ungarn. Cnobloch, the Austrian envoy to Budapest to the Austrian Foreign Minister. February 24, 1919. Also here, the draft of the ciphered reply March 6, 1919. Cnobloch refers to the planned involvement of the Poles in his March 4 and March 7 despatches. *NPA Fasz. 900.*

[211] *OL Cabinet Minutes,* December 29, 1918.

[212] *Ibid.,* February 28, 1919.

struggles against Italy over a host of disputes. The Károlyi government also jumped at the opportunity of exploiting this conflict and held talks with a view to forging links with the Italians as well.[213] Simultaneously with this, relations with the Holy See were restored. After some wrangling, the Cabinet endorsed the moving of the Viennese Nunciature to Budapest on March 17.

The victory of Soviet power, the pressing ahead of the Red Army in the direction of Galicia in the first few months of 1919 raised the question of possible rapprochement with Soviet Russia as well. In early March, after Kunfi and Kéri had returned from Switzerland (Kunfi attended a socialist congress in Bern, while Kéri was there on a diplomatic and journalistic mission), Károlyi considered this possibility, too. On the basis of the Bern congress and the talks which followed it, he edited a memorandum in which, among other things, he expounded that "greater attention must be paid to, on the one hand, the German Austrian state and through it our relationship with the German empire and, on the other, to Russia. For unless the domestic policy of the Entente states is radically transformed and the victory there of the forces of imperialism and capitalism drives both Germany as well as German Austria and Hungary into final ruin, then in this case a Russian–Hungarian–German block will automatically emerge..."[214] Buchinger was preparing for a trip to Soviet Russia as member of a study committee elected in Bern and asked Béla Kun, still under arrest at the time, for a letter of recommendation for his journey.[215] The idea of sending Kéri to Moscow also arose. The improved situation of communist leaders arrested at the end of February and the release of some of them were connected with these considerations.

The failure to reach agreement gave rise to the possibility of exerting influence over the population living in the seceding areas. "We have tried to reach the national minority masses after their leaders rejected our fraternal approach"— wrote Jászi later in a study on the subject.[216] By the term "reaching" Jászi meant the attempt to turn them against the occupiers. In order to accomplish this aim the government allocated substantial financial support; as early as December 28 the Cabinet decided that "the Cabinet Office provide the money required for propaganda purposes".[217] The propaganda campaign turned out to be a successful one. Workers, especially workers and peasants, reacted positively to slogans calling for social welfare demands, to agitation which often assumed a socialist character. The reason for this was that Hungary—thanks to the revolution—had made greater strides ahead in the realm of social welfare policy and democracy than the

[213] O. Charmant: "After the October Revolution", *Új Magyar Szemle*, 1/1920, pp. 1–8. Charmant, the Károlyi government's envoy to Vienna, advocated the idea of a Hungarian–Romanian–Italian alliance and, accordingly, urged rapprochement with Italy.

[214] *Levéltári Közlemények* (Archive Publications), 2/1969, p. 535. V. Székely: "Zsigmond Kunfi's Memorandum of February 1919 Concerning Hungary's Diplomatic Position."

[215] *Buchinger*, Vol. II., p. 67.

[216] O. Jászi: "Why Did Plans for a Danube Federation Fail?", *Látóhatár* (Horizon), 2/1953, p. 92.

[217] *OL K. 27. Cabinet Minutes*, December 28, 1918 (4) Support for the National Minority Movements.

neighbouring countries. Secession, the appearance of the Serbian, Romanian or Czech army signified a setback, the loss of revolutionary achievements.[218] (The dissolution of councils, the restriction of liberties, the curbing of salaries, the use of force to break strikes, the cutting off of benefits.) The loss of civil rights was coupled with economic shortages, including food, uneployment and forced recruitment into the new army. Poor provision and inadequate food supplies led to requisitioning; uneployment was not accompanied by unemployment benefit.

It was an advantage that links with the seeding areas continued to exist in many respects. Local organizations and groups of the Social Democratic Party, the trade unions and the sick-fund continued to function; the railway more or less remained the same and for the most part even public administration remained in place, with officials receiving wages or benefits from Budapest for quite some time after secession.[219] These links and the utilization of the one-time organizational framework enabled the Propaganda Committee, which was supported by the state, to continue its activity in the areas occupied by the Czech and Romanian army.[220]

[218] In his recollections László Rácz (Lipót Katz), one of the leaders of the working-class movement in Nagyvárad, describes how his brother, Béla Katz, who was a government commissioner for Nagyvárad and Bihar County at the beginning of 1919, compelled the big landowners to "temporarily" cede their land and ordered the utilization of ecclesiastical estates (hundreds of thousands of yokes of land and forests) for the benefit of both Hungarian and Romanian impoverished agricultural workers. "When ... the victorious Romanian royal army had marched in, the first thing they did was to drive the peasants from the episcopal forests and lands with force. As a result, 'the liberating Romanian brothers' were just as much hated by the Romanian poor peasants as by the Hungarian ones. Despite years of Romanian chauvinist propaganda... even years later peasant delegations kept going to Nagyvárad, looking for the "domnu workers' council" and asking that we serve justice and retrieve the episcopal forests and lands." (*Rácz*, p. 24.)

According to Jozef Sluka's recollection a revolutionary council was elected in Ruttka as early as October 26. "The council armed the workers, who then occupied the public buildings, the offices and the shops... The rich hid. They were terrified of the justified revenge of the poor. However, the armed workers demonstrated their maturity, they showed that being bloodthirsty was quite alien to their character." Sluka describes the council's early activity and concerning the events following the secession, he wrote the following: "One day the representatives of the Social Democratic Party's Central Committee appeared and presented the Kramář governments credentials. They wanted us to relinquish the sphere of authority which 'we are heedlessly usurping' in these heated days of change ... the most important task is 'to preserve law and order and calm' ... We have not relinquished... Armed legionaries came for us and took us to jail straight away. The members of the revolutionary workers council were immediately fired, many were imprisoned and persecuted." (*Együtt harcoltunk*, pp. 91–93.)

[219] On February 18 the Cabinet endorsed "the paying out of wages for Transylvanian civil servants and for the workers of state-owned factories", taking account of the fact that most officials had already been paid three months wages in January. At the same meeting it was decided that "the police officials and employees of Upper Hungary" be paid "the difference between their present wages and the wages they would receive from the Hungarian government". In response to a proposal submitted by Garami, the Cabinet meeting of February 14 decided that should "the employees of the Kassa-Oderberg railway be dismissed for refusal to take the oath for the Czecho-Slovak government, or because of their movement, the Hungarian state undertakes a guarantee to provide for them in such an event". *OL K. 27. Cabinet Minutes*, February 14, 1918. February 18, 24. (42, 46).

[220] On February 18 the Cabinet voted a sum of 350,000 crowns for the National Propaganda Committee with the stipulation that 100,000 crowns of this sum be spent on the Bratislava campaign. In

During the first few months of 1919 significant movements arose in the seceded areas—in Transylvania at the end of January, in Slovakia at the beginning of February and in the south at the end of February and the beginning of March.

The Romanian Prime Minister, Jonel Brătianu, accused the enemy—that is, the Hungarian government—before the Council of Ten in Paris with Bolshevik propaganda. ("The division of wealth and the abolition of rank had been promised; Wilson's policy had been proclaimed to be nothing but a capitalist policy; people had been told to kill officers and to do away with the governing classes."). Brătianu added that as a result of this propaganda campaign "100,000 workpeople strike and the news received from Transylvania was very disquieting".[221] However, Brătianu's charges, as far as the Budapest government was concerned, were unfounded. Insofar as Károlyi and the Berinkey government advocated social welfare demands it did so not because of "Bolshevik" considerations, but in the interests of Hungarian nationalist goals.[222] At the same time this was in harmony with the fact that the mass movement which flared up in the seceding areas—just as in Hungary—followed basically socialist goals. It was a result of this that in the course of strikes and other action solidarity was forged between workers of different nationalities; it was because of this that despite nationalist tendencies and provocation these movements enjoyed the support of socialists in Romania, Bohemia and Serbia as well.

If the fact that in this situation the wealthy classes and their representatives in Hungary sided with the occupiers and sought refuge with them is taken into consideration, then there can hardly be any doubt that these developments led to the dimininishing of mass support for the national bourgeoisie and to the clarification of the fronts.[223]

It was in such a situation that the Republic of Councils was proclaimed in Hungary on March 21, 1919. The Republic of Councils wished to resolve the

---

response to János Vass' reservations, Böhm admitted: "That they are making many mistakes, but they are doing a great deal of good, too. The movements in Transylvania and Upper Hungary are the result of their propaganda." *OL K. 27. Cabinet Minutes,* February 18, 1919. (7, 44).

[221] *Miller,* Vol. XIV., p. 175. Minutes of the meeting of the Council of Ten, February 1, 1918.

[222] Approving the proposal concerning the organization of the army, Károlyi said at the Cabinet meeting on February 18 in connection with the possibility of a "liberation campaign", that this would "require not only an army, but also a rousing ideological motivation. Total equality, land reform and a just distribution of wealth were such rousing motivations. If the industrial working class will liberate the oppressed people, it must be able to point out that it has such a country and government behind it which has accomplished this liberation work back home". *OL K. 27. Cabinet Minutes,* February 18, 1919. (23)

[223] In a speech to soldiers at Csucsa on March 15, Böhm described the situation as follows: "Let it make absolutely no difference to you, be they Romanian Boyars, be they Hungarian counter-revolutionaries, each must be fought with equal strength ... Do not feel anger towards the Romanian people, do not hate the Romanian people, but love them and love the British, the French and the Czechs, too, for it is not the people who are each other's enemies, but the ruling tyrants. It is the Romanian Boyars who want to strangle the Hungarian revolution, it is the Czech capitalists who want to take away the Hungarian mines. The people are brothers and when they have expelled their tyrants then the real Romanian people will also come and will extend their hands to the Hungarian people."

national minority issue, which the bourgeoisie had not been able to tackle along nationalistic lines in the spirit of equality and internationalism. After March 21 the national minority sections of the Communist Party and the Social Democratic Party merged. The Federation of International Groups was established. The outlines of socialist states and state formations in alliance with each other began to take shape. The sections of the International Federation contained potential future governments, which became obvious when the Slovak Republic of Council was formed.

The suppression of the dictatorship of the proletariat, the failure of expectations in regard to the German and Central European revolution, the fact that Hungary received no help from Soviet Russia in the summer of 1919, paved the way for the counter-revolutionary victory. The hope for the proletarian solution to the national minority issue remained unfulfilled. The restoration of capitalism and the resurgence of reaction once again unleashed nationalist feeling, which erupted with unprecedented strength. The united front of the Hungarian counter-revolutionaries and non-Hungarian anti-revolution interventionists—which held firm during the Republic of Councils—collapsed. Instead of the peaceful co-existence of peoples and alliance between those who depended on each other, rivalry flared up, with the succesful involvement of the masses. The new oppressors, in a reserved situation, wanted to continue to oppress, while the former oppressors—striving to keep the reserved situation—wanted to rule once again. The logic of events bred in hatred pointed irretrievably towards a new war.

SOURCES AND LITERATURE

Two in-depth studies have been published to date on the events immediately leading up to and the history of the bourgeois democratic revolution in Hungary.

It was during World War II that Sándor Juhász Nagy, the Minister of Justice for the Berinkey government, wrote *A magyar októberi forradalom története* (1918. október 31—1919. március 21.) (The History of the Hungarian October Revolution, October 31, 1918—March 21, 1919), Budapest 1945, a work based primarily on personal knowledge and impressions. A doctoral dissertation by Tibor Hajdu, *Az 1918-as magyarországi polgári demokratikus forradalom* (The 1918 Hungarian Bourgeois Revolution), Budapest 1968, was published on the occasion of the fiftieth anniversary of the revolution.

Recollections most of which contain accounts not only of the bourgeois democratic revolution and the events leading up to it, but of the history of the Republic of Councils as well, include Mihály Károlyi's *Egy egész világ ellen* (Against a Whole World), München 1923. (The new edition: Budapest 1965.) Károlyi's memoirs describe events up to October 31, 1918. For the manuscript of the unfinished second part, which discusses the period of the People's Republic, see Mihály Károlyi: *Az új Magyarországért* (For a New Hungary), Budapest 1968. Tivadar Batthyány represents the stance of the right wing of the Károlyi Party: *Beszámolóm I—II.* (My Account, Vols. I—II.), Budapest 1927. For the views of the radicals, see Oszkár Jászi's *Magyar kálvária, magyar feltámadás* (Hungarian Tribulations, Hungarian Resurrection), Wien 1920, a work which borders on the line of a memoir and a study. Mention must be given to the following recollections of social democrat leaders, e.g. Ernő Garami: *Forrongó Magyarország* (Agitated Hungary), Wien 1922; Vilmos Böhm: *Két forradalom tüzében* (In the Flame of Two Revolutions), München 1923 and Budapest 1946; Jakab Weltner: *Forradalom, bolsevizmus, emigráció* (Revolution, Bolshevism, Exile), Budapest 1929; Manó Buchinger: *Tanúvallomás. Az októberi forradalom tragédiája.* (Testimony. The Tragedy of the October Revolution), Budapest 1936; Idem: *Októberi forradalom — emigráció* (October Revolution—Exile), Budapest 1947. Béla Kun's writings on the history of the revolutions and the events leading up to them may be found in the following publications: Béla Kun: *A Magyar Tanácsköztársaságról. Válogatott beszédek és írások* (On the Republic of Councils. Selected Speeches and Writings), Budapest 1958. Idem: *Válogatott írások és beszédek I—II* (Selected Writings and Speeches, I—II), Budapest 1966. Idem: *Szocialista forradalom Magyarországon* (Socialist Revolution in Hungary), Budapest 1979. Of the recollections of communist authors, the following are of particularly high source value: József Lengyel: *Visegrádi utca* (Visegrád Street), Moskva 1932 and Budapest 1957, which the author has described as a historical report: a memoir by Gyula Hevesi: *Egy mérnök a forradalomban* (An Engineer in the Revolution), Budapest 1959 and 1965. Béla Szántó's account of the history of the revolutions, which is imbued with personal experiences, is also a noteworthy work. It can be found in manuscript at the Party History Institute Archives.

For a detailed account of the sources and bibliography of the history of the revolutions, see, András Siklós: *Az 1918—1919. évi magyarországi forradalmak. Források, feldolgozások* (The 1918—1919 Revolutions in Hungary. Sources and Studies), Budapest 1964.

1. POLITICAL CRISIS—REVOLUTIONARY SITUATION

CABINET CRISIS

The contemporary reports of the daily newspapers give detailed accounts of the Cabinet crisis in early October and the audiences and planning related to it. For his role in subsequent events, see József Szterényi: *Régmúlt idők emlékei. Politikai feljegyzések* (The Memoires of Bygone Times. Political Notes), Budapest 1925. Prince Lajos Windischgraetz's memoirs, which combine the real and the unreal, also deal with the Cabinet crisis and the history of the weeks leading up to the revolution: *Vom roten zum schwarzen Prinzen,* Wien 1920.

MIHÁLY KÁROLYI AND THE INDEPENDENCE AND '48 PARTY

The party's daily newspaper, *Magyarország* edited by Márton Lovászy, is a fundamental source of the Károlyi party's history. The party's programme was published in the July 19, 1916 issue of *Magyarország.* For the development and goals of the party see, the already cited works of M. Károlyi, T. Batthyány, and S. Juhász Nagy. Károlyi's speeches, articles and statements may be found in *Az új Magyarországért,* which has also been mentioned above. For a new in-depth study of Károlyi's life, see, Tibor Hajdu: *Károlyi Mihály* (Mihály Károlyi), Budapest 1978.

THE BOURGEOIS RADICALS

The 1914 programme of the National Bourgeois Radical Party may be found in *Neues Politisches Volksblatt* (June 21, 1914), in an abridged form in *Világ,* the daily newspaper of the radicals (June 7, 1914), and in Hungarian translation, in Gyula Mérei's *Polgári radikalizmus Magyarországon 1900—1919.* (Bourgeois Radicalism in Hungary 1900—1919), Budapest 1947. For the demands of 1918, see, Oszkár Jászi: *Mi a radikalizmus?* (What's Radicalism?), a pamphlet, Budapest 1918. Idem: *A Monarchia jövője. A dualizmus bukása és a Dunai Egyesült Államok* (The Future of the Monarchy. The Fall of Dualism and the Danubian United States), Budapest 1918. This book was later published under the title of *Magyarország jövője és a Dunai Egyesült Államok* (Hungary's Future and the Danubian United States). The title of the German edition: *Der Zusammenbruch des Dualismus und die Zukunft der Donaustaaten,* Wien 1918. For a more recent appraisal of Jászi's conception, see, Domokos Kosáry: "Ungarische Politische Bestrebungen und die Probleme der Monarchie im Zeitalter des Dualismus", *Acta Historica,* 1—2/1971 and Gyula Vargyai: *Nemzeti kérdés és integráció. Adalékok Jászi Oszkár nemzetiségi koncepciójának értékeléséhez* (The Nationality Issue and Integration. Contributions to the Appraisal of Oszkár Jászi's National Minority Concept), Pécs 1970; József Galántai: "A radikálisok és a nemzeti kérdés. Jászi Oszkár föderációs koncepciói az első világháború alatt" (The Radicals and the Nationality Issue. Oszkár Jászi's Federal Concepts during World War I), *Világosság* (Clarity), 1/1973. The minutes of the October 1918 congress have not survived, more precisely have not been found to date. For a detailed, albeit censored account, see, *Világ,* October 15, 1918.

THE HUNGARIAN SOCIAL DEMOCRATIC PARTY AND ITS LEFT WING OPPOSITION

For an account and assessment of the Social Democratic Party's activity and stance during World War I, see, Dezső Nemes: *A magyar munkásmozgalom történetéhez* (A Contribution to the History of the Hungarian Working Class Movement), Budapest 1974. A comprehensive view is published in *A magyar forradalmi munkásmozgalom története* (The History of the Revolutionary Hungarian Working Class Movement), Budapest 1972. For the most important documents, see, *A magyar munkásmozgalom történetének válogatott dokumentumai (MMTVD),* (Selected Documents from the History of the Hungarian Working Class Movement), Vols. 4/B and 5, Budapest 1956. For accounts and newspaper articles published on the occasion of Ervin Szabó's death, see László Remete (ed.)'s *Szabó Ervin 1877—1918* (Ervin Szabó, 1877—1918), Budapest 1968. The full text of the October 8 proclamation may be found in *Népszava*, while the minutes of the emergency conference which followed it, is in the appendix of the *MMTVD 4/B*. György Milei's "A hazai baloldali szocialista irányzatok a proletariátus feladatairól (1917 november—1918 november) (Domestic Left Wing Socialist Trends on the Tasks of the Proletariat, November 1917—November 1918) gives an account of the activity of the left wing, see *Párttörténeti Közlemények*, 4/1968.

THE HUNGARIAN COMMUNIST GROUP IN RUSSIA

The group's weekly, *Szociális Forradalom* is an important source of the activity of the Hungarian communist group in Soviet Russia. Unfortunately only incomplete copies have survived. For valuable documents pertaining to the group's activity, see, György Milei's writings in *Párttörténeti Közlemények*, 1/1958, 1/1962, 2/1964 and 3/1967. Idem: *A Kommunisták Magyarországi Pártjának megalakításáról* (On the Founding of the Hungarian Communist Party), which is a synthesis of the group's history, Budapest 1962 and 1972. The documents already published in *Párttörténeti Közlemények* and others can be found in *A magyar internacionalisták a Nagy Októberi Forradalomban és a polgárháborúban* (Hungarian Internationalists in the Great October Revolution and the Civil War), Budapest 1967, which is a collection of studies. Another noteworthy document pertaining to the activity of the communist group is Béla Kun's preface to Tibor Szamuely's *Riadó. Válogatott cikkek és beszédek* (Alert. Selected Articles and Speeches), Moskva 1932 and Budapest 1957, with the title "Emlékezés Szamuley Tiborra" (In Remembrance of Tibor Szamuely). Interesting facts may be found in Lajos Németh's *Egy internacionalista visszaemlékezése 1917—1919* (The Recollection of an Internationalist 1917—1919), Budapest 1972. György Szamuely published excerpts from the minutes of the October 24 conference—which existed in the Thirties, but has disappeared since—in a study entitled "A Kommunisták Magyarországi Pártjának előkészítése" (The Preparation of the Hungarian Communist Party), *Sarló és Kalapács*, 4/1932. For the text of the proclamations endorsed by the conference, see György Milei: "Az OK(b)P magyar csoportja a KMP megalakításáért" (The Hungarian Section of the Russian Communist Bolshevik Party for the Forming of the Communist Party of Hungary), *Párttörténeti Közlemények*, 2/1964.

THE LAST SESSION OF THE NATIONAL ASSEMBLY

The minutes of the National Assembly session beginning on October 16 are published in: *Az 1910. évi június hó 21-re hirdetett országgyűlés nyomtatványai. Képviselőházi Napló. XLI.* (The Publications of the National Assembly Convened for June 21, 1910. Parliamentary Proceedings, XLI), Budapest 1918. Contemporary newspaper reports also carry accounts of the sessions. For the background and interesting details of the assasination attempt on Tisza's life, see the above-mentioned recollections of József Lengyel and Gyula Hevesi.

2. A VICTORIOUS REVOLUTION—THE HUNGARIAN REPUBLIC

THE FINAL DAYS—THE VICTORY OF THE REVOLUTION

Freed of the burden of censorship, the daily newspapers carried detailed accounts of the events of October 30—31 and the events leading up to them. Also see the aforementioned memoirs of Károlyi, Batthyány, Garami, Böhm and Weltner. Of contemporary publications special mention must be given to the accounts, based on personal experiences, by Lajos Hatvany and Lajos Magyar. Lajos Hatvany: "Egy hónap története" (The Story of a Month), *Esztendő* (Year), December 1918. Lajos Magyar: *A magyar forradalom. Élmények a forradalom főhadiszállásán* (The Hungarian Revolution. Experiences at the

Headquarters of the Revolution), Budapest 1919. For a recent edition, see *Késői tudósítások* (Belated Reports), Budapest 1966. A wealth of material may be found in: A diadalmas forradalom könyve (The Victorious Revolution Book), Budapest 1918, which was edited by Oszkár Gellért and contains personal accounts by the leaders and participants of the revolution. László Bús Fekete's *Katona forradalmárok* (Revolutionary Soldiers), Budapest 1918, deals with the activity of the Soldiers' Council. The facts published in this book are supplemented by subsequent recollections of members of the Soldiers' Council, i.e. László Lengyel: "A katonatanácsról" (On the Soldiers' Council), *Társadalmi Szemle*, 10/1958; Tibor Sztanykovszky: "A katonatanácsról" (On the Soldiers' Council). In: *Nagy idők tanúi emlékeznek*. (The Witnesses of Great Times Remember), Budapest 1958. In his voluminous memoirs, Lukachich subsequently described and justified the role of the Budapest Garrison as well as the cause of his own behaviour in the revolution: *Magyarország megcsonkításának okai* (The Causes of Hungary's Dismemberment), Budapest 1932. Light is thrown on the same issue, though from another angle by Béla Szántó's aforementioned manuscript as well. Regarding the role of the Archduke Joseph, see his own succint notes which should not be taken at face value: *A világháború, amilyennek én láttam* (The World War, As I Saw It), Vol. VII., Budapest 1934. The files and minutes of the subsequent, rather contrived trials connected with the Tisza murder are kept at the PI Archives. Accounts of the events in the rural towns and villages may be found in the provincial press and publications on local history. The latter are listed, up until to 1961, in András Siklós' aforementioned historiography; for more recent works, see a joint study by Lajos Gecsényi and Ferenc Glatz: "1918—1919 évfordulója a helytörténeti irodalomban" (The Anniversary of 1918—1919 in Local History Literature), *Párttörténeti Közlemények*, 3/1970.

The minutes of Cabinet meetings constitute an important source of the history of the bourgeois revolution. Notes on the sessions of the National Council and Cabinet meetings have survived only in fragmented form. As regards the history of the revolution interesting information can be found in the documents pertaining to the subsequent political trials of the leaders and minor participants of the revolution. In addition to the Tisza Trial—which has already been mentioned—the so-called People's Commissars' Trial and the Károlyi Trial deserve special mention. The minutes of the People's Commissars' Trial are kept at the PI Archives, while the material pertaining to the Károlyi Trial is preserved in the Municipal Archives. For information on the records kept by the organs of central and provincial administration see A. Siklós' aforementioned work. Edited by József Farkas, *"Mindenki újakra készül..." Az 1918—19-es forradalmak irodalma* ("Everyone is Preparing for Something New..." The Literature of the 1918—19 Revolution), Budapest 1959, 1962, is a four-volume anthology, which is a comprehensive synthesis of recollections and documentary publications on the period. Vols. I and II deal with the literature and press publications pertaining to the revolution, which were published at the time of the bourgeois democratic revolution.

THE FIRST DAYS OF THE REVOLUTION
THE PROCLAMATION OF THE REPUBLIC

The first account of the rural mass movements of early November and the retaliation against them came from István Kató: "Az 1918-as novemberi parasztmozgalmak" (The Peasant Movements of November 1918), *Századok*, 3/1956. The data published in the latter is supplemented by Tibor Hajdu's aforementioned study. See also, Vera Szemere: *Az agrárkérdés 1918—1919-ben* (The Agrarian Issue in 1918—1919), Budapest 1963; Pál Schönwald: *A magyarországi 1918—1919-es polgári demokratikus forradalom állam és jogtörténeti kérdései* (The Constitutional and Legal History Issues of the 1918—1919 Hungarian Bourgeois Democratic Revolution), Budapest 1969. The latter also publishes the most detailed information. For the bombing at Facsád, see, Elemér Jakabffy—György Páll: *A bánsági magyarság húsz éve Romániában 1918—1938* (Twenty Years of the Hungarians from Bánság in Romania, 1918—1938), Budapest 1939, pp. 17—18. For the events in Látrány, see, Károly Mészáros: *Az őszirózsás forradalom és a Tanácsköztársaság parasztpolitikája* (The Frostflower Revolution and the Peasant Policy of the Republic of Councils), Budapest 1966, p. 29. The newspapers also carried detailed accounts of the events in Jósikafalva, (*Pesti Hírlap*, November 8, 15, 1918). The telegrammes which flooded the Ministry of the Interior by the hundred during the first days of the revolution (at present they are kept in the PI Archives) provide abundant proof in regard to the popular character of the revolution.

For the few days in which the National Council Bureau functioned and was dismantled, see Lajos Magyar's aforementioned account: *A magyar forradalom.* Tibor Hajdu's *Tanácsok Magyarországon 1918—1919-ben* (Councils in Hungary in 1918—1919), Budapest 1958, is a comprehensive analysis of the issue of the councils. Pál Schönwald's aforementioned work gives a detailed outline of the state organization, the legal system and legislation which emerged during the revolution.

The proclamation which announced Emperor Charles' retirement and the statement pertaining to Hungary were published in the November 12 and 16, 1918 issue of *Népszava* and other dailies. For the Upper House members and barons' visit to Eckartsau see, in addition to Mihály Károlyi's and Tivadar Batthyány's recollections, Gyula Wlassics' account, which glosses over events: "Az eckartsau-i nyilatkozat. A Király-kérdés" (The Eckartsau Statement. The Question of the King), *Új Magyar Szemle,* 1—2/1921. The memorandum, or rather a copy of it, produced by the University of Arts and Sciences' Faculty of Law and Political Science—which was handed over by the delegation—can be found among the files of the Károlyi Trial in the Municipal Archives. The minutes of the first, November 16 meeting of the Great National Council were published as an appendix to the diary of the National Assembly. The text of the plebiscitary decision was published by *Codex Hungaricus,* (Statutes of 1918), Budapest 1919.

3. HUNGARY'S SITUATION IN WORLD AFFAIRS
THE KÁROLYI GOVERNMENT'S FOREIGN POLICY

For archival material pertaining to the Károlyi government's foreign policy, see Vera Székely: "A polgári demokratikus köztársaság és a Tanácsköztársaság külképviseletének iratanyaga az Országos Levéltárban" (Records of the Diplomatic Representation of the Burgeois Democratic Republic and the Republic of Councils in the National Archives), *Levéltári Szemle* (Archival Review), 1/1969. For the organization of the Foreign Ministry, see Ferenc Harrer's memoirs: *Egy magyar polgár élete I.* (The Life of a Hungarian Citizen, Vol. I.), Budapest 1968. A. I. Mayer's *Politics and Diplomacy of Peacemaking,* New York 1967, is a new and notable work on the diplomacy of the victorious powers and its domestic roots. Information on the activity of the Balkans armistice committee may be obtained from AOK's confidential files which are kept at the Kriegsarchiv in Vienna. For the text of the preliminary conditions, ignored by Hungarian historiography up to this date, see B. Krizman: "The Belgrade Armistice of 13 November 1918", in: *The Slavonic and East European Review,* January 1970; Krizman's study describes Pašić and Vešnić's message as well as the subsequent manoeuvres of the Serbian army. For Franchet's plans and changes in the balance of power, see Azan's aforementioned biography and Franchet d'Espèrey's subsequent statement in Vol. II of the Batthyány memoirs. See also the following, more recent publications: Rogers Cros: *La victoire des Armées Alliées en Orient 1918,* Montpellier 1968; J. Bernachot: *Les Armées Françaises en Orient après l'armistice de 1918,* Paris 1970. Köves' despatch may be found in the files of both the Károlyi Trial and the Ministry of the Nationalities.

There are accounts of the Belgrade talks in the aforementioned memoirs of Károlyi, Jászi and Hatvany. See also Károlyi's English language memoirs: *Memoirs of Michael Károlyi,* London 1956 (In Hungarian: *Hit illúziók nélkül,* Budapest 1977). For a French account, see Azan's aforementioned biography and a study entitled "L'armistice avec la Hongrie", *L'Illustration,* November 5, 1921. For a Serb account, see D. Kalafatović: "Nasa primirja u 1918. godini", *Srpski Knjizevni Glasnik,* X–XIII/1923. The text of the Belgrade Military Agreement is published by an official publication compiled for the Paris Peace Conference: *Document concernant l'execution de l'armistice en Hongrie (novembre 1918—mars 1919.)* Budapest 1919. For the Hungarian translation see Nyékhegyi's aforementioned work, *A Diaz-féle fegyverszüneti szerződés* (The Diaz Armistice Agreement), Budapest 1922. The French draft of the memorandum read out by Károlyi may be found among the records of the Ministry of the Nationalities. Mária Ormos' "A belgrádi katonai konvencióról" (On the Belgrade Military Convention), *Történelmi Szemle* (Historical Review), 4/1979, is a more recent account of the Belgrade Armistice which is based on material from French archives and approaches the issue, one-sidedly, from the viewpoint of French politics only. For a comprehensive analysis of the armistice and foreign policy issues, see Zsuzsa L. Nagy: *A párizsi békekonferencia és Magyarország* (The Paris Peace Conference and Hungary), Budapest 1965. As the relevant material of British, French, Austrian and other archives has become accessible since the publication of this book, it has in many respects become outdated.

The story of the Vix mission has been the subject of several studies by Sándor Vadász, who based his work on French archive material. For his most detailed study, see "Vix és Károlyi" (Vix and Károlyi), *Hadtörténeti Közlemények* (Publications on Military History), 2/1969. Also based on French sources is Peter Pastor's "The Vix Mission in Hungary 1918—1919.: A Re-examination", *Slavic Review*, 3/1970. A few documents from French archives have also come to light: György Litván: "Documents des relations Franco-Hongroises des années 1917—1919" *Acta Historicc, 1–2/1975*. Lajos Arday's dissertation is based on material from British archives: *Angol—magyar viszony a polgári demokratikus forradalom idején az angol levéltári források tükrében* (British–Hungarian Relations During the Bourgeois Revolution, as Reflected by British Archival Sources), Manuscript, Budapest 1976. For the activity of Czechoslovak diplomacy, see Beneš aforementioned memoires: *Nemzetek forradalma...* On the stand of the Italian government, see L. Valiani: "La politica estera dei governi rivoluzionari ungheresi di 1918—1919", *Rivista Storica Italiana, 4/1966*. The text of the memoranda pertaining to Czechoslovak and Romanian demands is published by the aforementioned official publication: *Documents concernant....* The activity of Romanian diplomacy is discussed in depth by S. D. Spector in *Romania at the Paris Peace Conference. A Study of the Diplomacy of Ioan I. C. Brătianu*, New York 1962.

In addition to the aformentioned works of Károlyi, Batthyány and Juhász Nagy, the counter-revolutionary charges levelled at the Belgrade Convention and the Károlyi government's foreign policy (Nyékhegyi, Rubint, etc.) were discussed and refuted on behalf of the Octobrists in several studies by Géza Supka. For the most detailed work, see: *A nagy dráma* (The Great Drama), Miskolc 1924 and "Összeomlás" (Collapse), *Századunk* (Our Century), June—July 1931.

4. *THE DOMESTIC SITUATION*

THE ECONOMIC SITUATION
ECONOMIC-POLITICAL AND SOCIAL WELFARE POLICY MEASURES

There is no comprehensive, in-depth analysis of Hungary's economic situation and the economic policy of the period of the bourgeois democratic revolution. The vital source material for this topic being in the archives of the Ministry of Commerce, were destroyed during World War II. Owing to the lack of archival sources, the economics researcher is often forced to rely on press publications and later reports of various organizations. For a brief outline of the issue, see Iván T. Berend—Miklós Szuhay: *A tőkés gazdaság története Magyarországon 1848—1944* (The History of Capitalist Economy in Hungary, 1848—1944), Budapest 1973, and Tibor Hajdu's aforementioned book: *Az 1918-as magyarországi demokratikus forradalom*. The chapter on economic history, which has been attached to the end of this work also goes into detail. For a useful analysis of the financial situation, see Imre Láng's study "A Károlyi- és Berinkey-kormány pénzügyi politikája" (The Financial Policy of the Károlyi and Berinkey Governments), *Századok, 5–6/1960*. See also Antal Orbán's writing on cooperatives: "Fogyasztási szövetkezetek a polgári demokratikus forradalom idején" (Consumers' Cooperatives during the Bourgeois Democratic Revolution), *A Magyar Munkásmozgalmi Múzeum Évkönyve 1967/68* (The Yearbook of the Museum of the Hungarian Working Class Movement, 1967—68), Budapest 1969. Katalin Petrák's *Az első magyar munkáshatalom szociálpolitikája 1919* (The Social Welfare Policy of the First Hungarian Workers' Power, 1919), deals with the measures introduced by the bourgeois democratic revolution, giving a brief summary of each. Regarding the activity of the Ministry of Public Welfare, see Iván Bognár's carefully compiled study: "A Népjóléti Minisztérium és a Népjóléti Népbiztosság szervezete 1917—1919" (The Organization of the Ministry of Public Welfare and the Commissariat of Public Welfare, 1917—1919), *Levéltári Közlemények, 2/1966*.

THE UNRESOLVED LAND ISSUE

For a comprehensive analysis of the problems pertaining to the land question, see Vera Szemere's and Károly Mészáros' already mentioned books. Barna Buza describes his conceptions of land policy and their anti-revolutionary and peasant appeasing character in a brochure entitled *A kommunista összeesküvés* (The Communist Conspiracy), Budapest 1919 and in "Az októberi földreform" (The October Land Reform), an article was published in *Öt év múltán a Károlyi-korszak előzményei és céljai* (The Events Leading up to and Goals of the Károlyi Era After a Lapse of Five Years), Budapest 1923. Documents reflecting the stance of the Roman Catholic Church may be found in the Esztergom Primatial Archives, among János Csernoch' papers. The minutes of the conference held at the Ministry of Agriculture were published in the 48–49/1918 issue of *Köztelek* (Common Site). It was also published as an off-print: *Értekezlet a birtokreformról* (A Treatise on the Land Reform), Budapest 1918. The views of the georgists are expounded by Gyula J. Pikler in *Magyar földreform* (Hungarian Land Reform), Budapest 1919. For the social democrats' agrarian programme and its justification, see Jenő Varga's brochure: *Földosztás és földreform Magyarországon* (The Land Distribution and Land Reform in Hungary), Budapest 1919. For the situation of agricultural workers, see Jenő Hamburger: "A mezőgazdasági munkásság helyzete a Károlyi-forradalom alatt" (The Condition of the Agricultural Workforce Under the Károlyi Revolution), *Proletár* (Proletarian), September 2, 1920. Zsigmond Móricz's contemporary writing: "Népszavazás a földreformról" (Referendum on the Land Reform), was published in the January 1919 issue of *Esztendő*. A new edition of this is *Új világot teremtsünk* (Let Us Create a New World), Budapest 1953.

STRUGGLE AROUND THE DEMOBILIZATION
AND REORGANIZATION OF THE ARMY

For the demobilization and reorganization of the army, see Vilmos Böhm: *Két forradalom tüzében...* and József Breit's already mentioned works. For a new approach, see Károly Őry: "A katonapolitika és a hadseregszervezés főbb kérdései az októberi polgári demokratikus forradalom időszakában" (The Main Issues Pertaining to Military Policy and Army Organization During the Period of the October Bourgeois Democratic Revolution), *Hadtörténeti Közlemények*, 1/1970 and 1/1971. For a brief overview, see Ervin Liptai: *Vöröskatonák Előre! A Magyar Vöröshadsereg harcai 1919* (Forward, Red Soldiers! The Battles of the Hungarian Red Army 1919), Budapest 1969.

Linder expounds his conception regarding the demobilization of the army in detail in his book entitled *Kell-e katona? A militarizmus csődje* (Are Soldiers Necessary? The Failure of Militarism), Budapest 1919. For legislation pertaining to the reorganization of the army, see Pál Schönwald's aforementioned book.

5. THE DISSOLUTION OF THE MULTINATIONAL STATE

The records of Jászi's Ministry for the National Minorities of the National Archives serve as a fundamental source regarding the Károlyi government's national minority policy and the process of disintegration.

For the distribution according to mother tongue of the population of the seceded areas, see: "A magyar Szent Korona országainak 1910. évi népszámlálása. Hatodik rész. Végeredmények összefoglalása." (The 1910 Census of the Countries of the Holy Hungarian Crown. Part Six. The Summary of the Findings). *Magyar Statisztikai Közlemények, Új Sorozat* (Hungarian Statistics Publication, New Series, Vols. 42, 48, 52, 56, 61, 64). The summary data was published in Vol. 64, Budapest 1920.

CROATIA—SLAVONIA AND VOIVODINA

The secession of Voivodina is discussed in detail by László Kővágó: *A magyarországi délszlávok 1918—1919* (The South Slavs of Hungary in 1918—1919), Budapest 1964. Kővágó's in-depth work publishes the Novi Sad Skupstina's resolution of November 25. See also Péter Lőrinc and Toma Milenković's lecture delivered at the meeting of scholars held on the occasion of the 50th anniversary of the Republic of Councils (Péter Lőrinc: "A Vajdaság és Magyarország forradalmi kapcsolatai, 1919" (The Revolutionary Links Between Voivodina and Hungary, 1919); Toma Milenković: "Adalékok a szerb-bunyevác Agitációs Bizottságnak a nemzeti kérdésre vonatkozó álláspontjához" (Contributions to the Stance of the Serb-Catholic-Serbian Agitation Committee on the Nationality Issue), *A Magyar Tanácsköztársaság 50. évfordulójára* (The 50th Anniversary of the Hungarian Republic of Councils), Budapest 1970, pp. 388—396, 144—166. Several interesting documents are published in *A vajdasági munkásmozgalom szocialista szakasza (1890—1919)* (The Socialist Phase of the Working Class Movement in Voivodina, 1890—1919, A collection of Documents), Novi Sad 1953. For an in-depth analysis of the Pécs strike movement, see Gyula Hajdu's *Harcban elnyomók és megszállók ellen* (At War with Oppressors and Occupiers), Pécs 1957. For the events which took place in the Banat in 1918—1919, see Josef Gabriel's book entitled *Fünfzigjährige Geschichte der Banater Arbeiterbewegung*, Temesvár 1928.

SLOVAKIA

The text of the Turócszentmárton proclamation which announced the secession of Slovakia is published in *Kelet-Európa 1900—1945. 5/1* (Eastern Europe 1900—1945. 5/1.), Budapest 1970, a chrestomathy and in a study by Lajos Steier: "The Turócszentmárton Declaration", *Magyar Szemle* (Hungarian Review), 2/1928. Steier's revisionist and anti-Czech writing also discusses the debate over the authenticity of the declaration. For a detailed discussion of the military events, see László Fogarassy's manuscript which is preserved at the Military History Institute: *Az öthónapos fegyverszünet, adatok a Károlyi-kormány hadtörténetéhez* (The Five-Month Armistice, Data Pertaining to the Károlyi Government's Military History), Budapest 1968. In addition to Hungarian newspaper reports and Cabinet minutes, light is thrown on negotiations with Hodža by Hodža's own recollection: *Slovensky rozchod s mad'armi roku 1918*, Bratislava 1929. For a new Czech account of the events of 1918—1919, see: L. Tajták: Usilie mad'arskych vladnucich tried o vdrzanie Slovenska v ramci Mad'arska roku 1918." *Historicky Časopis*, 4/1966 and L. Holotik: "Oktobrová revolucia a revolucné hnutie na Slovensku koncom roku 1918", Ibid., 4/1967. In an independent publication Tajták analysed the Eastern Slovakian events of the revolution (*Národnodemokratická revolucia na Vychodnom Slovensku v roku 1918*, Bratislava 1972). In his study and book Tajták denounces the Károlyi government's policy, which insisted upon territorial integrity and expresses the belief that in this region the Slovak population also supported the idea of joining Czechoslovakia. Vaclav Karl also discusses the history of the occupation of Slovakia in a book which was also published in Hungarian: *A csehszlovák burzsoázia intervenciós háborúja a Magyar Tanácsköztársaság ellen 1919-ben* (The Interventionist War of the Czechoslovak Bourgeosie against the Hungarian Republic of Councils in 1919, Bratislava 1956.)

TRANSYLVANIA AND ROMANIANS LIVING IN HUNGARY

For the events in Transylvania at the end of 1918 and beginning of 1919, see István Apáthy's recollections: "Erdély az összeomlás után" (Transylvania After the Collapse), *Új Magyar Szemle*, December 1920. Jenő Kertész: "A tíz év előtti Erdély napjai" (Transylvanian Days Ten Years Ago), *Korunk*, 1, 2, 3/1929. For interesting data particularly on the behaviour of the leading Hungarian political stratum, see Imre Mikes: *Erdély útja Nagymagyarországtól — Nagyromániáig* (Transylvania's Path From Greater Hungary to Greater Romania), Brassov 1931, a book which is more journalistic than scholarly in character. Two studies were published in Hungary after World War II on the events of 1919 in Transylvania: Károly Gulya: "Az erdélyi nemzetiségi kérdés megoldására irányuló törekvések 1918—

1919-ben" (Efforts to Resolve the National Minority Issue in Transylvania in 1918—1919), *Acta Universitatis Szegediensis Acta Historica T. IX.*, Szeged 1961, and Zoltán Szász: "Az erdélyi román polgárság szerepéről 1918 őszén" (On the Role of the Romanian Bourgeoisie in Transylvania in the Autumn of 1918), *Századok*, 2/1972. Some noteworthy studies published in Romania in Hungarian: László Bányai: "A Nagy Októberi Szocialista Forradalom erdélyi hullámai" (The Impact on Transylvania of the Great October Socialist Revolution), *Korunk*, 10/1957. Victor Chereșteșiu: "Szocialisták és szociálsoviniszták a román munkásmozgalomban" (Socialists and Social Chauvinists in the Romanian Working Class Movement), Ibid., 12/1957. Constantin Daicoviciu, László Bányai, Victor Chereșteșiu, Vasile Liveanu: "A tömegek forradalmi harca — döntő tényező Erdély Romániával való egyesülésénél" (The Revolutionary Struggle of the Masses—A Decisive Factor in Transylvania's Union with Romania), Ibid., 1/1959. For the events of 1918 see also *Erdély története* (The History of Transylvania), a two-volume work edited by Miron Constantinescu, Bucharest 1964, and V. Liveanu's book entitled *1918. Din istoria luptelor revolutionare din Romania*, Bucharest 1960. More recent studies—in contrast with works published during the late Fifties and early Sixties which gave priority to class criteria—profess the primacy of the nationality criterion. From this point of departure they give a positive assessment, without reservation, to the trends advocating union. At the same time they conceal or denounce the stand taken by the one-time left wing of the Social Democratic Party and the communists who turned against royalist Romania and searched for another solution. This conception dominated the studies published on the occasion of the 50th anniversary: see *Revue Roumaine d'Histoire*, 6/1968 and *Unification of the Roumanian National State. The Union of Transylvania with Old Romania*, Bucharest 1971, an anthology; in both publications see, above all, M. Constantinescu's relevant studies. See, further, A. Porțeanu's lecture delivered at the meeting of scholars staged on the occasion of the 50th anniversary of the Republic of Councils: "Az 1918-as magyarországi polgári demokratikus forradalom és Erdély" (The 1918 Bourgeois Democratic Revolution in Hungary and Transylvania), in the aforementioned publication, *A Magyar Tanácsköztársaság 50. évfordulója*. The study compiled for the 1980 International Congress of Historians also moves along the above mentioned lines: Gheorghe Iancu: "Der leitende Regierungsrat und die Integration der Verwaltung und der Institutionen Transilvaniens in den rumänischen Einheitstaat (December 1918—April 1920). In: *Nouvelles Études d'Histoire 2*, Bucharest 1980, pp. 119-131. A bibliography published on the occasion of the 50th anniversary provides abundant information about the literature of the union: *Contribuții Bibliografice privind unirea Transilvaniei cu Romania*, Bucharest 1969.

The original copies of the joint November 1 appeal of the Romanian, Hungarian and Saxon National Council and of the November 9 message of the Romanian National Council may be found among the records of the Ministry of the Nationalities. For the Arad negotiations, see Jászi's account: *Visszaemlékezés a román nemzeti komitéval folytatott aradi tárgyalásaimra* (My Recollections of My Negotiations with the Romanian National Committee in Arad), Cluj-Kolozsvár 1921. The appeal for a federal state was published in the November 3, 1918 issue of *Világ*. The text of the Gyulafehérvár resolution is published in the aforementioned *Kelet-Európa 1900—1945* chrestomathy. It may also be found in Zsombor Szász's: "A gyulafehérvári rezolúciók" (The Gyulafehérvár Resolutions), *Magyar Szemle*, 4/1928. For a more recent Romanian analysis of the events at Gyulafehérvár, see I. Gheorgiu—C. Nuțu: *A gyulafehérvári nemzeti gyűlés December 1, 1918* (The Gyulafehérvár National Assembly, December 1, 1918) 1968, Bucharest. A professional account of the appearance of the Romanian army and the hostilities connected with it is given by G. D. Mărdărescu, the commander of the Transylvanian Romanian army in *Campania pentru desrobirea Ardealului și occuparea Budapestei. 1918—1920*, Bucharest 1921. A Hungarian account of the events is given by Károly Kratochvil and József Breit in their books which are imbued with anti-Károlyi government sentiments: *A székely hadosztály 1918—1919. évi bolsevistaellenes és ellenforradalmi harcai...* (The 1918—1919 Anti-Bolshevik and Counter-Revolutionary Battles of the Sekler Division...) Budapest 1938; József Breit: *A magyarországi 1918—1919. évi forradalmi mozgalmak és a vörös háború története* (The History of the 1918—1919 Revolutionary Movements in Hungary and the Red War). See also László Fogarassy's already mentioned manuscript entitled *The Five-Month Armistice*. The text of the Medgyes resolution of the Saxon National Assembly is published in F. Teusch's *Geschichte der Siebenbürger Sachsen*. Vol. IV., Hermannstadt 1926.

CARPATHO—UKRAINE

For the history between 1918—1919 of the Carpatho-Ukraine, see the works of Ukrainian historians, some of which have been published in Hungarian as well: M. Troján: "Bereg vármegye dolgozóinak harca a tanácshatalomért az 1918—1919-es években." (The Struggle of the Workers of Bereg County for Soviet Power in 1918—1919), *Századok*, 1–2/1964. B. Spivak, M. Troján: *Felejthetetlen 40 nap* (40 Unforgettable Days), Uzhorod 1969. For an overview of relevant works in Ukrainian, see M. Trojan: "A Kárpátokon túli ukrán történészek legújabb kutatásai" (The Most Recent Research of Subcarpathian Ukrainian Historians), *Századok*, 2/1963. "Az 1918—1919 évi magyarországi forradalmak története a szovjet történészek munkáiban" (The History of the Hungarian Revolutions of 1918—1919 in the Works of Soviet Historians), *Századok*, 2–3/1969. For an American assessment, see Paul Robert Magocsi's study entitled "The Ruthenian Decision to Unite with Czechoslovakia", *Slavic Review*, June 1975, pp. 360—381, and his book entitled *The Shaping of a National Identity, Subcarpathian Rus' 1848—1948*, Cambridge, Massachusetts, London 1978. The bibliography attached to this book contains over 2,000 titles. The substance of Magocsi's study is that for the Ruthenians unity with Czechoslovakia meant the optimum and most acceptable solution. More recent works by Hungarian historians deal mostly with the events leading up to the union. Ernő Gergely also deals with the period of the bourgeois democratic revolution in "Adalékok a nemzetiségi kérdés problémájához a magyarországi polgári demokratikus forradalom idején" (Contributions to the Problem of the Nationality Issue During the Hungarian Bourgeois Democratic Revolution), *A Magyar Munkásmozgalmi Múzeum Évkönyve. 1967—1968* (Yearbook of the Museum of the Hungarian Working Class Movement), Budapest 1969. Idem: "Az ukrán és a német kérdés a Magyar Tanácsköztársaság nemzetiségi politikájában" (The Ukrainian and German Question in the Nationality Policy of the Hungarian Republic of Councils), *Századok*, 2–3/1969. The text of Act X of 1918 is published by the official, publication of the Ministry of the Interior: *Az 1919. évi törvények gyűjteménye* (The Collection of Legislations Passed in 1919), Budapest 1919. The act is described and analysed by Pál Schönwald in his already mentioned work. For debates over autonomy, see *Ruszka–Krajna politikai jelentősége. Vitaülés az Országos Néptanulmányi Egyesületben 1919, február 23.* (The Political Importance of Ruszka–Krajna. A Debate at the National Public Education Association, February 23, 1919, Budapest 1919.)

WESTERN HUNGARY (BURGENLAND) AND GERMANS LIVING IN HUNGARY

Literature on the question of Burgenland is fairly extensive, albeit the majority of publications tend to deal with later developments, those which followed the period of the revolutions. For an analysis, among other things, the events of the bourgeois democratic revolution, see Katalin Soós: *A nyugat-magyarországi kérdés (1918—1919)* (The Western Hungarian (Burgenland) Issue, 1918—1919), Budapest 1962. For the history of the Southern Swabians, see Éva Madaras' study: "Adalékok a vajdasági németség politikai történetéhez (1918 október—1919 augusztus) (Contribution to the Political History of the Germans Living in Voivodina) (October 1918—August 1919) *Acta Universitatis Debreceniensis ... Series Historica V. 1966*. Owing to its reactionary criteria and nationalistic attitude, Ludmilla Schlereth's book, entitled *Die politische Entwicklung des Ungarländischen Deutschtums während der Revolution 1918/19*, München 1939, is of little use. For a detailed bibliography of the question, see László Fogarassy: "Bevezetés a burgenlandi kérdés forrásaiba és irodalmába" (An Introduction to the Sources and Literature of the Burgenland Issue), *Soproni Szemle* (Soproni Review), 2/1971. The people's law act regulating the right of the Germans to self-determination was published in the already mentioned official publication of the Ministry of the Interior.

6. THE COMMUNIST PARTY OF HUNGARY
AND THE COMMUNIST GROUPS OF NON-HUNGARIAN WORKERS

THE SOVIET GOVERNMENT'S APPEAL

For the Soviet government's appeal, see *Lenin Magyarországról* (Lenin on Hungary), Budapest 1965, a collection of documents. The articles quoted from the Soviet press appeared in the October 16,1918 issue of *Pravda* and the October 18 and 20,1918 issues of *Izvestia*.

THE FORMATION OF THE COMMUNIST PARTY OF HUNGARY

For an overview of the history of the formation of the party and of the party itself during the period of the bourgeois democratic revolution, see the already mentioned publications, *A magyar forradalmi munkásmozgalom története* and György Milei: *A Kommunisták Magyarországi Pártjának megalakításáról*. The more important documents were published in Vol. 5 of MMTVD and in the already mentioned works of Béla Kun. Béla Szántó' account, in manuscript form, as well as his book, written immediately after the defeat of the dictatorship of the proletariat, *A magyarországi proletariátus osztályharca és diktatúrája* (The Class Struggle and Dictatorship of the Proletariat in Hungary), Wien 1920, are also valuable source works. An anthology of recollections, *Nagy idők tanúi emlékeznek* (The Witnesses of Great Times Remember), Budapest 1958, as well as its revised edition, *Tanúságtevők. Visszaemlékezések a magyarországi 1918—1919-es forradalmak résztvevőitől* (Witnesses. Recollections of the Participants of the 1918—1919 Revolutions in Hungary), Budapest 1978, are also valuable contributions to the subject. The resolution of the November 4 Moscow conference is published by *A Magyar Internacionalisták a Nagy Októberi Szocialista Forradalomban és a polgárháborúban* (Hungarian Internationalists in the Great October Revolution and the Civil War), which has already been mentioned. An account of the founding of the party in Hungary is given by Béla Kun in his recollections: "Hogyan alakult meg a Kommunisták Magyarországi Pártja" (The Forming of the Communist Party of Hungary), *Új Előre 25 éves jubileumi albuma* ("New Advances" 25th Jubilee Album), New York 1927. It was also published with the title "Összehívjuk az alakuló ülést", (We Convene the Statutory Meeting), in the 11/1958 of the *Társadalmi Szemle*. See also, Béla Szántó: "Hogyan alakult meg a KMP?" (How was the Hungarian Communist Party Formed?), *Új Március* (New March), March 1928.

THE PARTY'S PROGRAMME AND ITS GOALS
THE ENLIGHTMENT AND ORGANIZATION OF THE MASSES

Most of the information regarding the party's programme may be found in the articles of *Vörös Újság* and contemporary party publications. For the history of *Vörös Újság*, see Béla Vágó's recollections: "A Vörös Újság első számáról" (Concerning the First Issue of Red News), *Új Március*, March 1928 and Pál Hajdu's account of his personal experiences: "A Vörös Újság" (The Red News), *Sarló és Kalapács*, 4/1934. An account of the formation of the Communist Young Workers' Association (KIMSZ). is given by László F. Boross in "A KIMSZ megalakulása és első lépései" (The Forming and First Steps of KIMSZ), *Sarló és Kalapács*, 1/1934. For a full-lenght study on the subject, see: László Svéd: *Utat tör az ifjú sereg* (The Young Legion Breaks Through), Budapest 1962. László Svéd also collected the most important documents of the young workers' movement in *A vörös lobogó alatt. Válogatott írások a magyar kommunista ifjúsági mozgalom történetéről 1917—1919* (Under the Red Flag. Selected Writings on the History of the Hungarian Communist Youth Movement 1917—1919), Budapest 1955. For the anti-communist arguments of the Social Democratic Party, see *Népszava* articles, particularly in the December 11, 15 and 19, 1918 issues and, further, the pamphlets "Mit kell tudnia minden munkásnak?" (What Should Every Worker Know?) and "Nyílt levél a magyar szociáldemokrata munkássághoz!" (Open Letter to the Hungarian Social Democratic Workforce!), which were published at the end of 1918 and a the beginning of 1919.

THE COMMUNIST GROUPS OF ROMANIAN, SOUTH SLAV, SLOVAK AND OTHER NON-HUNGARIAN WORKERS

For a comprehensive study of the formation and subsequent activity of the national minority groups, see László Kővágó: *Internacionalisták a Tanácsköztársaságért* (Internationalist for the Republic of Councils), Budapest 1969. For the events leading up to the formation of the national minority groups, see János Kende's dissertation: *A magyarországi Szociáldemokrata Párt nemzetiségi Politikája, 1903—1919* (The Nationality Policy of the Social Democratic, Party, 1903—1919), Budapest 1973.

LIST OF ABBREVIATIONS

A diadalmas forradalom könyve =
A diadalmas forradalom könyve. A népkormány tagjainak, a forradalom szereplőinek és 75 magyar írónak önvallomása. A forradalmi napok hiteles krónikája (The Victorious Revolution Book. Recollections of the Member of the People's Government, the Participants of the Revolution and 75 Hungarian Writers. The Authentic Chronicle of the Revolutionary Days), ed. Oszkár Gellért, Budapest 1918

A földmunkásmozgalom története =
József Takács: *A földmunkásmozgalom története. Harminc esztendő* (The History of the Agrarian Labour Movement. Thirty Years), Budapest 1926

A katonatanácsról =
Tibor Sztanykovszky: "A Katonatanácsról" (On the Soldiers' Council), in: *Nagy idők tanúi emlékeznek (1918—1919)* (The Witnesses of Great Times Remember), Budapest 1958

A magyar béketárgyalások =
A magyar béketárgyalások. Jelentés a magyar békeküldöttség működéséről Neuilly S/S-ben 1920 januárius—március havában (The Hungarian Peace Talks. A Report on the Activity of the Hungarian Peace Delegation in Neuilly S/S, in January—March 1920, Vol. I, Published by the Hungarian Royal Foreign Ministry), Budapest 1920

A magyar októberi forradalom története =
Sándor Juhász Nagy: *A magyar októberi forradalom története* (1918. október 31—1919. március 21) (The History of the Hungarian October Revolution, October 31, 1918—March 21, 1919), Budapest 1945

AOK =
K.u.K. Armeeoberkommando

A szakszervezeti mozgalom =
A szakszervezeti mozgalom Magyarországon 1917—1922. A Magyarországi Szakszervezeti Tanács jelentése (The Trade Union Movement in Hungary, 1917—1922. The Hungarian Trade Union Council Report), Budapest 1923

Az Erdélyi Föld Sorsa =
Dr. Miklós Móricz: *Az Erdélyi Föld Sorsa. Az 1921 évi román földreform* (The Fate of the Transylvanian Land. The 1921 Romanian Land Reform), Budapest 1932

Bajza =
József Bajza: *A horvát kérdés. Válogatott tanulmányok* (The Croat Question. Selected Studies), Budapest 1941

Batthyány =
Count Tivadar Batthyány: *Beszámolóm I–II.* (My Account, Vols. I–II), Budapest 1927

Bernachot =
Jean, General Bernachot: *Les Armées Françaises en Orient après l'Armistice de 1918*
Vol. I. L'Armée Française d'Orient, L'Armée de Hongrie (11 novembre 1918—10 septembre 1919)
Vol. II. L'Armée du Danube. L'Armée Française d'Orient (28 octobre 1918—25 janvier 1920), Paris 1970

Böhm =

Vilmos Böhm: *Két forradalom tüzében. Októberi for-radalom — Proletárdiktatúra — Ellenforradalom* (In the Flame of Two Revolutions. October Revolution—Dictatorship of the Proletariat—Counter-Revolution), Wien 1923

Böhm: *A háborús korszak bűnei* =

A háborús korszak bűnei. A nyomorúság Magyarországa. Böhm Vilmos Hadügyminiszter beszéde a budapesti Munkástanács 1919 február 24-iki ülésén (The Sins of the War Period. Impoverished Hungary. A Speech by the Minister of Defence Vilmos Böhm at the February 24, 1919 Meeting of the Budapest Workers' Council), Budapest 1919

Breit =

József Breit of Doberdó: *A magyarországi 1918/19. évi forradalmi mozgalmak és a vörös háború története. I. A Károlyi korszak főbb eseményei* (The History of the 1918—1919 Revolutionary Movements in Hungary and the Red War. Vol. I, The Main Events of the Károlyi Era), Budapest 1929

Buchinger =

Manó Buchinger: *Küzdelem a szocializmusért. Emlékek és élmények. II. Októberi forradalom — emigráció* (Struggle for Socialism. Memories and Experiences. Vol. II, October Revolution—Exile), Budapest 1946

Buza =

Barna Buza: *A kommunista összeesküvés. Hogy kezdődött a zsiványdiktatúra? Kommunizmus vagy földosztás?* (The Communist Conspiracy. How did the Dictatorship of Rogues Begin? Communism or Land Distribution?), Budapest 1919

Document =

Documents concernant l'exécution de l'armistice en Hongrie (novembre 1918—mars 1919), Budapest 1919

Együtt harcoltunk =

Együtt harcoltunk. Visszaemlékezések az 1919-es Szlovák és Magyar Tanácsköztársaságra (We Fought Together. Recollections of the 1919 Slovak and Hungarian Republic of Councils), Bratislava 1960

Erdély története =

Victor Cherestesiu, Cornelia Bodea, Bujor Surdu, Calmi Muresan, Constantin Nutu, Ákos Egyed, Miron Constantinescu, Vasile Curticepeanu: *Erdély története II.* (The History of Transylvania Vol. II), Bucharest 1964

Értekezlet =

"Értekezlet a birtokreformról. A Földművelésügyi Minisztériumban 1918. november 20-tól november '29-ig." (A Conference on Land Reform at the Ministry of Agriculture between November 20 and 29, 1918. Offprint from the 48 and 49/1918 issue of *Köztelek*) Budapest 1918

1910. évi népszámlálás =

"A Magyar Szent Korona országainak 1910. évi népszámlálása. Hatodik rész. Végeredmények összefoglalása" (The 1910 Census of the Countries of the Hungarian Holy Crown. Part Six. The Summary of the Findings, Published by the Royal Hungarian Central Statistic Office), *Magyar Statisztikai Közlemények, Új Sorozat* (Hungarian Statistics Publications, New Series, Vol. 64), Budapest 1920

Gheorgiu—Nutu =

I. Gheorghiu—C. Nutu: *A gyulafehérvári nemzeti gyűlés. 1918. december 1.* (The Gyulafehérvár National Assembly. December 1, 1918), Bucharest 1968

Hajdu =   Tibor Hajdu: *Az 1918-as magyarországi polgári demokratikus forradalom* (The 1918 Hungarian Bourgeois Democratic Revolution), Budapest 1968

HHStA =   Haus-, Hof- und Staatsarchiv, Wien

HL =   Hadtörténeti Levéltár (Military History Archives)

House =   *The Intimate Papers of Colonel House* (Arr. by Charles Seymour), Vols. I–IV, London 1928

Jakabffy =   Dr. Elemér Jakabffy: *Erdély statisztikája* (Transylvania's Statistics), Lugos 1923

Jászi =   Oszkár Jászi: *A Monarchia jövője. A dualizmus bukása és a Dunai Egyesült Államok* (The Future of the Monarchy. The Collapse of Dualism and the Danubian United States), Budapest 1918

Ježek =   Zdenek Ježek: *Ucast dobrovolniku v bojich o Slovensko a Tesinsko v letech 1918—1919,* Praha 1937

KA =   Kriegsarchiv, Wien

Károlyi 1923 =   Mihály Károlyi: *Egy egész világ ellen* (Against a Whole World), München 1923

Károlyi 1968 =   Mihály Károlyi: *Válogatott írások és beszédek 1908—1919* (For a New Hungary. Selected Writings and Speeches 1908—1919), Budapest 1968

Károlyi Mihályné =   Mrs. Mihály Károlyi: *Együtt a forradalomban. Emlékezések* (Together in the Revolution. Recollections), Budapest 1967

Katona forradalmárok =   László Bús Fekete: *Katona forradalmárok* (Soldier Revolutionaries), Budapest 1918

Képviselőházi napló =   *Az 1910—1915. évi országgyűlés képviselőházának naplója XLI. kötet* (Parliamentary Proceedings of the Lower House of the 1910—1915 National Assembly, Vol. XLI), Budapest 1918

Kratochvil =   Károly Kratochvil of Szent Kereszthegy: *A székely hadosztály 1918—19 évi bolsevistaellenes ellenforradalmi harcai a székely dicsőségért, Erdélyért, Magyarország területi épségéért és Európáért* (The 1918—19 Anti-Bolshevik Battles of the Sekler Division for Sekler Glory, for Transylvania, for Hungary's Territorial Integrity and for Europe), Budapest 1938

Lenin Magyarországról =   *Lenin Magyarországról II.* (Lenin on Hungary, II), rev. ed., Budapest 1964

Lukachich =   Baron Géza Lukachich: *Magyarország megcsonkításának okai* (The Causes of Hungary's Dismemberment), Budapest 1932

Mărdărescu =   G. D. Mărdărescu: *Campania pentru desrobirea Ardealului și occuparea Budapestei, 1918—1920,* Bucharest 1921

Mikes =   Imre Mikes: *Erdély útja Magyarországtól Romániáig, I–II.* (Transylvania's Path from Hungary to Greater Romania, Vols. I–II), Braşov 1931

Miller =   David Hunter Miller: *My Diary at the Peace Conference of Paris* 28. Vols., New York 1928

MKSM =   Militärkanzlei Seiner Majestät des Kaisers und Königs

MMTVD 5. =   *A magyar munkásmozgalom történetének válogatott dokumentumai. V. 1917. november 7—1919. március 21.* (Selected Documents from the History of the Hungarian Working Class Movement. Vol. V, November 7, 1917—March 21, 1919), Budapest 1956

Mohácsy =	Béla Mohácsy: *A magyar királyi államvasutak a világháború alatt* (The Royal Hungarian Railways in the World War), Budapest 1925
Nagy idők tanúi =	*Nagy idők tanúi emlékeznek (1918—1919)* (The Witnesses of Great Times Remember, 1918—1919), Comp. by Mrs. Ernő Lányi, Budapest 1958
Nemzetiségi kérdés =	A nemzetiségi kérdés a társadalmi és az egyéni fejlődés szempontjából. A Huszadik Század körkérdése (The Nationality Issue from the Viewpoint of Social and Individual Development. The Circular Question of *Huszadik Század*), Budapest 1919
OL =	Országos Levéltár (National Archives)
Opočenský =	Jan Opočenský: *Der Untergang Österreichs und die Entstehung des Tschechoslovakischen Staates*, Praha 1928
Ö—U. lezter Krieg =	*Österreich-Ungarns letzter Krieg 1914—1918, Bd. 1–7. Hrsg. Vom Österreichischen Bundesministerium für Landesverteidigung und vom Kriegsarchiv. Bd. 7: Das Kriegsjahr 1918,* Wien 1938
PI Archives =	MSZMP Központi Bizottsága Párttörténeti Intézet Archívuma (The Party History Institute Archives of the Hungarian Socialist Workers' Party Central Comittee)
Rácz =	László Rácz: *Porszem a viharban* (A Speck of Dust in the Storm), New York 1965
Schönwald =	Pál Schönwald: *A magyarországi 1918—1919-es polgári demokratikus forradalom állam és jogtörténeti kérdései* (Political Science and Legal History Issues of the 1918—1919 Hungarian Bourgeois Democratic Revolution), Budapest 1969
Statisztikai Évkönyv 1918 =	*Magyar Statisztikai Évkönyv. Úf folyam* (Hungarian Statistical Yearbook. New Series), Vols. XXIV, XXV, 1916, 1917, 1918, ed. and publ. by the Royal Hungarian Central Statistic Office, Budapest 1924
Steier =	Lajos Steier: *Ungarns Vergewaltigung. Oberungarn unter tschechischer Herrschaft,* Zürich—Leipzig—Wien 1929
Számvevőszék jelentése =	*A m. kir. Legfelsőbb Állami Számvevőszék jelentése a magyar államnak az 1918. évi november hó 1-től 1919. évi március hó 20-ig és 1919. évi március hó 21-től 1919. évi augusztus hó 6-ig terjedő időszakokban utalványozott kiadásairól és előírt bevételeiről szerkesztett kimutatáshoz* (The Report of the Royal Hungarian Supreme State Audit Office to the Hungarian State Concerning the Account Drawn up of the Expenditure and Revenues for the Periods Between November 1, 1918 and March 20, 1919, and March 21, 1919 and August 6, 1919), Budapest 1923
Szterényi =	Baron József Szterényi: *Régmúlt idők emlékei. Politikai feljegyzések* (The Memories of Bygone Times. Political Notes), Budapest 1925
Szücsi =	József Szücsi (Bajza): "Horvátország népessége." (Croatia's Population), Offprint from *Földrajzi Közlemények* (Geographical Publications), Vol. XLIV, 2—5) Budapest 1916

Teleszky =   Dr. János Teleszky: *A magyar állam pénzügyei a háború alatt* (The Financial Affairs of the Hungarian State During the War), Budapest 1927

Teutsch =   Friedrich Teutsch: *Geschichte der Siebenbürger Sachsen für das sächsische Volk. IV. Band. 1968—1919. Unter dem Dualismus*, Hermannstadt 1926

Varjassy =   Dr. Lajos Varjassy: *Gr. Károlyi Mihály—Kun Béla— Horthy Miklós. Az októberi forradalomtól a "bűnös" Budapest hódolatáig 1918—1919* (Count Mihály Károlyi—Béla Kun—Miklós Horthy. From the October Revolution to the Surrender of "Guilty" Budapest, 1918—1919), Timişoara 1932

Vitaülés =   *Ruszka-Krajna politikai jelentősége. Vitaülés az Orsz. Néptanulmányi Egyesületben 1919. február 23. Domokos László, György Endre, Podhradszky György, Szegedy Rezső, Vikár Béla nyilatkozatai* (The Political Importance of Ruszka-Krajna. A Debate at the National Public Education Association, February 23, 1919. Contributions by László Domokos, Endre György, György Podhradszky, Rezső Szegedy, Béla Vikár), Budapest 1919

Weltner =   Jakab Weltner: *Forradalom, bolsevizmus, emigráció* (Revolution, Bolshevism, Exile), Budapest 1929

GEOGRAPHICAL NAMES

Antalfa		Kovačica (SFRY)
Arad		Arad (RPR)
Balázsfalva	Blasendorf	Blaj (RPR)
Bánffyhunyad		Huiedin (RPR)
Beszterce	Bistriz	Bistriţa (RPR)
Brassó	Kronstadt	Braşov (RPR)
Csap		Cop (USSR)
Csíkszereda		Sereda Ciuculni (RPR)
Dés		Dej (RPR)
Déva	Diemrich	Deva (RPR)
Dévény	Theben	Devín (CSR)
Eperjes	Eperies	Prešov (CSR)
Érsekújvár	Neuhausel	Nové Zámky (CSR)
Fehértemplom	Weisskirchen	Biserica-Albă (RPR)
Gyimesbükk		Ghimeş-Făget (RPR)
Gyulafehérvár	Karlsburg	Alba Iulia (RPR)
Huszt		Chust (USSR)
Jászvásár		Iaşi (RPR)
Kassa	Kaschau	Košice (CSR)
Kolozsvár	Klausenburg	Cluj-Napoca (RPR)
Körösmező		Jasinja (USSR)
Kralován		Kral'ovany (CSR)
Lupény		Lupeni (RPR)
Malacka		Malacky (CSR)
Marosvásárhely	Neumarkt	Târgu-Murăsulni (RPR)
Máramarossziget	Marmarosch	Sigethul Marmatei (RPR)
Medgyes	Mediasch	Mediaş (RPR)
Munkács		Mukac'evo (USSR)
Nagybánya	Neustadt	Baia Mare (RPR)
Nagybecskerek	Gross Betschkerek	Zrenjanin (SFRY)
Nagykároly	Gross Karol	Carei (RPR)
Nagykikinda	Gross Kikinda	Kikinda (SFRY)
Nagyszombat	Tyrnau	Trnava (CSR)
Nagyszeben	Hermannstadt	Sibiu (RPR)
Nagyvárad	Grosswardein	Oradea (RPR)
Pancsova		Pančevo (SFRY)
Petrozsény		Petroşeni (RPR)
Pozsony	Pressburg	Bratislava (CSR)
Rimaszombat	Grossteffelsdorf	Rimavská Sobota (CSR)
Ruttka	Ruttek	Vrutky (CSR)
Sopron	Ödenburg	
Szabadka	Maria-Teresiopel	Subotica (SFRY)

Szakolca	Skalitz	Skalica (CSR)
Szatmárnémeti	Sathmar	Satu Mare (RPR)
Szászváros	Broos	Orăştie (RPR)
Szenic		Senica (CSR)
Temesvár	Temeschburg	Timişoara (RPR)
Tölgyesalja		Zádubnie (CSR)
Turócszentmárton	Sankt Martin	Turčiansky Svätý Martin (CSR)
Újvidék	Neusatz	Novi Sad (SFRY)
Ungvár		Uzhorod (USSR)
Uzsok		Užhok (CSR)
Vasvár	Eisenburg	
Versec	Werschetz	Vršac (SFRY)
Zám		Zam (RPR)
Zilah	Zillenmarkt	Zalău (RPR)
Zólyom	Altsohl	Zvolen (CSR)
Zsibó		Jibău (RPR)
Zsolna	Sillein	Žilina (CSR)